FROM CRISIS TO COMPLACENCY?

From Crisis
to Complacency?

Shaping Public Policy
in Britain

BRIAN W. HOGWOOD

OXFORD UNIVERSITY PRESS
1987

Oxford University Press, Walton Street, Oxford OX2 6DP

Oxford New York Toronto
Delhi Bombay Calcutta Madras Karachi
Petaling Jaya Singapore Hong Kong Tokyo
Nairobi Dar es Salaam Cape Town
Melbourne Auckland

and associated companies in
Beirut Berlin Ibadan Nicosia

Oxford is a trade mark of Oxford University Press

Published in the United States
by Oxford University Press, New York

British Library Cataloguing in Publication Data
Hogwood, Brian W.
From crisis to complacency?: Shaping public
policy in Britain.
1. Great Britain—Politics and government
—1979–
I. Title
354.4107'25   JN318
ISBN 0–19–827273–1
ISBN 0–19–827272–3 Pbk

Library of Congress Cataloging in Publication Data
Hogwood, Brian W.
From crisis to complacency?
Bibliography: p.
Includes index.
1. Great Britain—Politics and Government—
1945–   2. Political planning—Great Britain.
3. Policy sciences. I. Title
JN231.H64   1987   320.941   86–23918
ISBN 0–19–827273–1
ISBN 0–19–827272–3 (pbk.)

Set by Cambrian Typesetters, Frimley, Surrey
Printed and bound in
Great Britain by Biddles Ltd,
Guildford and King's Lynn

Contents

CONTENTS

For Alison
who is blissfully unaware of
the contents of this book

Acknowledgements

Chapter 2 has benefited from helpful comments by Jeremy Moon, who was kind enough to read a draft version of the chapter. Chapter 4 draws heavily on work I have conducted jointly with Tom Mackie on the comparative analysis of cabinet committees; Tom also commented on the draft chapter and encouraged me to make a necessary brutal excision. Although he will undoubtedly still be unhappy about its emphasis, chapter 5 on the legislative process has benefited from comments from Mark Franklin.

In this book, particularly in chapter 3, I have chosen to place a different emphasis on the variety of processes involved in shaping British public policy from that adopted by Jeremy Richardson and Grant Jordan. This book has, however, been immeasurably informed both by their insights into policy-making in Britain and by their continuing empirical work.

One of the most interesting conversations I have had about the subject-matter of this book, particularly that contained in chapters 1 and 3, was with Rod Rhodes at the PAC conference in York in September 1985. The discussion was a good advertisement for going to conferences but skipping some of the sessions. This book has benefited from that decision, and would undoubtedly have benefited more if I had followed up all his tips.

Chapter 1

Making Sense of Policy Activity

1.1 From crisis to complacency?

A child dies, killed by her own parents; a famine which has been developing for months is portrayed on television screens. The government suddenly devotes attention to an issue which had not until then been treated as a political priority, even if government already had some involvement in that area. This upsurge in interest might spur the government into some activity such as launching an inquiry into cases of child abuse or announcing aid allocations. Once the immediate political crisis is passed, the government loses interest, either taking no further action or allowing the programme established as a result of the crisis to struggle on with little political follow-through to see if it is actually working, until a further crisis gives prominence to policy problems. This is the cynical, rather caricature picture of government embodied in the question in the title of this book.

This book will examine how far that is an accurate characterization of the policy process in practice in Britain. From the start, though, we should be cautious about assuming that there is necessarily one type of process or 'policy style' that will adequately describe all policy activity in Britain across policy areas and across time (cf. Jordan and Richardson, 1982). In particular, we should not confuse the public prominence of political activities with intensity of government concern; as will become clear, much of the most important discussion about shaping public policy in Britain takes place in private.

1.2 What is public policy?

What kind of issues are covered by the term 'public policy'? Two different stories which appeared in the press on 14 October 1985 illustrate the range of considerations with which any analysis of the British public policy process must be concerned.

The first story concerned the cabinet infighting during the annual public expenditure decision-making leading to the Autumn Statement (see chapter 6 on budgeting). The Chancellor of the Exchequer, Nigel Lawson, was trying to cut £3bn from the bids made by ministers to bring expenditure within a ceiling of £139 billion (*The Times*, 14 October 1985). There was speculation that defence and social security would be frozen or cut, while law and order could hope for increased spending following a speech by Mrs Thatcher at the Conservative Party Conference the previous week. This is public policy rounded to the nearest ten million pounds.

The second story concerned Mrs Elizabeth Fairhurst's meat and vegetable pies (*Financial Times*, 14 October 1985). The Finance Act 1984 imposed Value Added Tax (VAT) on any supply of hot food for consumption off the premises; cold food was zero rated. The officials at the Customs and Excise had realized that what counted as hot was not self-evident so they defined hot food as 'that heated and supplied at a temperature above the ambient air temperature for the purpose of enabling it to be consumed at such a temperature'. However, the case of Mrs Fairhurst's meat and vegetable pies raised the question of when hot pies were actually sold hot for that purpose. The shop baked pies on the premises. Mrs Fairhurst:

told the tribunal that after removing the hot pies from her oven she puts them in trays from which clients would be served . . .

Mr Kenneth Pimblett, the proprietor, said the shop was a traditional bakery and that it was a matter of chance if the pies were not cooled to room temperature when sold. He said the pies were quite palatable when cold. Alternatively, customers would re-heat them at home.

The pies were baked on the premises, he said, purely for marketing reasons. The baking produced an agreeable smell and atmosphere and demonstrated the pies to be fresh.

A regular client was a Mrs Wood, a Customs officer who lived locally. She saw that at lunchtime there was often a rush of office workers and school children who would buy pies almost as soon as these were removed from the oven, before they had cooled, and often would eat them immediately.

Mrs Fairhurst, cross-examined, said clients specifically asked for hot pies.

The tribunal decided her pies were more palatable when hot, or at least warm, and that some clients liked to eat the pies before these had gone cold.

It decided every pie satisfied the statutory test of being heated to enable it to be consumed hot and it therefore upheld the Customs and Excise case that part of the meat pies should be subject to 15 per cent VAT.

Customs officers in January had analysed the sales pattern on several days between noon and 1 pm, having decided sales at other times should be zero-rated.

On their sample's basis they decided 11.94 per cent of total sales should be liable to VAT. The tribunal upheld this figure and the procedure which produced it.

This is public policy to the second decimal place.

The word 'policy' is part of the everyday language of newspapers and television. Even a casual study of news items with the word 'policy' in them will reveal that the word is being used in different ways, from a broad label such as 'environmental' policy to the consequences of specific actions taken by government. Politicians rarely make these distinctions explicit, but Roy Hattersley, Labour's Shadow Chancellor of the Exchequer, complained that in costing Labour's programme at £24bn the Treasury had a 'habit of assuming that the aim has become a policy and that the policy will be implemented in a single year' (*Financial Times*, 11 March 1986). He was therefore distinguishing three quite different meanings of policy.

Pointing to differences of usage might seem to be just academic nit-picking—of course we all know what public policy is. However, take this comment by a local authority education official:

It might help here to consider the question of what we actually mean by government policy. Is it the manifesto promise? Is it the thrust of policy given vague shape by the rhetoric of campaigning political leaders? Or is it the hard factual stuff of an Act of Parliament?

I confess that I am by no means sure what does constitute government policy, although for the last nine years of my professional life the matter has been of the utmost practical importance. (Turner, 1980.)

If someone actually involved in administering policy does not know what is meant by government policy, what hope is there for outsiders?

A good start is to take a careful look at all the different ways in which the word 'policy' can be used (Hogwood and Gunn, 1984, 13–19). For example, we often find references to social policy, economic policy, foreign policy, or, more narrowly, housing policy, education policy, etc. These are both commonly used and common-sense *labels*, though when we start to analyse them we find it difficult to draw sharp boundaries between them (for example, between industry policy and trade policy and between trade policy and foreign policy). These labels can be used to cover both existing government activities in that sphere and potential innovations or alternatives. Clearly, there are variations in the extent to which the government is already involved in a policy area. Social security is an example of a policy area where the government is already involved in almost every conceivable type of benefit and where policy proposals will inevitably involve replacing or changing existing activities. Leisure and recreation is one field where there is in principle scope for greater government involvement in activities where it has not previously intervened.

We are all familiar, particularly during the party conference season, with expressions such as 'Conservative policy is to promote freedom' or 'Labour policy is to reduce inequality'. This is *policy as aspiration* or *policy as general purpose*. This is a perfectly legitimate everyday use of the word 'policy', but it says nothing about how the desired state of affairs is to be achieved or the purpose fulfilled. This is true also of 'statements of government policy' on occasions such as the Queen's Speech at the beginning of each annual Parliamentary Session. For example, the Queen's Speech at the beginning of the new Conservative government in May 1979 included this passage on Northern Ireland:

In Northern Ireland my Government will strive to restore peace and security and to promote the social and economic welfare of the Province. They will seek an acceptable way of restoring to the people of Northern Ireland more control over their own affairs. (*HC Deb.*, 15 May 1979.)

Put in this way, expressions of purpose may seem very woolly, but the idea of objectives is at the heart of much of the writing on management and policy analysis. Almost by definition, policy is concerned with *purposive* action, that is action which is designed to carry out certain objectives. Of course, the objectives may be unclear, contradictory, or unfulfilled in practice. Different people may have different motives in developing policies. Some motives (such as self-glorification) may be considered disreputable, but the idea of motiveless policies is literally incomprehensible. Public policies in modern Britain are not things that just happen, they are the results of conscious action. This is not to deny the scope for interpreting what might underlie the action, or for unintended outcomes. Further, in a book primarily concerned with descriptive analysis, we should avoid assuming that analysis starting from the definition of objectives is an accurate description of how policies actually evolve. One contradiction which can arise because parties alternate in office or individual parties change their emphasis is that government as the party in office may have a stated purpose and intentions which are substantially different from what the government as the whole set of organizations engaged in delivering public policies is actually doing. The bulk of policy delivery at any given time reflects the political priorities and legislation of previous governments.

We can talk of any political organization, whether interest group, political party, or government itself, having *policy proposals* in the sense of statements of specific actions they would like to see undertaken by government. For example, the 1985 Labour Party Conference passed a resolution calling for the appointment of a minister for conservation responsible for all aspects of environmental policy, including the abolition of hunting with dogs and the establishment of a national environmental protection agency to enforce legislation.

It is common to hear the publication of a White Paper described as an announcement of government policy. However, such *government 'decisions'* may still require to be enacted as law. As both the 1974–9 Labour government with its frequent minority status and even the 1979 Conservative government with its supposedly comfortable majority have found, this cannot always be taken for granted. Even when enacted, such decisions still have to be implemented or enforced, perhaps by bodies other than central government itself. 'Policy' in its broadest sense should be differentiated from a 'decision'; a decision is simply a particular choice among competing alternatives. Although we often speak of a 'decision-making' stage in the policy process, referring to a decision about alternatives made by 'key' decision-makers, important decisions affecting policy are in fact made at all stages. The decision about whether or not to treat an issue seriously in the first place or decisions about how to implement it are often at least as important as any formal decision by, say, the Cabinet.

A policy acquires a different formal status when it is legitimated, for example, by being embodied in an Act of Parliament or statutory instrument to permit or require an activity to take place. Here policy receives *formal authorization*. When an Act of Parliament is passed it is common to hear this referred to as a policy having been carried out or 'implemented'. However, this is very misleading, since all that has happened at this stage is that a bit of paper has been signed. Funds still have to be spent and perhaps staff hired before any of the activities envisaged in the Act can take place. To quote again from the education official referred to earlier:

What then of the final category of government policy—the Act of Parliament? Is not this a clearly defined directive for the administrator? Alas no! To give two examples—freedom of parental choice of schools was enshrined in the 1944 Education Act but in practice it never existed. More recently, access to public buildings for the disabled has been the subject of legislation, but in practice once more little or nothing has been done. (Turner, 1980.)

This is not to argue that the passage of legislation is unimportant— it is an important legitimating stage in the policy process (see 5.9).

For policies to impinge on citizens, they have to be delivered through an organizational structure with staffing and a budget. This leads on to the concept of *policy as a programme*—a defined and relatively specific sphere of government activity involving a particular package of legislation, organization, and resources. Thus we can talk of a school meals programme, which involves a specific piece of legislation, various resources, and the manpower to deliver the programme. Government housing policy (policy as label) can be said to consist of a number of programmes such as the provision of council houses, a housing improvement programme, a mortgage interest subsidy programme, and so on. The British style of legislation and budgeting tends to result in less clearly definable packages than is the case in the United States. Programmes may also become intertwined at the point of delivery. We may want to distinguish between policy as a purpose or objective and alternative programmes which might carry out that objective. For example, a policy of encouraging industry to invest in areas of high unemployment might be pursued through a programme of investment grants or through a programme of tax reliefs.

Ultimately, policy can be seen as what government actually delivers as opposed to promises or has formal authorization for.

Such *outputs* take many forms—the payment of cash benefits, the delivery of goods or services, the enforcement of rules, the invocation of symbols, or the collection of taxes. The form of outputs varies between policy areas. It is sometimes difficult to determine what the final 'output' of government policy is. For example, in education there is a tendency to talk in terms of money, teachers, school buildings. It might be better to call these 'intermediate outputs', since they contribute to the final output of teaching but are not themselves that output. Outputs in practice may not conform to stated intentions; for example, if in practice the government is not taking the necessary steps to ensure access for the disabled this calls into question the extent to which it is meaningful to talk of providing full access for the disabled as being 'policy' when this is not in fact happening.

Another way of looking at policy is in terms of its *outcomes*, that is, in terms of what is actually achieved. The distinction between *outputs* (the activities of government at the point of delivery) and *outcomes* (the impact of those activities) is often slurred over, and is sometimes difficult to make in practice, but it is an important one. Thinking of policy in terms of outcomes may enable us to make some assessment about whether the stated purpose of a policy appears to be what the policy is actually achieving as a result of the way it was designed. Focusing on the impact of policies also serves as a reminder that policy delivery and impact are rarely a matter of a straight-line relationship between a single policy instrument or organization interacting with its environment to produce a clear-cut impact. There are frequently a number of organizations operating in the same policy area. In addition, there may be spillovers from other policy areas which impact on the same targets, thus producing interaction effects. The overall outcome will be the product of the outputs of these organizations and their effect on the environment, which may well depend on the reaction of the citizens at whom they are targeted. This *product* of the impact need not necessarily reflect the sum of the purposes of the organizations concerned or of the original decision-makers. Some aspects of the impact may be entirely unintended; a good example of this is the evolution of the 'poverty trap' in Britain as the result of the separate development of a large number of policy instruments designed to assist the poor and of the personal taxation system.

All policies involve assumptions about what governments can do and what the consequences of these actions will be. These assumptions are rarely spelt out, but *policies imply a theory* or model about what the relevant factors are and how changes in government activity would affect them. If we think of policy in terms of the theory which appears to underlie it, we can see that failure of a policy can arise (1) from the government's failure to carry out in full or in the expected form the activities assumed, or (2) because the activities, even if carried out, fail to have the consequences expected according to the theory, or (3) because there are other influences, perhaps the effects of other government activities, which were not taken into account in the development of policy ideas. Because the implicit policy theories are rarely spelled out, one of our tasks in studying public policy is to try to tease out the theories underlying policies and examine the internal consistency of the resulting model and the apparent validity of its assumptions.

Finally, we can think of *policy as a process* by which proposals are transformed into activities. This way of thinking about policy helps to pull together all the above different ways of looking at policy. One theme is implicit in the title of this book: policy-making is a process which develops over time from the raising of the issue, discussion of it, and subsequent government action or inaction. The process approach emphasizes that policy can be shaped at all stages of the policy process. It focuses on the actual behaviour of organizations rather than simply on what is proposed or intended. Although we are interested in policy proposals, we are also concerned with what governments actually do, rather than only with what governments say they are going to do, or even what is on the statute book. The study of policy is also concerned with what governments do not do—by not taking up an issue or by not following through a decision—as well as with what government spends money on. Policy as inaction is much more difficult to pin down and measure than policy as action (see 2.8).

Studying policy-making by tracking through the ways in which issues are processed provides a markedly different perspective from one which looks at British government through chapters on the formal institutions of government—the government, the civil service, the House of Commons, the House of Lords—or even one which recognizes the importance of other organizations and has a separate chapter on interest groups. This is certainly not to argue that institutions are unimportant; indeed, one of the key elements of a policy approach to studying British government is that policy-making is not just about political actors as individuals but as members of organizations. In this book institutions are mentioned, but in terms of the role which they play at different stages of the policy process. Perhaps the simplest way to describe the concerns of the book is to say that it is concerned with what government does, in terms of what policies it produces and the processes by which those policies are shaped, rather than with how government is elected or how its membership is determined.

1.3 The policy process in the political system

In the last section it was pointed out that one of the ways in which we could think of policy was as a process and that this was worth exploring further because it had advantages in drawing together all the other ways in which the word 'policy' is used and showing the relationship between them. The idea of policy as a process is closely related to the idea of political activity taking place within a political system rather than simply in terms of 'government'. The idea of a political system has increasingly been used since the mid-1960s as a framework for analysing decision-making and policy-making (see e.g. Burch and Wood, 1983).

The main features of the political system model are:

1. The *political system* (which is a broader concept than just the government and the legislature) is embedded in a social and economic *environment* and interacts with it (see Fig. 1.1).
2. The political system receives *inputs* (articulation of demands, resources, supports) from the social and economic environment. Because demands are always larger than available resources, generalized support from citizens for methods of allocating resources to demands is crucial, even if citizens do not agree with many of the specific actions of government.
3. The *decision-making process* within the political system converts these inputs into *outputs* in the form of goods, services, laws, and so on.
4. *Feedback* from the social and economic environment may lead to a further round of inputs.

At this high level of generalization, the systems framework does

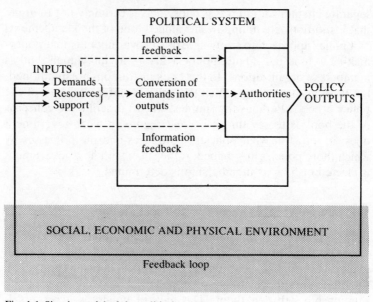

Fig. 1.1 Simple model of the political system
Derived from Easton (1965)

have some value in that it points to *the relationship* between demands, the political system, the outputs of the system, and the impact of these outputs in terms of stabilizing the environment or setting off new demands. It also provides us with a framework in which we can try to understand how changes in the social and economic environment are followed by changes in the outputs of government and in the structure of the political system. The framework also stresses the cyclical nature of much policy-making: policies produce impacts which may in turn set off new demands or stronger or weaker support for government.

However, as an aid to understanding the functions of the state in a country like Britain, the systems model suffers from a number of defects. First, the framework says nothing about *how* inputs are transformed into outputs. It treats the decision-making process as a 'black box'. It tells us nothing about the distribution of power or the substance of policies. The model, as such, does not tell us, for example, whether specific groups suffer because their wants are continually ignored. Secondly, the model operates at too high a level of generality—if we changed the labels in Fig. 1.1 it could be a sausage machine. Burch and Wood (1983) specifically make the analogy to a factory production process. Having stated that the political system maintains its existence by responding to the changes in the environment, it has relatively little to tell us about which changes matter politically and why particular policies are evolved in response to them. Thirdly, the logical ordering of the systems framework might seem to imply that decision-making only follows on and reflects demand articulation. In practice, political demands may be shaped or even created by political leaders (Ham and Hill, 1984, 15). Using the systems framework at this level of generality as a model for describing the British public policy process is a bit like painting by numbers without the numbers.

One way of moving away from the systems model as sausage machine is to develop it in more detail in terms of the *organizations* involved. For example, in looking at education we could fill in the diagram by listing the large number of sources of demands, such as parents, councillors, teachers, MPs, industrialists, and so on. We could list the major departments engaged in the decision-making process, including the Department of Education and Science, the Scottish and Welsh Offices, and, in the mid-1980s, the Manpower Services Commission and the Department of Employment. Education departments in local authorities would have to be included as participants in the decision-making process, rather than simply agents who provide the outputs of the system.

If you attempted to draw in all these organizations and their links, the diagram would very quickly become complex. One feature which would emerge quite quickly would be that organizations can be involved both in delivery and in making demands. For example, education outputs are delivered by teachers, but teachers' unions are directly involved in making demands on the political system, and are also involved in the decision-making process, both through their representation on committees and through more informal mechanisms of consultation. Such a diagram, whether for education or any other policy area, would also reveal that there is a multiplicity of participants even at a single stage. In other words, it is not a matter of demands being channelled through one organization, with that organization only being involved in making demands. Organizations, whether governmental or non-governmental, are typically involved at several stages of the policy process; for example, 'pressure groups' will not just be involved at demand articulation stage. However, developing the systems framework in this way, while leading to a more detailed understanding of a particular policy area, does not enable any general insights or provide a framework for comparing the treatment of different demands or different policy areas.

An alternative (but not incompatible) way of developing the systems model is to break down the process by which inputs are converted into outputs into stages. There are different ways of listing stages, but they all bear some resemblance to Fig. 1.2 (cf. Rose, 1973). The numbers next to each stage refer to the chapters of this book. The use of a policy process framework has both advantages and limitations. Here we are concerned not simply with the intellectual advantages and limitations of the model of the policy process viewed in the abstract, but with how useful it is in studying what British government actually does.

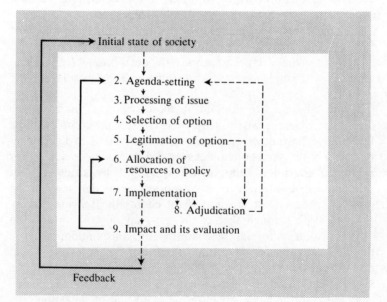

Fig. 1.2 The policy process

First, as with the political system model, the process model has the advantage of showing the interaction between political organizations and the social and economic environment in which they operate. Secondly, an undoubted advantage of the process model is that it is *dynamic*. It does not abstract government activity from the sequence of events nor does it assume that policy is determined at one point in time. This is an improvement on a decision-making framework focusing on a 'policy-making' stage and perhaps on the steps leading up to it. The 'decision-making' focus implies a division between politics and administration which is not appropriate, since politics clearly enters into the implementation stage. In contrast, a process approach stresses that policies are not advocated, adopted, implemented, and evaluated at a single point in time. The process model is concerned with the *consequences* of a policy and not simply with what led to the adoption of the policy. This concern with consequences includes the consequences for future government decisions in the policy area concerned. We may be interested in only part of the process in a particular study, but it always helps to see it in context.

However, in the real world it is not easy to characterize policy in terms of simple cycles of the policy process feeding neatly back into new cycles. The policy process in relation to specific decisions may be truncated and within any policy area at any one time specific issues may be at different stages of the policy process. It may prove difficult to characterize a particular event as unambiguously related to one stage of one cycle in the policy process. Further, a process model provides us with a framework into which we can fit information about influences on a policy and how those influences relate to each other. However, this does not tell us which of the multitude of possible influences are worth examining in the first place. Finally, when viewing the whole range of government activity we have to remember that the bulk of it at any given time is routine, and therefore concerned only with the implementation and impact stages.

Burch and Wood (1983, 15) argue that there are problems with the policy cycle approach which make it unattractive. First, they argue that the emphasis on phases suggests some kind of chronological sequence which is inevitably involved in policy-making. They believe that the process is more fluid than this suggests. However, it is argued here that this implies caution in using a process framework rather than abandoning it. Burch and Wood also argue that:

Perhaps more important, the policy cycle approach is somewhat neutral in its attitude towards the role of government. It does not centre on government but rather on particular policies, so that it does not fully allow for the positive, shaping role of public agencies, which we see as an important characteristic of 'big' government in the modern age.

However, it is surely a virtue rather than a disadvantage that the process framework does not presume in advance that government bodies in the narrow sense have a determining role in shaping public policies. The process approach helps to get the role of government bodies in policy-making in perspective. While 'big' government does imply that government is involved in a broader range of activities, this does not imply that it is necessarily able to engage in a 'positive, shaping role'. Indeed, some commentators have suggested that modern government is *less* able to determine the outcome of public policy because of the way in which it relies on others for its success (see e.g. King, 1976). Burch and Wood take the definitional point that government involvement is by definition necessary for something to constitute a public policy and elevate this to the assumption (which they make explicit) that government plays the central shaping role. It is entirely appropriate to have a central *focus* on government role, providing that this is in some kind of perspective: since the role played by government may vary from policy area to policy area or issue to issue, the policy process can provide a framework for *comparing* the role of government.

1.4 Different perspectives on policy

Fig. 1.3 would suggest that we can identify different levels of generalization about policy, from dealing with an individual policy issue, to all issues in a policy area, to possible generalizations about British public policy as a whole, either in terms of common patterns among issues or in terms of determining priorities among them. This picture has some merit if only to prevent us overgeneralizing from limited information, but, as we shall see, it does imply an over-neat picture of different levels fitting inside each other.

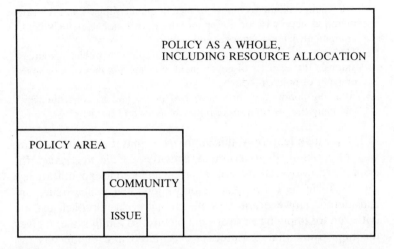

Fig. 1.3 Different levels of generalization about policy

1.4.1 The political system and allocation between policies

At the highest level of aggregation we could use the model of the political system to draw attention to the importance of features of the social and economic environment which appear relevant to policy-making, including economic resources, their growth and distribution, and their association with political demands and resources. The relevant environment would include Britain's position as a medium-sized country with a relatively open economy. Within the political system features of the formal institutions which potentially apply to all issues could be identified, as could mechanisms such as political parties and interest groups and their political support as well as active or passive political support for the political system as a whole.

The level of total resources and their allocation through the political system is one crucial feature of policy which can best be seen from this perspective. Burch and Wood (1983) suggest that a more pertinent alternative than the policy cycle approach outlined in the last section is what they call the 'Policy Approach', implying active government, characterized in terms of three main procedures:

1. *Acquiring resources*: the extraction and gathering in of public resources from the wider political, economic and social systems.

They define public resources to include public support and the raw materials necessary for the operation of government, namely land, equipment, labour, finance, and capital.

2. *Dividing resources*: the division or allocation of public resources amongst the agencies of government in terms of policy programmes or types of policy products.

3. *Applying policy*: the carrying out of policy and its consequences, including the distribution of policy benefits and burdens.

The positive feature of this approach is that it provides a useful way of looking at government activities *in the aggregate*, for example, how overall levels of taxation and public expenditure are set. This can be overlooked if only individual policy issues are considered. However, just as the policy cycle approach can be criticized for implying an over-neat picture, so can this one: it gives the impression that resources are acquired and divided as the result of aggregate sets of decisions. In contrast, the conventional wisdom about how governments make budgets emphasizes the extent to which in any given year changes are marginal and reflect the accumulation of commitments to individual programmes (see chapter 6). Thus, government rarely makes decisions 'in the aggregate' even on budgeting. Issues are *not* processed or considered in the aggregate—though aggregate or cumulative factors may provide the context in which those issues are considered. Taking an aggregate picture does not necessarily describe a process which is itself operating at aggregate level. The policy cycle approach and the Burch and Wood approach should be seen as complementary, rather than rivals. The process approach provides a framework for examining what happens to particular issues. The so-called 'Policy Approach' emphasizes the role of resources and helps to give a perspective on government activity in the aggregate.

1.4.2 Differences between policy areas

What constitutes a policy area is not necessarily self-evident or self-defining. However, in looking at common-sense labels, such as health, defence, agriculture, and so on, we can find differences in characteristics between policy areas and a degree of shared characteristics within them. For example, most health policy issues, whether concerned with hospitals, dental treatment, or pharmacies, have a number of characteristics which they share, including the involvement of professions and quasi-professions and a type of policy output which involves the delivery of goods and services to individual citizens. Similarly, social security involves the provision of cash benefits, whether in respect of children or old-age pensioners. Both health and social security policy differ in turn from defence as a policy area. We would expect that these differences might be reflected in the politics surrounding different policy areas. For example, professional bodies are important in health care but much less significant in social security policy; defence policy is likely to be much more a matter for internal processing by government rather than domestic interest groups.

Though the picture is far from being a neat one, increasingly since the 1950s these broad policy areas have been reflected in the coverage of single, large Whitehall departments. However, as we noted in section 1.2, 'policy as a label' does not necessarily produce exclusive and self-contained areas. An issue might be labelled as a poverty problem or a housing one, a health problem or a social work one. Some policy areas are intrinsically overlapping, such as industrial policy, trade policy, and foreign policy.

In addition to nature of employee, nature of output, and nature of target population, international interpenetration is a factor in variation between policy areas. Two broad forms of international penetration can be identified. First, there is interaction arising from international institutions of which Britain is a member, such as NATO or the European Communities, or through a process of direct governmental bargaining with other governments or foreign bodies. Here the British government is explicitly involved in taking decisions, but not unilaterally. This type of interaction is most obviously relevant to defence and foreign affairs, but applies to an increasingly wide range of domestic policy areas, such as agriculture, particularly through our membership of the European Communities. The second type of interpenetration reflects the varying permeability of domestic policy areas to outside influences which are not the direct result of decisions by the British government in conjunction with other governments. No domestic policy area is totally insulated, but clearly policy areas such as social security and health are much less directly impacted than energy policy, which is affected by international prices and supply of a number of internationally traded fuels.

Fig. 1.4 reflects the fact that government departments vary according to the extent of 'openness' to direct domestic pressures outside government and to the extent of openness to international pressures. Defence policy is *relatively* closed to domestic pressures outside government, but is fundamentally subject to international penetration. For departments with a low degree of international interpenetration the occasional international repercussions of their actions may be neglected (e.g. fees for overseas students), and the international negotiating aspects of their work (outside the European Communities at least) may be mediated through the Foreign Office rather than directly.

1.4.3 'Policy communities' as a focus

It has been suggested that much of the political processing of issues takes place not at the level of policy area or department, but in more delimited 'policy communities' (Richardson and Jordan, 1979; Jordan and Richardson, 1982; Sharpe, 1985). For example, Jordan and Richardson (1982, 94) argue that:

Within the general setting of the departmental sectors, there is a tendency for policy communities to emerge. The policy community in any area is an imprecise structure likely to alter from time to time and from particular issue to issue, yet it is worth identifying as a *community*: in other words, it has continuity, implicit authority structures.

Jordan and Richardson (1982) suggest that policy communities operate at the level or detail covered by an Assistant Secretary or Under-Secretary in the civil service, that is, below the top ranks of Permanent Secretary and Deputy Secretary. Such policy communities may on occasion overlap policy areas or sectors. Membership of policy communities may overlap and there will be many linkages between the various policy communities in each sector.

A crucial feature of the idea of policy communities is that the community consists not simply of civil servants and ministers but of relevant 'recognized' interest groups and of other governmental bodies, both appointed and elected local authorities. Parliament is notably not a member of these communities, in contrast to the

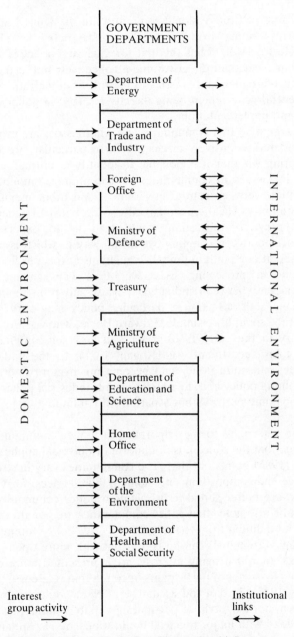

Fig. 1.4 Relative openness to domestic and international influences

central role of Congressional committees in the United States in the corresponding 'iron triangles' or 'issue networks' (Jordan, 1981; Heclo, 1978). Thus the unit for analysing policy is seen as much narrower than the government collectively but at the same time much broader, since it stresses the role of organizations other than central government being directly engaged in policy formulation and implementation.

The argument that communities are where issues are processed is considered extensively in chapter 3. In particular, we will be considering whether it is possible to identify a 'normal' style of processing issues in communities by consultation amounting to negotiation between central government and other members of the community. The discussion of differences between policy areas in the previous subsection would lead us to expect some differences between communities in the way in which issues are processed at one point in time. We might also expect to find some variations in processing style over time between individual ministers and between individual parties and prime ministers. Processing style affecting a particular policy may vary over a longer time span; for example, Edward Boyle, who was Education Secretary in the early 1960s, remarked how self-contained the work of his department was (Kogan, 1971); by the mid-1980s, however, education policy had become much more intertwined with training policy and, to a lesser extent, industrial policy. Such variations may occur within a pattern of continuing or recurring features.

Those who point to the importance of policy communities do not argue that the concept is of uniform or universal applicability. Sharpe (1985) points out that 'The communities vary in strength, influence and composition since some public services, for various reasons, are better suited to attracting a policy community than others'; he also notes that policy communities are not always able to present a united front to the outside world. Policy communities (or 'subgovernments') can be contrasted with more open 'policy networks' in which many interests are represented more evenly than the closed set of participants in communities (Benson, 1982; Rhodes, 1985). Jordan and Richardson (1982), while arguing that there is a 'normal' style of negotiating within communities, note that policies with major financial implications are less suitable for 'in sector' treatment, that some issues such as defence and foreign affairs do not involve much organized group deliberation, that some issues such as some manifesto commitments are regarded as 'non-negotiable', and that Parliament as a whole does play an important role on some moral and constitutional issues. Jordan and Richardson nevertheless stress similarities between the processing of some of these types of issues and processing through communities and regard them as deviations from a norm of negotiation through policy communities.

The relative significance of 'sectorization' at policy area or departmental level and policy communities as a narrower focus is ambiguous in some of the writing on this theme (see Jordan and Richardson, 1982). One possible interpretation is that community is the main focus for consultation between civil servants, interest groups, local authorities, and other government bodies, while department or policy area is the main unit for negotiations *within* central government. Even within one department there may be considerable variation in whether there are clearly separate communities or clearly interacting ones. We can retain the idea of a policy area, where it does not coincide with departmental boundaries, as patterns of overlap and frequent interaction by members of policy communities, as well as point to objective interactions, such as those between schools and universities, and to similarities which make it administratively convenient to group communities together.

The concepts of sectors and communities are helpful in stressing the disaggregated nature of much policy processing but it is important also to stress aggregative aspects—the common social, economic, and political environment, budgeting (chapter 6), and decision-making in the cabinet system (chapter 4). While encouraging us to focus on a set of recurring relationships which cross formal organizational boundaries and even the boundary between governmental and non-governmental bodies, the concept of policy community may imply a degree of containment of issues within limited communities which is greater than that which actually exists. A number of issues will even overlap policy areas, either because there is a wide area of overlap of interest (e.g. trade and foreign policy) or because of what at first sight appear to be fortuitous coincidences or clashes of interest. For example, when the Home Office disclosed at the end of 1985 that it was considering a policy of restricting government contracts to companies which could prove that they employed a representative proportion of black people, the proposal was publicly denounced by an employment minister as contrary to government policy of reducing burdens on business. Where such patterns of overlap recur, a policy community may develop, but unless we are to stretch the concept of policy community to cover everything, there are clearly many issues which cannot be neatly fitted into the concept.

Does this mean that we have to abandon the concepts of policy sectors and policy communities? Far from it; it simply means that we should adopt a more subtle delimitation, recognizing that at the margins there will be overlaps of interest with other policy areas, some recurring, some *ad hoc*, but with a more or less exclusive 'core' set of issues at the centre of the policy space. The extent of overlap or core will vary from policy area to policy area and across time. For 'core' issues we can often identify policy communities of governmental and non-governmental actors, normally involving more than one government organization. Thus, for 'core' issues these policy communities will be more or less exclusively involved in discussing policy changes and implementing them. For peripheral issues, particularly those overlapping with other policy systems, other sets of actors may be involved. Again, there can be conflict, competition, or co-ordination, though for such overlapping issues we would expect there to be a greater tendency to conflict and competition compared to those for 'core' issues.

1.4.4 Issues as a focus

While the idea of policy community may help us to identify recurring patterns, it is important to remember that political issues are the raw material which is being processed and processing style may vary between issues according to type of issue or for *ad hoc* reasons relating to how the issue has arisen and whose interests it affects. Chapter 2 analyses the different types of issues that arise and the different ways in which issues can get on to the political agenda.

Attempting to identify neat self-contained issues each of which are processed through their own policy cycle may present a misleading picture of how issues get shunted aside and tangled up together. The 'garbage can' model draws attention to situations where the raising of an issue provides an opportunity for other problems to be considered. In other words, at any given time there will be a number of different issues floating around, some problems looking for a solution, some pet solutions looking for a problem. The raising of a new issue may result in some of these other issues being dumped in the same decisional 'garbage can' because some angle or relationship with the new issue is perceived:

Suppose we view a choice activity as a garbage can into which various problems and solutions are dumped by participants. The mix of garbage in a single can depend partly on the labels attached to the alternative cans; but it also depends on what garbage is being produced at the moment, on the mix of cans available, and on the speed with which garbage is collected and removed from the scene. (March and Olsen, 1976, 26.)

This model suggests that issues are often not processed in a neat way: they attach themselves or have attached to them a whole set of other issues whose relationships to the immediate issue are not always obvious. Thus the 'garbage can' model, where it is applicable, casts doubt on the neatness of the idea of issue, of the policy process, and of policy community.

The processing of policy issues cannot be abstracted from their timing. To focus on the policy process as a policy cycle rather than as a one-off linear policy sequence emphasizes this. There can be a change of definition or perception of a policy problem across a series of cycles, whether from previous cycles which were truncated because the issue never got to the stage of leading to an implemented policy or as a consequence of the effects of a fully implemented policy.

Past policies have implications both for the process by which new policies might come into being and for the substance of future policy because of the inheritance of past policies (Hogwood and Peters, 1983; Wildavsky, 1980, ch. 3). Previous policies result in pre-existing clientele and service providers and their political spokesmen. To a considerable extent, the policy community and the policy sector in many policy areas will be the creation of previous policies. Both these process consequences and the features of the past policies themselves may constrain would-be policy reformers from the range of options which is taken seriously—policy advocates are not starting with a clean policy slate. This is particularly the case with policies with 'stock' effects, for example, in housing, where the physical fabric and the patterns of tenure reflect the accumulated effects of past policies. Even if a party did not want to introduce mortgage tax relief in its present form and scale, the existence of a large section of the population which currently benefits from it may mean that the party is reluctant to advocate its abolition, as is the Labour Party. Thus, an issue involving the reversal of an already existing policy is not symmetrical to the issue which involved establishing that policy in the first place.

Issues, then, cannot be viewed simply as free-standing, one-off events. The remaining chapters of this book, in looking at the various stages of the policy process as set out in Fig. 1.2, use the process approach as a framework for examining what are often recurring patterns and influences at aggregate level rather than implying that policy-making is as neat as the figure taken on its own would imply.

Chapter 2

How Issues Emerge (or do not)

2.1 Issues in political debate

This chapter explores the concept of political issues and the implications of differences between types of issues for the nature of political debate before going on to examine why some issues do appear to be taken seriously by policy-makers while others are not.

One of the problems in trying to move from a casual discussion of day-to-day political debate to a more analytical approach is the bewildering array of terms which crop up to describe political debate. A number of these terms are listed below, together with some of their implications, but many of them are used in media coverage or general conversation in a fairly loose way—or one term may deliberately be used rather than another because of its pejorative implications:

issue: used here as a generic term; implies a reasonably structured political debate.

problem: something calling for attention, which may or may not have led to debate about options.

question: similar to problem, but may imply greater lack of agreement about what ought to be done.

scandal: implies dereliction of duty by government, either in terms of policy (e.g. treatment of the mentally ill) or personal conduct (e.g. Watergate, Poulson). The implication is that remedial action should be taken. Clearly, much more value-laden than 'issue'.

controversy, conflict, and debate: terms which imply a structuring of the issue into alternative options and strong disagreement about appropriate course of action.

It is not worth dwelling on the subtleties of differences of meaning among these various terms because of the loose way they are used. However, it is an interesting exercise to collect uses of such terms in statements by politicians and interest groups and in newspaper coverage, and to analyse these in terms of the extent to which value-laden words are used in describing the nature of the issue in a conscious or unconscious attempt to shape the way it will be considered and the extent to which the issue is already structured in terms of the options available and agreement or disagreement about what the government ought to do.

Some political issues arise as matters requiring immediate public attention. Examples here would include the nineteen people who died of food poisoning at the Stanley Royd psychiatric hospital in Wakefield, West Yorkshire, in summer 1984, which resulted in a government inquiry, and a request from the Under-Secretary of State for Health to the Blackpool Wyre and Fylde Health Authority to inquire into allegations about standards of care at the Inglehurst Nursing Home in Blackpool after former staff members complained in summer 1984 about squalor and neglect of patients.

An all too frequently recurring issue of an international kind is a famine due to a specific drought or war or natural disaster; in the autumn of 1984 there was considerable concern about famine conditions in Ethiopia. This short-term concern about the immediate problem can be contrasted with the long-term issue of poverty and underdevelopment from which many of the countries affected suffer.

Other issues reflect longer-term social concerns, often institutionalized in the form of lobbies, for example, for the disabled or the homeless. Immediate issues may reflect or lead to longer-term ones: for example, child deaths leading to review of appropriate conduct for social workers; cases of foetuses supposedly born alive helping to maintain the longer-term issue of abortion law. Another example is the way in which the Confederation of Health Service Employees (COHSE) attempted to link the deaths at the Stanley Royd hospital mentioned above to 'cuts' in staff and equipment in the National Health Service. Moon and Richardson (1984b) describe how groups whose primary existence had nothing to do with unemployment as such have tried to 'piggy-back' on the unemployment issue in an attempt to give added impetus to their own issues, including energy conservation and Sunday trading.

Another distinction is between 'one-off' and 'recurring' issues. One-off issues are those which arise once and, either because they are dealt with by government or interest is lost in them, no longer receive public attention, for example, whether or not to have a decimal currency. Recurring issues reflect either fluctuations in public (which may be a limited public) interest, for example, poverty, prosecution of shoplifters; or fluctuations in the circumstances giving rise to the problem, for example, accelerating inflation, snow on roads, the third London airport, famines; or a mixture of fluctuations in the scale of the problem and fluctuations in public concern, such as the problems of the 'inner city' (see also 2.5).

2.2 Direct and indirect conflict over issues

While it is useful in trying to understand politics to tease out some analytically useful distinctions about issues, in practice it is often unclear what exactly the issue or problem being talked about is. Similarly, what to one set of participants in a public debate is a matter of pragmatic decision-making on a specific issue may be elevated by others into a great issue of principle, for example, banning dogs from public parks in Burnley.

In principle, we can, however, draw a distinction between direct and indirect conflict over issues. *Direct opposition* is characterized by two or more groups or individuals holding opposite or incompatible positions about the same issue; for example, the Labour party arguing for greater nationalization, while the Conservative government is selling off existing nationalized industries. Such issues are relatively simple and often have a great deal of political drama and rhetoric surrounding them. However, more complex but equally important are issues where *indirect opposition* occurs when the demands by one group can only be satisfied at the expense of the satisfaction of the demands of another group. For example, demands for greater exploitation of energy resources might only be possible at the expense of demands for greater protection of the environment. Issues are always competing with each other for attention and for the resources to enable the demand associated with them to be carried out (see 2.4 and chapter 6 on allocating resources to policies), and in that sense all political demands are in indirect opposition.

While most political issues are debated in terms of specific courses of action which it is urged the government should or should not take, underpinning these and often appearing in the political rhetoric is an appeal to particular values—such as freedom, equality, the importance of governments taking decisions according to proper procedures—as being the ones which ought to determine the outcome of the issue.

Again, we can, at least in principle, separate disagreements about the interpretation of the *same* value and disagreements about the priority to be accorded to different values. For example, freedom is a value which might be appealed to by both sides in an argument. Airlines might argue for their freedom of the skies, but people living near airports might appeal to their freedom to live in peace and quiet. In other cases, such as equality *relative* to freedom, to earn or own what you want may be accorded different relative priority by different groups. Similarly, the concept of fairness for all may be put forward as a justification for bans on discrimination against coloured people or women, but will be opposed by those who argue that the most important value is freedom for individuals to associate with whoever they wish.

Thus, even though there may be general agreement about the desirability of values such as order, freedom, equality, and justice, they:

do not provide clear guidelines that can easily be applied to resolve public policy issues. Rather, they as frequently help to increase the intensity of disagreement among groups involved in those issues as they do to reach an acceptable position. (Coplin and O'Leary, 1978, 15.)

The term issue has been confined here to circumstances where there is disagreement about the desirability of a state of affairs. If there is total agreement about a matter then there is no political issue. Those who have studied political behaviour may, however, have come across the concept of 'valence issues' as used by Butler and Stokes (1969). In contrast to *position* issues like nationalization where there are disagreements, they mean by *valence issues* ones where there is a virtual consensus in the electorate, and indeed among the parties as well. For example:

there is no body of opinion in the country that favours economic distress, and thereby cancels some of the votes of those who want better times; the whole weight of opinion lies on the side of prosperity and growth . . . parties attempt to associate themselves in the public's mind with conditions, such as good times, which are universally favoured, and to disassociate themselves from conditions, such as economic distress, which are universally deplored. (Butler and Stokes, 1969, 236.)

In other words, valence issues are what Americans would call 'motherhood and apple pie' issues—everyone is in favour of them.

Such matters only become issues in the sense used here if disagreement about them arises in terms of who is most suited to pursue them or perceived trade-offs between valence issues. For example, inflation becomes a political issue not because one party favours it and the other does not, but because there are disagreements about what means can or should be used to secure the agreed aim of reduced inflation, and also disagreement about which party is best fitted to secure this end.

Similarly, there is consensus about the desirability of both low inflation and unemployment, but there may be disagreement about any perceived *trade-off* between them. For example, a social survey conducted in 1983 showed that when asked 'If the government had to choose between keeping down inflation or keeping down unemployment, to which do you think it should give the highest priority?', 69 per cent answered unemployment and 27 per cent answered inflation (Harrison, 1984, 60). Even among Conservative identifiers the proportion was 52 per cent answering unemployment and 44 per cent inflation. However, among strong Conservative party supporters the proportion was 45 per cent answering unemployment and 50 per cent answering inflation. For its part, the Conservative government continued to declare that its attempt to reduce inflation had priority, though in the autumn of 1984 it voiced increased concern about unemployment.

There is also the possibility of disagreement about the trade-off *over time* in the treatment of a particular issue—for example, the Conservative government is willing to tolerate high levels of unemployment now, even though it is seen as the most important political issue, in the hope that this will lead to lower levels in the future, though it has developed special policies to meet the accusation that nothing was being done about unemployment (Richardson and Moon, 1984).

2.3 Issues of self-interest and societal values

Continuing on this theme of exploring analytically useful classifications which are sometimes difficult to observe in practice, we can distinguish between issues of self-interest and those concerned with more general values about how society should work. Issues of self-interest are clearly those where individuals or groups directly affected attempt to secure policy decisions favourable to their interests, whether financial or otherwise. Business lobbying for a special reduced interest rate clearly falls into this category, as do students campaigning for higher grants. At the other extreme are issues which are not immediately related to the interests of a specific group but are concerned with more general values about society such as freedom, equality, the importance of proper procedures for deciding issues. In practice, of course, these broader values are often invoked to try to enlist the support of others not directly affected by self-interest, whether or not the groups involved actually feel such values are at stake (Coplin and O'Leary, 1978, 13). An example of a group directly affected which is trying to appeal to broader values are lecturers and students campaigning against cuts in higher education.

2.4 Classifying the nature of issues

This section offers a classification which summarizes the ways in which issues differ in the range of options available to the government, the scope available for bargaining between interested parties, and the possible outcomes for those who are involved in arguing about the issues (see Table 2.1). It should be stressed that which category an issue falls into will in part be subjective; for example, whether or not putting VAT on books is seen as an issue of principle or of redistribution, whether an issue is seen as a zero sum or positive sum issue. This perception will also depend on the breadth of perspective in considering an issue: are we talking about closing a ward in a hospital or the future of the National Health Service? Are we talking about dividing up a larger public expenditure cake or also about the increases in taxation which may be necessary to finance it? The last example in particular emphasizes that the nature of an issue can be transformed if it is broken into a chain of separate decisions rather than a global one.

The subjective element in defining issues raises the possibility that different participants may differ about the nature of the issue they are debating. Nevertheless, the classification does help to relate the characteristics of issues to features of the politics of the process by which their resolution will be attempted and to the set of likely outcomes for the participants.

Table 2.1 Types of issues

	Principle	Lumpy	Cuts/ Redistribution	Increases
Range of options open to government	Yes/No	Location	Finely divisible but constrained	Finely divisible
Scope for bargaining	Minimal	Minimal (except for log-rolling)	Bargaining about relative cuts (negative or zero sum)	Bargaining about relative growth (positive sum)
Outcome for participants	Win or lose	Win or lose	Differential misery	Differential benefits

All-or-nothing issues (issues of principle)

Many constitutional, religious, or moral issues are of this nature. In its crudest form there are only two alternatives available: Northern Ireland is either part of the Republic of Ireland or it is not; abortion is either legal or it is not. Clearly the scope for bargaining and compromise in such issues is limited, which is why such issues are often those that recur most frequently in British politics, are the most heated, and are those which the British government seems least capable of resolving. Some commentators have argued that the reason why the British government has failed to come up with a satisfactory solution in Northern Ireland is that there is *no* solution which would please both main groups in the province in the long term.

Obviously, the extent to which something is an all-or-nothing issues is partly a matter of individual attitudes: some people may find the idea of abortion distasteful but be prepared to accept its legalization in certain circumstances and subject to certain safeguards. For others, however, it is an all-or-nothing issue— either you win the issue completely or you lose completely. The strong inclination to bargain on issues came into evidence in the debate on a private members' bill on abortion in 1975.

The greater the number of all-or-nothing issues, the greater the strain on the political system and the greater its need for additional supports (see the discussion on the role of 'supports' in the political system in 1.3). Such issues may also cause strains within political parties: it is interesting to note that many of the occasions when party discipline has been suspended and a free vote allowed have been all-or-nothing issues: either moral ones, such as the legalization of homosexuality and abortion, or 'either/or' political ones, such as whether we should stay in the Common Market, whether or not to vote 'yes' in the devolution referendum.

Lumpy goods

This is a type of issue which is similar to all-or-nothing issues in that the output cannot readily be subdivided and shared, but it is different in that it is to do with the distribution of assets rather than moral or constitutional issues. A lumpy good is something like an airport, power station, or steelworks which cannot readily be shared out and distributed evenly. Thus in competing for such goods (or campaigning to avoid them), the stakes are high. A government may occasionally try to resolve an issue by subdividing a lumpy good, leading to suboptimal results. For example, in 1958 the Conservative government announced the construction not of one large fully-continuous steel plant but of two smaller 'semi-continuous' mills at Llanwern in South Wales and at Ravenscraig in Scotland. Similarly, the 1964–9 Labour government approved the construction of three aluminium smelters, one in Wales, one in Scotland, and one in the north of England (see Dell, 1973, 109–21). The closure or threatened closure of the plants in Scotland have subsequently caused political headaches for government. Although an individual lumpy good cannot readily be shared out, *log-rolling* can lead to deals being made about the distribution of a collection of lumpy goods, such as the designation of enterprise zones or freeports.

Wherever possible, some political entrepreneur will seek to turn both all-or-nothing issues and lumpy goods into bargaining issues.

Zero or negative sum issues

Here we are concerned with distribution within a fixed or reducing total of resources *relative to commitments*. What is at stake are resources for different purposes. This can involve expenditure allocations, changes in taxation, or changes in the balance between taxation and expenditure. We are assuming that there is considerable scope for bargaining about the exact size of each share (that is, what is at stake are not lumpy goods). However, because of the assumption about a fixed or declining ceiling, an increase in allocation to one purpose can only be obtained at the price of a reduction for another. Compromise is possible, and, indeed, necessary, but the bargaining is likely to be fierce, since each group will be attempting to maintain at least its existing position. It should be emphasized that we are talking about constraints on resources relative to commitments—the amount of resources available may actually be increasing, but if an increasing amount is committed, say by automatic welfare benefits, then the bargainable amount may effectively be reduced. This constitutes a description of public expenditure decision-making at both central and local levels since the mid-1970s. Political systems are poor at the explicit allocation of losses.

Positive sum issues

Again we are concerned with allocation between competing purposes or groups. Now, however, there is the possibility of some groups increasing their total without other groups suffering, or even of increases all round. Clearly, it is easier to bargain in situations when what is at stake are variations in growth rates rather than the size of cuts. This described the way public expenditure decisions were often made until the late 1960s. There are also recorded cases of a previously agreed ceiling being raised by the Cabinet to accommodate otherwise irreconcilable claims. However, nostalgia for the 'politics of a golden age' is not sufficient to secure the conditions for its operation.

2.5 What are policy agendas?

The traditional approach to studying British politics not only neglected what happened to decisions after they were made, but also tended to take for granted the issues on which decisions were made. Yet clearly issues or potential issues vary considerably in the extent to which government explicitly takes a decision on them, even if that decision is to do nothing. Accordingly, it is important to study this first important hurdle in the process of transforming ideas or demands into government action.

Here the concept of a 'policy agenda' can be useful. Definitions of what constitutes the 'policy agenda' vary: for our purposes, the agenda can be defined as those demands made upon government to which policy-makers choose or feel obliged to pay serious attention. This definition of the policy agenda is accordingly a narrower concept than all demands made upon government, but a wider one than the issues on which governments actually act in terms of passing laws or spending money; the consequence of giving attention to an issue may simply be to decide to do nothing or to postpone taking action.

'Policy agendas' are abstract concepts; there are no generally agreed lists which we can look up to see what is on a particular policy agenda at any given time. Yet we can get some idea of the political salience of issues by examining party manifestos, Queen's Speeches, and media coverage of issues. Although abstract, the concept of policy agendas is a useful one because it focuses on why some issues are given serious attention and others are not and why, having been given such attention, they are acted on in a different way:

Thousands of demands are made on government each year, but only a small proportion of these demands are taken on board by the political system and *possibly* acted on. Most are stillborn or suffer a premature death. (Richardson and Jordan, 1979.)

A distinction can be made between 'systemic' policy agendas and 'institutional' policy agendas (see Cobb and Elder, 1972). *Systemic policy agendas* consist of all the issues which are generally perceived in a particular policy community as deserving public attention and involve matters which are within the jurisdictions of government institutions or are appropriate for them to take decisions on. There will be as many systemic agendas as there are 'political systems' or 'subsystems'. Thus one can point to a British policy agenda, a Scottish policy agenda, and perhaps a West-Central Scotland policy agenda—unemployment, vandalism, housing, etc. These systemic policy agendas are essentially discussion agendas.

Institutional agendas, on the other hand, are composed of those problems to which public officials and politicians in specific government bodies give attention. Thus an issue in West-Central Scotland, such as a possible closure of the Ravenscraig steel plant, may be on the policy agenda of the regional council, the district councils, various Scottish-level bodies, Whitehall departments, or combinations of these. Thus if those raising an issue are concerned with potential action rather than simply general discussion, they must ensure that the problem gets on the relevant institutional agendas and not simply the systemic agenda.

Agendas can be divided into 'recurring' and 'new' items. *Recurring* items are those which appear regularly on policy agendas, such as public expenditure allocations, increases of nominal tax allowances, and social security benefits. Some items may appear on a *cyclical* basis rather than an annual basis: statutory or quasi-statutory incomes policies, 'the urban problem', the control of public expenditure. This reflects the cyclical nature of some of the problems or cycles of interest in persistent problems (see 2.1 above).

New items arise from crises, new situations, or situations newly perceived. For example, the 'energy crisis' of 1973–4 had elements of all these. Alternatively, a new item may emerge more gradually, as with concern for the 'environment' (see Brookes *et al.*, 1976; Solesbury, 1976; Sandbach, 1980). New items either disappear from the policy agenda or become recurring items. The items may disappear because they are shelved when political demands evaporate after a crisis passes, because of boredom with repeated raising of the issue, or because government action to deal with the issue meets the demands. New items may become recurrent items because government response is inadequate, because the situation continuously alters, or because the issue becomes *institutionalized* and therefore is continuously on the agenda of the service-providing agency and recurs as a budget item.

The number of genuinely new agenda items in Western societies is decreasing and this trend is likely to continue (Hogwood and Peters, 1983). In other words, policy agendas increasingly consist of the same items coming up again or of items concerned with the effects of existing policies. Three reasons for this can be suggested:

1. There are relatively few areas in which the government does not now have some involvement.
2. Existing policy itself leads to issues.
3. The pressure of commitments or resources means that new demands which require expenditure will be less likely to get serious attention.

It would be dangerous to allow the concept of an 'agenda item' to make us think that issues come neatly packaged, occur once, and then either are or are not placed on a policy agenda. In fact, issues may be intertwined with each other or may be transformed over the years. For example, previously separate issues affecting landscape, roads, and pollution are now much more likely to be perceived as being interrelated under the general heading of 'the environment' (Brookes *et al.*, 1976). Issues with contrasting implications may also become intertwined, such as the tension between energy demands and environmental considerations. An item may be submerged or achieve little priority until a crisis enables it to achieve prominence. An item may disappear only to reappear later in a different guise. Items which are solutions to possible problems or vice versa may have to wait until the relevant solution or problem (or one to which they can attach themselves) emerges before they receive serious attention. So, we are rarely talking about an issue suddenly emerging and immediately getting on a policy agenda through a single route.

2.6 How issues get on policy agendas

Issues can get on policy agendas in a variety of ways, and these vary in the degree of initiative by the policy-makers or the extent to which they are merely in response to events or pressures. As well as affecting whether or not an issue gets placed on the agenda at all, these routes can affect the priority given to an issue by policy-makers and therefore the attention and resources devoted to it. It is important to remember that politicians' time is limited and the attention span of the media is often short, so issues are continually competing with each other and with new issues for attention.

Clearly the various routes listed below are not mutually exclusive. Indeed, when the initiative comes from outside a government department, an issue may require to arrive through more than one route before a decision-maker takes the issue seriously. It is important to pay attention to who sponsor issues as well as the channels by which they arrive on the agenda. The question of why some issues are given serious attention by decision-makers and others are not is one of the central points of contention in the literature on community power, which will be touched on in 2.8.

A *crisis* may result in attention suddenly being devoted to an issue, including bringing an issue off the 'back-burner' into the forefront of public attention. An example of this would be the poisonous wastes issue in Britain, which had been under government examination off and on since the early 1960s, but led to legislation only in 1972 following the discovery of cyanide waste in a derelict brickyard used by children as a playground (Kimber *et al.*, 1974). Timing and recurrability of crises are important. The Bradford fire disaster in 1985, coinciding with incidents of football hooliganism in Britain and by British fans at the Hysel stadium disaster in Belgium led to an upsurge in political interest, including the involvement of the prime minister.

Political leaders and parties may themselves take the initiative in placing an item on the policy agenda. For example, Robinson and Sandford (1983, 220) found that political parties were by far the most important source for placing proposals for new taxes on the political agenda (see also 6.3). When a party comes into office, the relevant sections of the party manifesto move from the systemic agenda firmly on to the departmental agenda. In party terms this is most likely to be significant at an election when the party achieves office after being in opposition. At elections when the party is in power, the government's agenda will at least in part dictate the contents of the party's manifesto, rather than simply vice versa (see Rose, 1984, 57–60). At the time of a general election, civil servants will prepare two (and in future perhaps more!) sets of briefings for ministers after the election. However, manifesto commitments account for only a proportion of the government's agenda. Using one partial indicator of the government's agenda, Rose (1984, 70) found that only around 10 per cent of legislation came from manifesto initiatives (see Table 2.2). The lack of a reliable parliamentary majority did not appear to affect this

Table 2.2 Sources of government legislative initiatives (%)

Source of initiative	Conservative 1970–4	Labour 1974–9
Ongoing Whitehall events	81	75
Reaction to events	11	11
Manifesto initiative	8	13

Source: Rose (1984, 70) Table 4.5.

proportion adversely, with the Labour government of 1974–9 having a substantially higher proportion of manifesto initiatives than the Conservative government of 1970–4.

These figures should be treated with some caution as an indicator of the overall role of manifestos, since some manifesto proposals may be pursued by non-legislative means (such as circular 10/65 on comprehensive education issued by the Labour government in 1965) or, as Rose points out, through a reallocation of public expenditure priorities. Further, Rose's analysis refers only to specific identifiable proposals in the manifesto, and the broader framework of the manifesto stance and the surrounding debate at the time of the general election may affect the other sources of initiative. First, civil servants and interest groups may only press suggestions under 'ongoing Whitehall initiatives' which they think would fit in with or at least not contradict the stances taken in the party manifesto. Secondly, the content of the legislation arising from the Whitehall process or reaction to events may be affected by the party's stance.

Rose points out that only 16 per cent of initiatives arising from the 'ongoing Whitehall process' led to divisions by the opposition at second or third reading under the 1970–4 Conservative government, and only 15 per cent under the 1974–9 Labour government; there were divisions on only 21 per cent of legislation arising from reaction to events under both governments. The symbolic rather than substantive nature of such divisions when the government has an overall majority does make the significance of these figures difficult to interpret, but they do indicate that the broad party shaping of the agenda of government issues and how these issues are processed is confined to a minority of issues.

There are differences between policy areas in the extent to which items are placed on the agenda by politicians; Edward Boyle, a former Conservative education minister, stated that overwhelmingly the biggest number of major issues originated from the 'education world', that is, those working in or administering education, rather than party, Cabinet, prime minister, or MPs, but that education was different from some other subjects in this (Kogan, 1971, 89).

Individual ministers can also play a role in setting and maintaining the agendas of their departments. Although ministers cannot hope to take the initiative across the whole range of a department's functions, they can ensure that one or two key issues are raised or, once raised, kept to the forefront of their department's attention. One of the difficulties facing individual ministers in trying to redirect the agenda of their department is that they are likely to be reshuffled within a period of a few years. Civil servants recognize that the personalities of individual ministers can make a difference. For example, in the briefings, already referred to, prepared at the time of general elections, there may be not just one set of briefings based on the assumption that the existing government might be returned, but one based on the assumption that the existing minister would stay in post and one on the assumption that another minister from the same party might be appointed.

Agenda-setting is also one of the few political activities where individual back-benchers may play a crucial role. An example here would be the private members' bill introduced by Austin Mitchell MP in 1983 to scrap the solicitors' monopoly on conveyancing; this received overwhelming support for its second reading in the House of Commons. The bill was withdrawn when the government itself gave an undertaking to bring in legislation to end the monopoly. Similarly, the decision in 1963 by John Stonehouse MP to introduce a private member's bill on the abolition of Retail Price Maintenance led to the government giving the issue serious attention, leading to the adoption of the proposal (Bruce-Gardyne and Lawson, 1976).

Non-elected public officials may take the initiative in raising an issue. Because of the myth of ministerial responsibility we rarely know the details of such cases, but one well-documented case is the way in which Jack Beddoe, an Under-Secretary at the Ministry of Housing and Local Government, ensured that water reorganization was firmly placed on the policy agenda (see Jordan, Richardson, and Kimber, 1977; see for other examples Richardson and Jordan, 1979, 93–6). More generally, each department has a 'departmental agenda' of issues which it would like taken up.

One of the major roles of *interest groups* is to attempt to get issues affecting their members on the policy agenda. Another is to react to issues raised by others which affect their members. Indeed some pressure groups, for example on the issue of membership of the European Communities, were set up, both for and against, in reaction to the issue being raised. The term 'pressure group' might

seem to imply that the role of groups is largely to make demands
on the political system. In other words, that they are concerned
largely with the initial stages of the policy process. This would be a
misleading impression, since an active interest group will seek to
be actively involved at all stages of the policy process. Even in the
initial stages, it may be misleading to talk in terms of pressure or
demands. The initiative for a new policy may come from
government and the group invited to comment on it. The
government may even invite groups to make demands. For
example, the Sector Working Parties under the 1974–9 Labour
government's 'industrial strategy' included industrial and union
representatives, and they were to examine their industry and
identify action to be taken by firms and by government. In such
cases, the idea of groups having to force issues to the attention of
government is inappropriate. In other cases, of course, particularly
where demands are unusual or non-routine, this problem of
attracting serious government attention may be the first hurdle.
The chances of a group's request being taken seriously depend on
the extent to which it is regarded by the government as a
'legitimate' group, and this will also be important at the later
stages of processing of the issue (the importance of 'legitimacy' is
considered in 3.3).

A highly important and growing feature of the interest group
scene has been the organization of state employees involved in the
delivery of public policy into unions or professional bodies which
not only seek to carry out collective bargaining on behalf of their
members, but seek to influence the direction of public policy,
including the one they are paid to deliver. For example, under the
1974–9 Labour government the Confederation of Health Service
Employees (COHSE) agitated for the phasing out of private pay
beds in National Health Service hospitals.

Various forms of *protest activity* may also serve to highlight
problems, and are likely to be used by groups and individuals not
institutionalized into the Whitehall interest group bargaining
communities. In the early 1980s largely peaceful protests about
nuclear power suceeded in placing the issue on the systemic
agenda, and protest about nuclear arms succeeded in placing the
issue of unilateral disarmament on the systemic agenda and that of
the Labour Party after a gap of over a decade. In neither case is
there much indication that protest has succeeded in getting the

Conservative government to alter its views, though it now takes more seriously the issues as perceived by the protestors. Leaving aside outright terrorism of the type used by the IRA and INLA to attempt to highlight the issue of British withdrawal from Northern Ireland, various forms of criminal activity may be used by protestors. For example, the Animal Liberation Front has carried out raids on laboratories where animals are used in experiments. Protest activity may lack a clear focus: the urban riots of 1981 and 1985 in Britain were accompanied by criticisms of policing, racialism, unemployment, housing, and leisure facilities.

The attention given by *press and television* to which 'facts' they look at and how they present them obviously affects which issues get on the policy agenda. Investigative journalism also plays a part, as in the campaign by the *Sunday Times* on compensation for children crippled at birth because their mothers had taken the drug thalidomide during pregnancy. Because of its large audiences and visual impact, television is a particlarly effective medium: the then prime minister, James Callaghan, is reputed to have been stimulated into an interest in possible government roles in promoting microtechnology after seeing a BBC *Horizon* programme. The famine in Ethiopia only became a political issue in late 1984 after a television news item showed pictures of some of the victims, though the problem had already been known to government. However, television is not necessarily the best system for 'early warning indicators' of possible problems or opportunities (Weiner, 1976).

From the perspective of individual government organizations, much of their institutional agenda will be determined by *intergovernmental* agenda-setting by which one government body raises an issue for another government body (for example, circulars from central government departments to local authorities, planning applications from the Atomic Energy Authority to drill test bores for a feasibility study on atomic waste disposal). In turn central government may consider an issue because it has been raised by local authority associations.

As we shall see in chapter 8, an increasingly important source of issues which the government has to deal with are the *courts*, both British and European.

International emulation may lead to an issue being taken up in another country, either to avoid a similar disaster, for example, the Three-Mile Island incident, the Bhopal disaster, or to copy policies which are considered desirable—historically this was true of some Welfare State policies. In the 1980s privatization and deregulation were issues which the British government was involved both in importing and exporting.

A crisis, then, is only one of a number of ways in which an issue gets on to policy agendas. It is the route which perhaps receives the most public attention, but a whole range of often specialized issues are constantly being raised in a less public manner.

2.7 Factors influencing whether an issue gets on the agenda

Given that these are the major routes by which issues are raised, it is clear that some issues (and some ways in which issues are 'packaged' in an attempt to receive attention) are more likely to be successful in getting on the policy agenda than others. Exploitation of these characteristics may assist 'outsider' groups or those on the threshold of recognition by government to get serious attention for their cause. A number of factors which seem to affect the chance of an issue getting on the political agenda are considered in this section.

Whether issues have what Solesbury (1976) calls *particularity*, in other words that they can be clearly exemplified by particular occurrences or events, can be crucial in triggering political interest. Thus where there is a widespread actual or potential problem, it may be too abstract or hypothetical until attention focuses on particular examples or incidents; for example, the Torrey Canyon (marine pollution), the Poulson trial (public corruption), and the example of poisonous wastes disposal mentioned earlier. Media-related events such as the publication of reports can be contrived, but an even bigger impact can be made if, say, the relevant interest group guides the media to individuals epitomizing the issue they are campaigning about (e.g. child poverty, damp housing). Symbolic events, such as the dumping of non-returnable bottles on the manufacturer's doorstep by Friends of the Earth, can also be contrived. Given the importance of television, issues which can be presented in a highly visible form (e.g. oil on the beaches, petrol bombs in the streets) are likely to make a large impact.

Clearly, an issue with which a large proportion of the population can *identify* (mortgage interest rates, old-age pensions) is likely to be picked up quickly and treated seriously by government departments responsible. Alternatively, issues which have considerable *human interest* or other form of appeal are likely to receive attention even from those not directly affected (e.g. cruelty to children or animals).

If an issue is to be treated seriously or even discussed at all, it must have basic *legitimacy*, that is be generally recognized as an appropriate topic for action (or in some cases cessation of action) by government. Legitimacy will depend in part on the source of the demand as well as its content.

The extent to which an issue can be *politicized*, for example, along party political lines or by association with powerful groups like trade unions, will clearly assist it in achieving media coverage. However, this may only be sufficient for the issue to be present on the systemic agenda, and may not ensure that it is taken seriously by a government ideologically opposed to the way in which the issue has been posed.

Finally, some issues receive attention because they are *'fashionable'*, receiving a lot of concentrated discussion and attention, before perhaps fading away. 'Microelectronics' is an issue which is currently not merely important but also 'fashionable'. 'Inner city' policy has gone through cycles of interest which are only weakly related to objective indicators of the state of the inner cities. There can be a 'snowballing' effect whereby an issue receives greater attention as one actor reacts, positively or negatively, to the agenda-setting initiative of another.

2.8 Why some issues do not get on agendas

Just as interesting as why some issues do get on the policy agenda is why some do not. Here we need to distinguish between issues which are the subject of open debate and those which are on institutional agendas. Because of the relatively closed nature of the policy process in British central government it is possible for there to be little public debate but for the issue to be getting serious attention in private from decision-makers; this was true of nuclear power policy until the late 1970s, when the debate began to go public.

There may be a number of reasons why some issues do not get on the agenda, why once they get there they receive relatively low priority, or why they get on the policy agenda in a way perverse to the intention of the group campaigning for change. Examples of 'perverse' agenda-setting include the campaign in the late 1970s by the Paedophile Information Exchange to reduce the current age of consent, which was followed by public outcry and police investigations into members of the group. Another example is the perception of the problem posed by urban riots as being one of law and order.

Where an issue is highly complex or technical it may receive little public attention, and where the government itself is not particularly interested nothing may be done, or the problem may even be allowed to worsen; this is arguably true of the 'poverty trap'. These considerations will be reinforced where demands may be poorly articulated by the group affected (e.g. the poor), and where the number affected is small or dispersed. In some cases, the group affected may have little public sympathy or may be actively despised, for example, the 'undeserving' poor, homosexuals, at least in the past.

On some (non-)issues there may be a consensus which results in views opposing this consensus receiving little attention; for example, advocacy of the complete abolition of private ownership in Britain. Some analysts would argue that such a consensus may be false, and that the social or political structure may result in some issues being ignored or suppressed. A particular firm may be so dominant in a town that individuals affected by pollution from it may not even attempt to raise this as a political issue because they know that they would fail to get the issue taken up (see Crenson, 1971). An alternative explanation would be that at least some of those suffering from the adverse effects of pollution may feel that the benefits of continuing employment are more important. It is notoriously difficult to secure agreement among political scientists about why some issues are taken up and others not, and whether this structuring of the agenda constitutes the exercise of power or not (compare Lukes, 1974 with Polsby, 1980). Cases where an issue is never raised or when raised is never actively pursued are sometimes referred to as 'non-decisions'.

The view that the social or political structure leads to some issues being ignored is particularly associated with Marxist or 'ruling class' theorists, but is by no means confined to them. For example, Stringer and Richardson (1980, 24) argue that:

some 'problems' fail to reach the policy agenda, fail to be 'defined' as problems, because of the way in which data on that policy area are collected, analysed and presented (or not presented, as the case may be).

In other words, there can be political reasons, or reasons of organizational advantage, for the way data are collected or published. In turn, the way in which data are made available has implications for agenda setting:

In any debate about air pollution, or drug abuse, it is difficult to argue that there is a serious problem requiring government action if the 'official' figures show otherwise. This is not to suggest some greater conspiracy designed to fool the public into thinking that everything is satisfactory. There are often practical considerations which to some extent prohibit the collection of more accurate information. (Stringer and Richardson, 1980, 25.)

For example, information collection may not be adapted to changing circumstances. However, it would be naïve to believe that all such cases are due to 'practical considerations'.

Naturally, a government department will develop systems for monitoring data which advance the interests of the department, for example, those that indicate rising 'demand' for its services. Conversely, data which would throw up problems whose consideration might work against the department's interests might be neglected or even suppressed by the department. Thus there are favourable problems (= opportunities) and unwanted problems from the perspective of particular public organizations.

Chapter 3

Processing the Agenda

Studies of foreign policy-making in Britain or indeed of policy-making in general have too often assumed that all policies are managed in a similar fashion, and so have generalized from the more important decisions to the less important. (Wallace, 1975, 5.)

3.1 Maintaining issues on the agenda

This chapter examines what happens to issues between the time they succeed in getting on the policy agenda and the time at which the government makes a decision not to take action or to take action in a particular form. The processing of issues involves the appraising of options and discussions with interest groups, and the chapter examines the extent to which this takes place within relatively closed communities.

It goes almost without saying that the first consideration of those who have been successful in getting an issue on the policy agenda is to keep it there. The euphoria and political mobilization in getting initial attention, when stress tends to be laid on the advantages and potential for dealing with the issue, may disappear once the snags and costs of dealing with the issue become clearer (Downs, 1972).

Thus one kind of processing is that an issue is processed *off* the agenda. This can result in various ways:

—announcing once apparent political pressures have died down that it is proposed to take no action;
—announcing a detailed investigation after which no action may be taken (discussed in 3.4);
—allowing the issue to be considered at length but with little sense of urgency, so that a decision is never made to move from no-decision to decision, and the issue can be said almost to have 'evaporated' from the agenda.

Given the constant competition for political attention for issues—old ones, recurring ones, new ones—and given the competition for the other scarce resources of legislative time and finance, an issue will need continuing rather than merely initial support for it to receive priority or even maintain a place on the agenda at all. Where the issue is one to which the department or ministers are themselves strongly committed, the maintenance or development of the issue is reasonably assured. In the absence of this type of inside backing, however, those promoting the issue may have to take continuing action to maintain pressure for the development of the issue. Much of this pressure may be exercised by private lobbying of departments, through inspiring questions on progress in the House of Commons, or through the actual or potential use of publicity to make a fuss about lack of progress. Caution should be exercised in the use of the last option, however, since political embarrassment to a minister or department is unlikely to secure their active co-operation in producing the policy most favourable to those pressing for change.

3.2 Types of processing

3.2.1 The main categories of processing

Once issues are on the political agenda in Britain, they are processed in a variety of different ways, though some are clearly more common than others. Table 3.1 lists the main categories of processing in approximately descending order of the extent of central government direction to the process. Given the variety of different forms of processing, it is difficult to separate out changes across time (for example, whether the Thatcher government has a distinctive style) from differences which may exist at any given time. The government and individual ministers will vary substantially in the extent to which they have clear objectives for particular policy areas. However, this variation across time and between ministers has to confront continuing 'objective' features, such as whether affected interests can effectively exercise a potential veto over the implementation of government policies.

On some issues the government may seek to *impose* its policy, without having to bargain away any aspects of its preferred policy.

Table 3.1 Main types of processing

Imposition
Internalized within government
Processable through consultation (see Table 3.2)
Policy emerges from practice
Non-internalizable

A precondition of this style is, of course, that the government already has a clearly worked-out policy of its own. A second precondition is that the government actually has the power to implement its preferred policy. In practice, the issue of objective constraints is far from clear-cut, since the potential veto power or obstructive capacity of opponents is in part a matter of perception, and governments may be able to overcome opposition if they are prepared to bear the financial costs and political risks, as with the 1984–5 miners' strike. The Anglo-Irish agreement of 1985 was arrived at without consultation of representatives of the majority community, though the minority community was indirectly consulted through its links with the government of the Irish republic. However, because on many issues there are groups whose opinion matters in political debate and which may control information and other resources needed by government, the opportunities for outright policy imposition are limited (Jordan, 1985, 19). Even where the government could unilaterally achieve what it wants, it may deliberately choose to engage in consensus building.

Some issues are processed in a way that is relatively *internalized within Whitehall*. This is true of a number of aspects of foreign affairs and defence (discussed in more detail in 3.5) and of some aspects of economic policy. Here the policy process does involve discussions *within* Whitehall, but with little or no direct participation by groups, though their views and anticipated reactions and those of Parliament may provide part of the background taken into account in considering the options.

Consultation is a pervasive (though not universal) feature of the policy process in Britain. However, to describe consultation as the 'norm' could be misleading in two ways. (1) It implies that other forms of processing are in some sense deviant, whereas they may in fact be the normal way of processing certain types of issues; it is more useful to try to identify the factors underlying variation rather than to focus on one pattern which is actually 'abnormal' for some kinds of issues. (2) 'Consultation' covers an extremely wide range of practices, both in terms of the number of organizations being consulted and in terms of the role of government in taking and implementing decisions after consultation (see Table 3.2). Consultation can range from cosmetic ritual to meaningful bargaining between government and group. Given the variety of relationships which can be covered by the word 'consultation', this does raise the question whether like other terms (often with value connotations) which are subject to a number of interpretations, such as 'democracy' or 'representative', it has become a word which of itself conveys little substantive meaning (i.e. is empty of content as a word). To adapt a phrase used by Wildavsky (1973) about planning, 'If consultation is everything, maybe it's nothing'. Accordingly, it will be necessary to 'unpack' the concept of consultation and this is done in 3.2.2.

For a number of policies which gradually evolve over time at grass-roots level, it may be inappropriate to identify the process as one of explicit consideration at national level during the crucial stages of development. Rather the situation is one where *policy*

Table 3.2 Processable through consultation

Participants	Role of govenment in consulting			
	Referee	Corporatist	Negotiate a. principle b. details	Cosmetic
Policy community 1. Single (recognized) group	X			
2. Multiple groups (a) multilateral discussions				
(b) serial bilateral		X		
Cross-community				
'Open' consultation 1. Government initiated		X		
2. Blown open	X			

Note: X represents impossible or unlikely combinations.

emerges from practice. Such development may take place within the framework of existing legislation or be subsequently facilitated or endorsed by central government decision, but the crucial stages of development take place through practice at the point of delivery, with dissemination of ideas through professional links including those between professionals in different local authorities, between members of the same profession in the private and public sectors, and between those at local level and those in central government bodies (see Dunleavy, 1982).

A number of issues are in practice *non-internalizable* in the sense of not being suitable for negotiation and compromise among Whitehall departments or between departments and groups. This can arise in two ways. The first is the all-or-nothing type of issue discussed in 2.4, where there is limited room for compromise and strong feelings on both sides, often within the government party. In such cases, government is normally happy that issues should be processed by such methods as parliamentary decision or a referendum, since there is limited scope for arriving at a generally accepted result through bargaining with groups. A second category of non-internalizable issues is where attempts at bargaining break down, as when there is failure to agree or renew an incomes policy with trade unions. In such cases government has to decide whether to seek to impose a policy or abandon the search for one.

3.2.2 Varieties of consultation

In 3.2.1 it was argued that consultation covered a wide range of practices, and this section outlines the main types of variation. Table 3.2 has two dimensions. The first, shown by the rows in the table, indicates the number of participants. The second indicates the government's role in consulting these participants. Some combinations, such as open consultation and corporatism, are logically impossible or highly unlikely.

Where the government has no clear policy goal, it may act as a *referee* (Jordan, 1985). Rather than being a direct 'combatant', the government is open to competing group bids, though it may prefer the groups themselves to arrive at a consensus and may facilitate the emergence of such a consensus. An example of an issue on which the government had no strong views of its own and acted as a referee was the proposal to change the date at which car registration prefix letters were changed each year. The old system (itself switched in 1967 from January at the request of the industry) provided for the change to be made in August of each year. The change of letter led to a bunching of car sales in August each year, during the holiday period for both British car manufacturers and dealers. One consequence was to provide an opportunity for foreign car manufacturers, for whom it was the poorest sales month on the continent, to import cars to meet the seasonal bulge in demand in Britain. The government did have an interest in changing the system, since the Department of Transport's centre in Swansea was unable to cope with the 370,000 registrations, over 20 per cent of the annual total, in August, when staff holidays were at their peak. By November 1985 both motor manufacturers and dealers were split on the options, which included abolishing an annual letter change date, reverting to a change in January, and switching to October. Police and consumer protection organizations favoured the retention of an annual letter change. In March 1986 the government announced that from 1987 the annual changeover date would be switched to October. Here consultation is clearly taking place, with the views of groups being the prime determinant of the policy outcome, but it is different from the type of process involved when the government does have views of its own on the issue.

Corporatism is a term with rather more meanings than there are people who have written about it (see Jordan, 1981). The term is at times used so loosely that it would cover most of the range of types of 'consultation' considered in this section. However, the term is probably most useful if we confine its use in the British context to its original relatively narrow meaning, namely that interest organizations and government jointly determine policy and that policy is actually implemented through the organizational structure of the interest organizations. Undoubtedly one can find policies in Britain which conform or approximate to this concept including some attempts at incomes policies and to a weaker extent the operation of manpower policy through the Manpower Services Commission. The most notable form of corporatist-style policy-making is 'self-regulation' of professions, trades, and financial institutions. The history of British policy is also littered with what can be regarded as examples of failed corporatism, including incomes policies and the 'tripartism' of the 1974 Labour government's industrial strategy. A corporatist style of policy processing depends on a set of assumptions that only occasionally apply in British politics: (1) that the views and objectives of government and the one or more sets of interest organizations are sufficiently close for them to arrive at agreement on policy; (2) that government will be capable of delivering its side of any such agreement (which depends on whether it has control over Parliament and over events); (3) that the interest organizations can actually control the detailed decisions of their members either through ability to issue instructions, disciplinary mechanisms, or dissemination of professional values. It is this last condition which is frequently lacking. For example, the Trades Union Congress is palpably unable to control the reaction of trade union members at factory floor level; Sector Working Parties may exort changes for their industry, but investment decisions are taken at the level of the firm, albeit in the context of government incentives. However, it is precisely because corporatism occurs only in certain circumstances that it can help us to understand British public policy. If we try to stretch the concept to cover every occasion when interest groups sit down with government and try to agree on a policy then we have lost the value of the insights which the concept might provide.

Thus it can be seen that the idea of *government as negotiator* is not identical to that of corporatist arrangements. The idea of negotiation implies that the government does have a view about what it would like to achieve, but is prepared to bargain about the policy to secure the agreement of groups or at least to minimize their opposition. Government may engage in negotiation either because it feels that an agreed policy will be easier to legislate or implement, that it will suffer fewer adverse political consequences, or because it prefers a consensual style of policy-making. However, government is not simply an equal partner in such bargaining. Government, in particular central government, has access to powers of legitimation and the right to extract resources which mark it out as a distinctive set of political actors (see also Rhodes, 1985). Central government departments are not just another collection of 'groups'. Further, it is important to distinguish between negotiations of principle or of some substance on a policy and those which are concerned about the details of administration of a policy line determined by government. If there is indeed a 'logic of negotiation' (Jordan and Richardson, 1982), it is often because groups do what they can to ameliorate what they regard as the worst features of government plans. In some cases government may be highly dependent on others for the effective implementation of policy. As Jordan (1985) points out:

In such circumstances a range of outcomes can result in the Government *satisficing* with symbolic action, or entering serious negotiation, or turning the attainable into an objective . . . Recent British examples of 'wanting what they can get' include the Government's presentation of their deal with China over Hong Kong—and the presentation of the slide to the pound to dollar parity.

Even when consultation does take place, it may be *cosmetic* only. As will be noted in the next section and in chapter 8, government departments are increasingly required to consult affected groups or other government bodies before announcing a decision. There are also political advantages in being seen to listen to the views of those affected. However, these pressures place a premium on the procedures and the appearance of consultation rather than the extent to which government is influenced by the expression of the views of others. The recognition of the requirement for consultation may take on the quality of a ritual incantation which indicates its lack of substance, as in a speech by Kenneth Clarke, the Employment Minister, to the 1985 Conservative Conference when he said:

We will call upon trades union opinion, we will have green papers, we will consult, we will have white papers and we will not shrink from introducing further legislation to protect and maintain the rights of individual trades unionists within their trade union movement.

Turning to the second dimension of Table 3.2, that of the number of participants, we can see that at one extreme the government may be engaged in discussions with only one recognized group (though there may be other groups which are excluded from discussions). This has traditionally been the case in agriculture, where the farmers were the sole relevant group, though by the mid-1980s there were signs that the policy community was opening up to allow conservation groups to participate.

Rather more policy communities consist of a number of different groups. It is obviously important to distinguish between circumstances where those groups share a common set of objectives and those where the groups themselves disagree. Multilateral discussions between government and groups are much more likely in the former case, while where there is disagreement the government may prefer 'serial bilateral negotiations'. Clearly, where there is disagreement among groups the government's own scope for maneouvre is increased, except in cases where all groups are intransigent and each separately has an effective power of veto. Where a number of groups are involved, their participation in the consultation process may be skewed, with some groups being engaged in meaningful consultation, while other groups are asked to state their views for cosmetic reasons. Different groups may also have different potential for assisting or thwarting government intentions. Occasions when consultation is 'skewed' are discussed in more detail in 3.3.4.

Issues vary in the extent to which they are processed through individual sectors or existing policy communities. Some issues are processed through *ad hoc* issue networks, resulting in the involvement of a larger number of participants, both government departments and non-governmental organizations. An example here is the Westland affair in 1985, which involved both the Ministry of Defence and the Department of Trade and Industry. Such cross-community processing is most likely in one of two circumstances. The first is where there is a clash between the priorities of two different departments or policy communities. In such cases it is likely that the issue will be pulled in to the centre for resolution through Cabinet or cabinet committee.

The second is where an issue is marginal and relatively neglected by the department which at first sight would be responsible for it. This provides an opportunity for a 'pre-emptive strike' by another government organization to develop its own interests. Examples include the launching of the Technical and Vocational Education Initiative (TVEI) by the Manpower Services Commission in 1982 (not the Department of Education and Science), and the launching by the Department of the Environment (rather than the Department of Industry) of local enterprise agencies. Two features are notable about both these examples. First is the lack of a defensive reaction by the minister heading the department which was 'attacked' (Sir Keith Joseph in both cases). The second is the pilot or developmental nature of the initiatives as originally launched.

Moon and Richardson (1984a) suggest that the TVEI experiment is of wider interest to observers of the UK policy style, suggesting that radical innovation is possible even in a period of resource squeeze. The view taken here is that the TVEI type of initiative depends on a set of circumstances and issue characteristics which, while not unique, cannot be generalized to the British policy process more broadly.

The opposite extreme from single-group policy communities is 'open consultation', where a large and varied collection of groups, or even the general public, are able to participate, or at least have the opportunity of formally recording their views. In some cases, the widespread participation may be initiated by government because of the broad-ranging impact of proposals, as with the proposed introduction of value added tax and the 1985 social security proposals. In the case of the social security proposals the government even placed advertisements inviting the general public to submit their comments. In other cases, such as nuclear power, the issue may have been 'blown open' and the government no longer able to contain it within a closed policy community. Wide-ranging consultation is, of course, no guarantee that all views will be given equal weighting.

The next section examines a number of different aspects of consultation practices in the British policy process, including the extent to which it is a common practice, the role of formal and informal consultation, and the skewing of political influence in the policy process.

3.3 Consultation practices in Britain

3.3.1 Consultation as due process?

Issues do vary in the way in which they are processed, but for a wide range of issues the involvement of interest groups in discussions with government departments is a key feature. The amount of consultation varies according to department, the style of different officials, and even in some cases the style of individual ministers.

No interest group which knows its business will simply sit on its hands after it has articulated its demands and let the government get on with it. The group will seek to be actively involved in the appraisal of policy options and in the selection of the final decision. Ideally, it will want to get itself in a position where it can effectively veto an option which it particularly dislikes, though this is not a position which the interest group can necessarily achieve. It is perhaps worth distinguishing between 'political' veto power and 'objective' ability to obstruct implementation. In Britain, discussions are typically private, either through consultative committees, or informally in contacts with ministers and civil servants. This aspect of government–interest group relations highlights the danger of viewing the policy process on a particular issue in isolation. Groups are only likely to be in a favourable position to influence options on an individual issue if this is the product of long-term association over previous related issues.

Group activity is not simply a matter of groups putting pressure on government but is a two-way process. Analysis of relations between groups and government must recognize that each has something that the other needs. There are certain things that interest groups or other government bodies clearly seek from central government. First, groups will want advance information about any proposed policy changes. This will give time for internal consultation within the group, formulation of view, and, if necessary, mobilization of political resources. Secondly, a group will seek participation in decisions, both the ability to affect the general thrust of policy and the *details* of the proposal. Thirdly, a group will seek the sympathetic administration of law where there is discretion; for example, the Association of University Teachers negotiated with the Inland Revenue a tax allowance for book purchases. A group may also be looking for legitimation of self-regulation, for example in the professions and for City institutions.

Perhaps less obviously, government also needs certain things from interest groups. First, the government itself may need information from groups, for example about investment intentions from the Confederation of British Industry (CBI). Secondly, the government will seek the co-operation of group leaders to influence their membership. However, the leaders may not always be able to deliver, for example, the Trades Union Congress on incomes policy. Thirdly, government will seek the explicit or implied 'consent' of a group to its proposals where the interest group is generally seen to be legitimate. Finally, the government may recognize the importance (positive or negative) of the group in administering policy, for example, doctors in the National Health Service or trade unions and industrial relations legislation.

If politics can be viewed as a game, then there are clearly 'rules of the game' (cf. Rhodes, 1981). Government, however, is not just another actor but can in part write the rules of the game, determine who can play, and even (in the case of both local authorities and 'campaign' groups or research bodies) create or abolish the people with whom it is 'playing'. In the case of group–government relations, as in central–local relations, one of the most important rules of the game is that of 'consultation'. In countries with written constitutions, greater emphasis may be placed on whether policies or their enforcement have conformed with constitutional and legal requirements. In Britain it is virtually part of our constitution that groups affected by government proposals should be asked for their opinion on them and that the government should consider altering proposals in the light of representations made by the groups. Indeed, the obligation to consult has been established in a number of court cases (see 8.2). Often the requirement to consult certain specified organizations is written into legislation, but this is not the important point.

In return for being consulted the implication is that the group accepts the government's right to make a decision on the matter. If this is contested, then the right to consultation in future may be withdrawn. Further, consultation is a two-way rule—it is not the done thing unreasonably to refuse to be consulted. However, groups have to avoid appearing to be co-opted by government by agreeing to consultation on matters to which they are fundamentally opposed. After all, government engages in consultation at least in part as a commitment-generating strategy.

Like any 'rule of the game', we can best gain an idea of the significance of the 'rule' about consultation when it is broken. The vehement reaction of affected groups when the government announces a proposal without having discussed the substance and detail of it with them in advance indicates the general expectation that the government will normally conform to the rule. For example, the British Medical Association (BMA) and the Association of the British Pharmaceutical Indusry (ABPI) protested vehemently when the government announced in 1984 a provisional list of drugs which doctors would be allowed to prescribe on the

NHS (with other drugs therefore excluded). Even though the contents of the list were subject to representations, the doctors and the drug companies were clearly affronted that they had not been consulted before public announcement of the proposal. The drug industry ran a large-scale press campaign at the beginning of 1985, with full-page adverts in the national press, but this indicates more about their fears that the normal private routes of contact with government were not sufficient on this occasion as it does about the (un)proven effectiveness of such press campaigns as an indirect means of affecting government. Even as a means of influencing Conservative backbench MPs the campaign appeared to be ineffective or even counter-productive because of the crudity of the associated letter campaign and the scare message of the adverts. This campaign was a classic 'fire-brigade' campaign, engaged in as a last resort when normal private channels to government seemed unlikely to produce the desired result.

The greater emphasis which the British government places on consultation with relevant groups than on the legitimating role of Parliament was shown by the strange affair of the Butter Prices Order in 1981 (*The Times*, 10 July 1981). Officials used the wrong list of organizations to be consulted, headed Butter Prices Order, but not covering as many organizations as it should have done, before laying before Parliament an order to raise the legal ceiling on butter prices. After complaints from some interested organizations that they had not been consulted, the Order was cancelled, despite the fact that it had already been laid before Parliament.

3.3.2 Formal and informal consultation

It is difficult to generalize about the scale of formal consultation practices even within departments, but most sections of Whitehall departments maintain lists of interest groups to be consulted on general or on specific matters (Jordan, 1985). Some lists are organized according to the Act to which they relate, while others are organized by section of the department. Some lists contain the names of individuals or individual firms as well as interest groups as such. Some lists are essentially mailing lists for circulars and reports, while other, shorter lists in the same department contain the more influential bodies. As Jordan (1985) points out, 'The existence of two lists does make fairly explicit what is usually

unstated—that there are many more passive recipients of information than active consultees'. Not all departments do maintain
written lists; such departments nevertheless have a clear idea of
the bodies which need to be consulted, adjusted according to
issue.

In some cases there is a specific statutory requirement that
consultation should take place before the introduction of statutory
instruments, and departments will maintain lists of organizations
for this purpose. Other legislation may impose a broader statutory
requirement on consultation, for example, on the Health and
Safety Commission. However, the selection of groups to be
consulted is usually at the discretion of the department or agency
concerned (Jordan, 1985). Lists of organizations to be consulted
are also maintained even when there is no statutory obligation to
consult—indeed, it is important to place the statutory requirements
and the maintenance of formal lists in context as the partial
formalization of a much wider practice.

Consultations involving very large numbers of groups or peak
organizations such as the TUC or the CBI may appear impressive.
For example, the views of 800 different trade and professional
bodies were received on the introduction of VAT and meetings
were held with over 200 groups (Johnstone, 1975), and 6,000
responses were received in response to the 1985 social security
review. However, more typical are meetings with a much smaller
number of organizations, often with highly specialized interests.

Where consultation has become routinized, it is also often
formalized in the sense of a consultative or advisory committee
being established with representatives from recognized interests.
These meet more or less frequently, and will obviously discuss any
new issues under consideration by government as well as points
about existing policy. However, the existence of these committees
should be regarded as complementary to more informal consultation, rather than a replacement for them. Particularly where
groups are antagonistic to each other, the department may find it
easier to bargain *bilaterally* with each of them, rather than
collectively. These committees have now had the label 'quango'
conferred upon them, and because they are alleged to represent a
source of ministerial patronage many of them were abolished in
the early 1980s (see Hood, 1981). However, this can be expected
to make relatively little difference to the importance of consultation

in the processing of issues. Informal consultations, that is outside the framework of committees, continue to take place. In other words, some of the formal settings of consultation may have disappeared but routinized consultation remains.

Some issues, particularly those associated with budgeting, occur on a regular, normally annual, basis (see 6.5), and formal procedures may be established for consulting groups in advance of government decision. Examples here are the annual farm price review and discussions with local authorities in advance of the announcement of the rate support grant settlement each November.

Focusing on 'events' in consultation where a group is formally asked for its opinion may obscure an important feature which tends to develop from routinized consultation: consultation takes place not simply on major issues but on a whole range of matters, including details of existing policies (as with the butter price increase discussed above). Officials of major interest groups may be in almost daily contact with civil servants in the relevant department. Thus consultations about the processing of issues have to be seen in the context of this long-term and continuous interaction.

Thus, in examining the options open to government, the relevant department will normally consult the relevant group or other government bodies and invite them for discussions. In the case of completely new issues in which the government has not previously been involved, it may not be immediately clear which groups are the relevant ones or whether they understand the normal rules of secrecy and bargaining. In such cases, the groups need to be socialized into the normal ethic and etiquette of consultation. However, in chapter 2 it was urged that the extent to which government is likely to be dealing with completely new issues and therefore with completely new groups is small and likely to diminish further (see also Hogwood and Peters, 1983).

Contacts between the staff of interest groups and civil servants are much more frequent than those between office-bearers and ministers. Indeed, one of the key resources required by interest groups is adequate staffing, which some of the less well-off groups may have difficulty in achieving. This may be offset for some of the 'campaigning groups' by a greater degree of personal commitment (even here a 'career structure' has emerged). Particularly in the discussion between full-time staff and civil servants where a 'negotiating' style has been practised over the years, there may be an atmosphere of mutual accommodation and discretion. Both sides will be anxious to avoid 'public fuss'. Civil servants will often be on good terms with their 'opposite numbers' in interest groups, and may have frequent informal consultations with them over the phone on a routine basis, not just when an important policy proposal comes up.

In some cases these opposite numbers might actually have had civil service experience, particularly for 'interest' rather than campaigning organizations. For example, the former head of the Office of Fair Trading, Sir John Methven, went on to become Director General of the Confederation of British Industry. A civil servant in the Ministry of Agriculture and Fisheries went on to become an official in the National Farmers Union. A particularly interesting indirect exchange (though not involving an interest group as such) occurred in March 1985, when the new Chief of Defence Procurement was Mr Peter Levene, until then chairman and managing director of United Scientific Holdings, a big defence contractor. His replacement as chairman of United Scientific Holdings was none other than Sir Frank Cooper, former Permanent Secretary at the Ministry of Defence. In September 1984 the Commons Treasury and Civil Service Committee had already argued for an extension from two to five years of the period before which a retiring senior civil servant could take up a private sector appointment closely related to his previous job.

3.3.3 Consultation as negotiation

The term 'consultation' can be misleading if it is taken to mean simply that groups are invited along to the department to air their views, they then go away, and the government makes up its mind. Rather, it would be better in some cases to regard the process as one of negotiating or bargaining in which compromise is sought on both sides. Jordan and Richardson (1982) regard this as the normal British policy style. Here meaningful negotiation, in the sense of central government directly trading what it would prefer for the co-operation of affected interest groups or other central bodies, is regarded as only one style of 'consultation', which in turn is only one main type, arguably the main type, of processing of issues in Britain. Further, within consultation as negotiation

there is a need to distinguish between negotiation over fundamental points and negotiation on points of detail.

Resolution of disagreements relating to an issue is unlikely to
take place in a single meeting. Rather, there is likely to be a series
of meetings gradually moving on to matters of detail. For the
group the advantage is securing the influence on the shape of the
proposals; for the government the advantage is that it receives the
'consent' of the group, whose leadership must sell the proposal to
members. This process of mutual accommodation takes place in
secret rather than in open forum. The reason for this is that stances
taken as bargaining positions might be confused with issues of
principle, and a willingness to compromise might be interpreted as
a defeat or climb-down.

There may be a desire on the part of both government and
groups to internalize the processing of issues within a structured
policy community. For departments this introduces greater predictability to the negotiating process and co-opts potential objectors.
For groups this reinforces their 'legitimate' role and increases the
predictability of the environment in which they operate. There are
advantages and disadvantages for both departments and groups in
this mutual co-optation when it does occur. For both sets of
participants there is the ease of procedures, and almost a cosiness
of personal relationships. However, from the perspective of
government as a whole there is a danger of the 'capture' of
departments by the lobby, while for groups there is a danger that
they may be turned into a instrument of government on corporatist
lines, and the group may be deflected from the wishes of its
membership.

While this emphasis on compromise and give and take is
important in understanding the role of consultations in processing
issues, it should not be assumed that agreement can always be
reached between departments and groups. However, even in such
cases the government is likely to offer consultations on the details
of its proposal. In doing so, of course, it will be able to say that it
has consulted the relevant groups and adjusted its proposals to
meet their objections. Faced with such a refusal to compromise on
the underlying principle of an issue, the group faces both a short-
term and a long-term dilemma. In the short term, if it negotiates
on detail with the government the group may become associated
with a proposal it dislikes; on the other hand, such negotiations

may help to ameliorate some of what are considered to be the worst features of the proposal. In the longer term, the group has to set the possibility that outright opposition to a proposal may prevent it being pursued by government against the possible longer-term damage that it might do to its influence on government.

3.3.4 Skewed consultation

Focusing on consultation as negotiation may lead us to overlook the fact that patterns of representation may often be lopsided, in part because of resources available to groups for bargaining, and in part because of the discretion of government in choosing with whom it will negotiate. For example, the tobacco manufacturers bargain directly with the Department of Health and Social Security about tobacco advertising and tobacco sponsorship of sports events. The Health Education Council (a government advisory body) and Action on Smoking and Health (ASH), a government-funded 'pressure group', make representations to the government but are not engaged in 'bargaining' since they have no bargainable resources except for use of publicity. This illustration is notable for the role of the government in creating two of the participants, HEC and ASH, which were putting pressure on it; government can create countervailing pressure organizations.

The concept of the 'legitimacy' of groups reflects the crucial importance in Britain of receiving official recognition as a group which must be consulted on relevant issues. A number of considerations determine whether a group will be recognized as 'legitimate', and its political muscle is not irrelevant. Obviously, the extent to which the group is representative of those whose interests it claims to be advancing is very important. Also important are the nature of the demands advanced and the manner in which they are advanced. It is particularly *interest* groups rather than promotional groups (especially those campaigning for change rather than the status quo) with which government departments have close consultations (see Davies, 1985, ch. 2). Extreme demands advanced in a strident way are not a recipe for being regarded as a candidate for consultation. Obviously, a group may occasionally be allowed to be obstructive and still be invited to consultations in future, but persistent obstruction would lead to withdrawal of the cachet of recognition as a legitimate group.

Being accepted as a legitimate group implies a willingness by the group to discuss and compromise even when it disagrees with a proposed policy and to do so largely in confidence. A group which persistently brags about concessions which it has wrung from civil servants is likely to find it more difficult to obtain such concessions in future.

It should be noted that being accepted as a 'legitimate' group is not an absolute concept, but one that relates to individual policy arenas. For example, it used to be that in consultations about lorry regulations only groups related to the road haulage industry were regarded as legitimate. Now, however, environmental groups have been recognized to have a legitimate interest in the matter (Richardson and Jordan, 1979, 83). Jordan (1985) refers to the Scottish Development Department consulting more groups than formerly 'with the mobilisation of new groups, governmental agencies and a new awareness of groups and government departments of the need to speak for their interests—for example it was claimed that the Department of Agriculture and Fisheries is increasingly concerned about the loss of agricultural land'. However, Friends of the Earth is not 'part of the club' on pesticides, whereas farmers and the chemical industry are (Davies, 1985, 42).

Obviously, it is much easier for established groups to be accepted as legitimate than new ones. However, with the right kind of persistence, groups previously regarded as fringe or freaky may come to be regarded as constructive and legitimate. For example, Friends of the Earth has now been brought into departmental consultations and working parties. In the case of a new policy issue, such as enterprise zones, a group which subsequently emerges as relevant may be omitted through a failure by the department to anticipate their interest rather than through an attempt to keep them out of the consultative process (Jordan, 1985).

A change in political party or prime minister may affect the acceptability of a group. Mrs Whitehouse's National Viewers and Listeners Association was given a respectful hearing by the Home Office after Mrs Thatcher took office, whereas previously the Home Office had been almost totally unwilling to listen or take into account what the association was saying (Davies, 1985, 118). Trade unions by contrast feel relatively neglected by the Conservative government (see also 6.5).

At local level group activity can also be divided into 'acceptable' or 'established' groups which are consulted by local government and 'unacceptable' ones which are not. This is similar to the distinction between 'legitimate' groups and others in activity directed at central government. Of course, a change in political office may produce a change in what is considered an acceptable group; the Labour administration of the GLC under Ken Livingstone accorded much greater influence to feminist and minority organizations.

Accordingly, in most cases where an issue arises in central government, the department will have had previous contact with groups concerned with the issue. It will thus already have a view on which are the relevant and legitimate groups—that is those recognized as representative and responsible, willing to bargain and compromise. Thus, the process of consultation here becomes routinized, with group representatives having a good idea of the best tactics to pursue and the limits of the pressure they can hope to exercise on the department.

However, inclusion on a list does not ensure equality of access. Trade unions and consumer groups as well as trade associations may be included, but as Jordan (1985, 16) points out:

Even where groups such as consumers are admitted to the consultative process, organisational weakness might mean that they fail fully to exploit their access. Accordingly the actual consultation pattern—even where not consciously contrived or manipulated—is likely to reflect subconscious or accidental bias.

Even when the department is keen to consult, there may be practical problems on the group side. Jordan (1985, 17) points out that 'Many groups are understaffed to meet the burden of consultation'. As a result, groups may decline the opportunity to be consulted. In other cases, the group may be unable to offer definitive comments in time because of the requirements for internal formulation of an official view. In such cases, the 'informal views of an officer' might be sought. Group resources devoted to relations with government departments are unlikely to be evenly distributed across all groups in a particular policy area. Some groups, such as some 'campaigning' groups, may suffer from low absolute resources, while others, such as many individual trade unions, although with substantial income may not treat back-up for consultations with government as a priority. Groups are also likely to differ on their ability to 'deliver' their membership on the basis of discussions which their officers or officials have held with government. Jordan (1985, 17) notes that the preparation of legislation 'involves large numbers of groups—though for many the involvement is restricted to pro forma or cosmetic consultation'.

3.4 Open consultation and committees of inquiry

British politics has often witnessed apparently greater openness of issue processing than is implied by the idea of closed policy communities. Sometimes this open discussion turns out not to amount to much. For example, the 'great debate' on education of the late 1970s, with its open public meetings, soon reverted to discussion between government and affected groups, though by the mid-1980s there was almost a state of trench warfare between government and the teaching unions and an increasing intrusion by the Manpower Services Commission into education during school years. More generally, and with varying degrees of significance, governments have since the mid-1960s made increasing use of 'Green Papers', setting out the government's views and sometimes alternative options and providing a period for debate and submissions before the government makes its decision.

In some cases the government may not be able to prevent debate about an issue broadening out from the closed policy community already involved. However, as in the case of the nuclear energy debate, there can be advantages to government in such public discussion. Williams (1980, 313), writing of the public nuclear debate of the mid-1970s and of the Windscale inquiry in particular, notes:

From the perspective of government the public nuclear debate of the mid-seventies could be viewed as having facilitated the discharge of two distinctively different functions. First, a controlled debate bringing in Parliament and with a good availability of information and adequate opportunities for involvement—itself quite different from participation—was a politically attractive way of accommodating conflict. The ensuing delay in making decisions had then to be tolerated as a necessary cost of securing at least a grudging, and of particular importance, non-violent acceptance. Second, public debate was also a genuine means, in circumstances involving at least some uncertainty, of getting all relevant questions identified if not answered, and of testing BNFL's case. The first of these functions no doubt amounted to a form of manipulation, but government is in part about that.

However, public discussion does not preclude additional private discussion between government departments and affected interests, nor does it prevent government, if it can manage it politically, from circumscribing some aspects of a policy sector as suitable for open processing and others as more appropriate for internalized processing. Williams notes of the nuclear power decisions that:

it was noticeable that the public debate was not allowed by Benn to embrace the new re-examination of thermal reactor policy when this took place in 1976–7. This was understandable given the nuclear construction industry's desperate need for work, but hardly in keeping with the minister's declared objectives in regard to public involvement.

For some, but not most, issues, the government sets up a Royal Commission or a committee of inquiry or appoints consultants to examine the issue and report back, perhaps making recommendations. Recent British governments have made less use of Royal Commissions since their heyday in the mid-1960s. An interesting innovation was the establishment in 1983–4 of four committees to consider related issues of social security, three chaired directly by government ministers.

Commissions can fulfil a number of purposes, including the collection of information, making broad or specific recommendations about policy, postponing decisions on embarrassing questions, providing 'independent' backing for a decision the government wants to take, gaining a broad perspective on a situation, and an educational role in bringing to the attention of the public some of the issues involved in a particular policy area (see Chapman, 1973, 194; Cartwright, 1974, 101–4; Rhodes, 1975). The roles actually performed by the committee may not always be those intended by the government; the inquiry chairman may set the pace, as with the Beveridge Report of 1942.

Because commissions are normally independent of government (though with their membership and terms of reference set by the government of the day) they have the potential for taking a fresh look at problems and attempting to build a consensus in a way that may not be possible for partisan political figures. Unfortunately, this freshness to a problem may also be associated with little previous knowledge of it, and one of the criticisms made of commissions by past members is that they were only just coming to grips with the issues when they had to report and were disbanded.

There can be problems in collecting information to be analysed by commissions. The extensive use of oral evidence by commissions has come under criticism for taking up considerable time but adding little to what could be more quickly obtained by other methods (Bulmer, 1982, 106–7). There are difficulties in meshing the time scale of conducting social science research with the time by which a final report has to be completed (see Bulmer, 1982, ch. 5). Inadequate resources may be provided to conduct appropriate research either by the commission's own staff or contracted out. There are also the usual problems of communicating what is required for social scientists and of social scientists presenting ideas and findings to commission members (see also Prest, 1980). Much of the information collected by commissions actually comes from government departments.

From the point of view of commission members, one of the main areas of concern is the way in which action by government on recommendations is delayed or recommendations are ignored or rejected (see Bulmer, 1982, 124–5). However, even when recommendations are not directly acted on, commission reports may have a broader effect on the way in which an issue is perceived by those interested in it (Vickers, 1965).

To an extent, commissions and committees do result in relatively greater openness in the processing of an issue, taking it out of a purely private interest-group–government dialogue. However, those making representations to a commission are often the same groups as would have made private representations to government departments—and, indeed, do so after the report of the commission is published. The same civil servant who acted as secretary to the committee may subsequently meet the same interest-groups to receive their comments on the report for which they gave evidence (Hogwood, 1979b). Inquiry committees are not a substitute for conventional consultation but an addition to it.

A potential for greater openness in those making representations on an issue is also provided by major planning inquiries, such as those into an application by British Nuclear Fuels to expand its facilities at Windscale (now Sellafield), by the National Coal Board to develop coal mines in the Vale of Belvoir, and by the

Central Electricity Generating Board (CEGB) to construct a water-cooled nuclear power reactor at Sizewell. Although technically concerned with land use issues, such inquiries provide an opportunity for wider policy issues to be aired. However, the cost of legal representation or expert advice may mean lopsided opportunities for objectors at inquiries, giving a potential advantage to well-funded private firms or public bodies with access to specialists. Opportunities for public airing of issues are greatest where there is a split in the 'policy community' itself, as at the Sizewell inquiry, where the South of Scotland Electricity Board favoured the advanced gas cooled reactor to the pressurized water reactor preferred by the CEGB. One result of major planning inquiries has been delays in the taking and implementation of decisions on major projects. In an attempt to short-circuit such delays and the extended public controversy given an arena in inquiries, the Conservative government has since 1979 made greater use of special development orders. The government has made it clear that there will be no planning inquiry into the Channel Tunnel project to avoid the inevitable delays and even possible resulting cancellation of the project.

3.5 Foreign policy: executive prerogative or blurred distinction?

Developments in trade, economics, defence, research, immigration, and the wide range of concerns of international organizations of which Britain is a member have all served to blur the distinction between foreign and domestic policy (see Wallace, 1975; Barber, 1976). However, while this does mean an increasing role for groups in providing an input on issues with an international dimension, it has not led to a total fragmentation of international issues into sectors or communites. Rather, one consequence of this blurring and the linking of different issues with a foreign dimension has been to push issues increasingly towards the centre in the sense of the network of interdepartmental committees and the Cabinet Office (Wallace, 1975, 271). Foreign and defence policy also involve different implementation considerations from most aspects of domestic policy (see 7.4). As was noted in section 1.4, the varying openness of different domestic policy sectors is itself a source of variations in the way policies are processed.

Foreign policy-making, while it may impinge on the concerns of domestic policy communities, cannot be analysed in terms of a policy community whose settled membership and relative autonomy from other aspects of government provides government decision-makers with a degree of predictability about the actions and reactions of non-government actors. As Wallace (1975, 6) points out:

in the extent to which governmental actors are involved in situations which they neither fully understand nor control, foreign policy-making differs in degree from most areas of domestic policy-making. Shared values and assumptions, long experience of dealing with each other, and a common acceptance of certain written and unwritten rules of the game make it possible for ministers and officials responsible for health services or education to deal with doctors' or teachers' organizations with a reasonable degree of certainty about their reactions to various proposals and a reasonable expectation that third parties will not directly intrude into this relationship. In foreign policy, even when a clear decision has been taken, unexpected responses from foreign governments, the interaction of a specific relationship with wider international developments, may rapidly outdate the policy decided upon or force the reopening of a settled question. Such a degree of uncertainty, it may be suggested, obtains in domestic matters only in economic and industrial policy.

Urgent matters or crises, not allowing time for preliminary work at lower levels, are also more common in foreign affairs than in domestic politics (Wallace, 1975, 74). Two additional features of foreign and defence policy also serve to reduce the scope for informed public debate and influence by groups. The first is the government's relative freedom from the need to gain parliamentary sanction; although it will be argued in chapter 5 that the government largely controls the legislative process, the need for legislative sanction does provide a degree of public exposure and timetabling constraints. Secondly and relatedly, foreign and defence matters have been subject to even greater secrecy than domestic ones.

Not all aspects of foreign policy-making have the same features and same types of participants; there can, for example, be important differences between overseas aid, defence and security, and foreign economic and commerical policy. Wallace (1975, 13) suggests that foreign policy can be divided into three layers. First, there are 'high policy' issues—those seen by policy-makers as affecting Britain's fundamental standing in the world. The bottom layer consists of 'low policy' issues—those in which few political values and few domestic issues are seen to be at stake; for example, detailed and routine transactions between friendly governments, regular conversations with distant countries, technical agreements on matters to which governments attach little political significance. High and low policy issues are both seen as largely matters for the executive, that is ministers and officials, though except for crises there may be constraints from party and interest groups. However, for the middle layer of 'sectoral policy' issues—those that are perceived as affecting only certain sections of society—the involvement of groups outside the executive is considerably greater.

High policy issues closely involve the prime minister and the senior members of the Cabinet as well as senior officials of the Cabinet Office and the major departments. In crises, decisions are likely to be taken by the prime minister and a very small group of ministerial colleagues and official advisers as described in 4.6. On other issues, such as joining the European Communities, the debate may widen. Peak organizations such as the TUC and the CBI are likely to be consulted. There may be widespread debate among the public and in Parliament, but the outcome is likely to be settled within the cabinet structure (it is important to distinguish between wide debate and wide participation in decision-making or decision influence). Decisions about Britain's nuclear deterrent are good examples of decisions taken within the executive, often in conditions of secrecy. There are indeed vigorous campaigning groups on such issues, but the Campaign for Nuclear Disarmament (CND) is a classic example of an 'outsider' group, whose views are quite simply rejected by government. By contrast, the decision about remaining in the European Communities was finally determined not by the executive, and not by 'policy communities' either—unusually, it went to a referendum.

Sectoral issues involve senior officials and in most cases departmental ministers. Issues involving several departments are overseen by a cabinet committee and by a parallel steering committee of officials. Here the interest groups are the sectoral organizations concerned with the particular area of policy; for example, on issues concerning tariffs and quotas for cotton goods, the various textile associations and some sections of the aid lobby. In foreign affairs as in domestic politics, on some issues there are countervailing groups, in some single interests, in some reinforcing multiple groups. On some issues, the links between departments in different countries may be stronger in policy approach and publicly expressed support than those between departments in any one country's government (Wallace, 1975, 270); this was certainly true of the Westland affair in 1985–6, when the Ministry of Defence mobilized its counterparts in other European countries against the line taken by the Department of Trade and Industry. Parliamentary interest in sectoral issues in foreign policy, when raised, tends to be at the level of the interested backbench committees rather than of the parties as a whole, and views frequently cross party lines.

Many of the details of external relations, such as a request for aid from a particular African country, are handled almost entirely within the executive, and then at a relatively junior level (first secretaries and counsellors in the Foreign and Commonwealth Office and principals and assistant secretaries in Home departments), with senior officials and ministers being only intermittently involved. Gray and Jenkins (1985) suggest that it was the treatment of the Falklands issue as a 'low policy' issue, and the failure to treat it as a high politics one that contributed to the British government's mishandling of the run-up to the war in 1982.

There are differences between the processing of defence policy issues and other foreign policy matters. Because of its cost, defence is much more closely constrained by the budgetary process, and as a result subjected to a regular and detailed scrutiny which does not apply in most other areas of external policy (Wallace, 1975, 121). On manpower, the absence of conscription (itself a policy decision) makes implication of decisions for morale and therefore recruitment important. These budgetary and cost constraints 'tie defence policy more closely to domestic politics than most other areas of external policy, requiring policy-makers to pay careful attention to carrying party and public opinion with them' (Wallace, 1975, 121). The cost and lengthening lead time of defence equipment have led to a more explicit planning approach in defence policy than in most areas of foreign or domestic policy, though this has not prevented continuing problems of delay and cost escalation, as with the Nimrod early warning radar system in the mid-1980s. Wallace (1975, 132) argues that it is difficult to discern anything resembling a military-industrial complex in

Britain in the sense of a powerful lobby linking the armed services with defence industries, pressing for a larger defence effort and a security-orientated foreign policy. The relationship between government and industry is close on procurement matters, but the Ministry of Defence appears to have the decisive say.

Costs and cost escalation have led to collaboration in procurement with foreign governments. This inevitably also has domestic industrial policy implications, as over the rescue of Westland helicopters in 1985–6, when the Department of Trade and Industry and the Ministry of Defence were in dispute. The symbolic aspects of high technology policy mean that defence procurement also gets tangled up with domestic industrial and science policy. However, there is relative harmony between the Foreign Office and the Ministry of Defence compared to the corresponding departments in other countries, for example, the United States. Within the Ministry of Defence attempts to overcome interservice rivalries have developed from the integration of the previously separate ministries for each armed service in 1962 to the abolition of separate junior ministers for each service.

Foreign and defence policy are much less likely to involve open consultation or genuine public debate than even most domestic matters. There is a lack of use of 'Green Papers' in foreign policy to explore alternatives publicly. Internal re-examinations of foreign policy are not always published. Even more than most domestic policy the foreign policy process is not a parliamentary one, and 'parliamentary confrontation takes place too often on unreal issues' (Wallace, 1975, 279).

Foreign policy, then, cannot itself be characterized as having a single 'policy style'. For a range of sectoral issues dealing with the international dimension or domestic interests the processing of issues will be similar to consultation in policy communities, though the overlapping nature of issues with an international dimension is likely to pull many of them into interdepartmental committees rather than allow them to be dealt with solely within separate sectors. For a number of high and low policy issues, however, the processing of the issue will be handled largely within the executive, with little direct consultation of groups. The very fact that foreign policy involves dealing with foreigners introduces uncertainty into both the processing of issues and the final outcomes of decisions.

3.6 Processing issues within Whitehall

Looking at the relationship of groups and departments does provide us with an important part of the picture, but what goes on inside Whitehall also matters. Of particular importance is who is involved in drawing up and filtering the options on which a decision is based. Former Labour minister Tony Benn (in Young and Sloman, 1982, 19–20) has argued that the options presented will reflect not the manifesto of the party in power but the 'policy of the outgoing government, minus the mistakes that the civil service thought the outgoing government made'. Conservative critics such as Nicholas Ridley (in Niskanen, 1973) have also referred to what they see as the obstructive role of the civil service. Most former and present ministers, however, express satisfaction with their senior civil servants (see Young and Sloman, 1982; RIPA, 1980). One interpretation is that the potential clash is between politicians with 'radical ideas', whether of the left or right, and civil servants as the advocates of continuity and of a concern with the practicality of policies. A number of ex-ministers and other commentators have noted that the advice coming from civil servants often reflects a 'departmental view' which persists over changes in minister and party in power (see, for example, Young and Sloman, 1982, 21–5). A quite contradictory criticism was made in the House of Commons on 11 November 1985 by Michael Meacher, a former Benn supporter, who argued that advice to ministers from civil servants was being increasingly tailored to what it was known that ministers wanted to hear. For this reason, the full range of independent and objective advice was no longer reaching ministers.

A broader criticism is that ministers are not always presented with all the options open to them, reflecting a penchant among civil servants for funnelling advice through a single source. To a large extent the remedy for being offered only a single option lies in the minister's own hands. Roy Jenkins (1971) found in the Home Office that he was presented with a single set of advice channelled through his Permanent Secretary, but he altered that system. If a minister makes it clear that he wants to be presented with options rather than a single departmental view and to have direct access to civil servants a couple of levels down the hierarchy he will be able to do so. The appointment of a limited number of political advisers has made relatively little difference to the continuing role of the civil service as the main source of information and advice. Mrs Thatcher has not been keen on her ministers having a large number of political advisers, though she maintains a Policy Unit of nine at No. 10.

However, it remains true that on many issues in both central and local government the role of ministers or councillors in the processing of issues is often confined to an acceptance or rejection of a single option presented to them by officials, or looking at a very limited range of options. Even where a number of options are presented, this may give little opportunity to consider these options because of shortage of time or because ministers have not had an opportunity to watch the arguments develop (see Cardona, 1981). On foreign affairs, Wallace (1975, 278) noted that ministers may be unaware of the debate about alternatives going on below them. By the time proposals reach the minister's desk the differences will have been filtered out into an acceptable compromise.

Issues do not always come departmentally packaged, and the processing of issues will frequently involve a number of departments. Differences of opinion between departments occasionally lead to sharp disagreements, and these disputes naturally receive the most publicity. Differences between departments also have to be seen in the broader context of competition among them for legislative and financial resources. However, disagreements on individual issues will be dealt with within the context of a concern with long-term relations, particularly on the civil service side. There is a general concern to minimize public row and avoid issues going to Cabinet, since if they do so this may lead to outside scrutiny (outside the affected departments, that is) of the issue and the unravelling of such agreement as they had been able to come to.

Some ex-ministers, notably Benn (1980), have argued that civil servants mobilize other departments against their minister and that civil servants from different departments do deals with each other and then present the compromise as advice to their ministers. Particularly important in this are interdepartmental committees, some of them shadowing cabinet committees of ministers (which are dealt with in 4.6). The role of interdepartmental committees is disputed. Such committees are often described as simply working for ministers and making recommendations or identifying options for cabinet committees (Morrison, 1954, 26; Wilson, 1976, 101). However, other ministers have argued that their role is more considerable. Crossman (1975, 200) argues, for instance, that:

> very often the whole job is pre-cooked in the official committees to a point from which it is extremely difficult to reach any other conclusion than that already determined by the officials in advance . . . I have yet to see a Minister prevail against an inter-departmental official paper without the backing of a Prime Minister, a First Secretary or the Chancellor.

These suspicions of interdepartmental committees seemed to be fairly widespread amongst Labour ministers in the late 1960s who suspected that information was exchanged and compromises worked out contrary to their wishes. However, the consequence of this was a loss of trust between themselves and their department. Officials became unwilling to take decisions at all and far too much was referred to ministers. This points to one of the reasons why there are so many of these committees in the first place—to ease the burden on ministers. In the particular case of Tony Benn in the 1974–6 Wilson government, the picture was complicated by the fact that he clearly lacked the confidence of the prime minister; his civil servants could not be sure that he would be able to carry the day for the department and therefore attempted to do what they considered to be the best deal with other departments (see Young and Sloman, 1982, 29–30). The problem cannot be solved by forbidding civil servants to make deals with other departments. The scale of government activities, and in particular those with interdepartmental implications, precludes ministers from discussing among themselves all the options.

A number of departments may be involved in the implementation of some policies because of functional interaction, or because special arrangements are made for administration of the policy in Scotland, Wales, and Northern Ireland. In such cases there will be a number of sets of committees with varying combinations of representatives from the departments or agencies sponsored by them. In addition, one department may be designated the 'lead' department. This department is given the responsibility for drawing together any proposals for changes in policy, but only after consultation with other departments involved. For example, the Department of Trade and Industry is the lead department for regional policy, even though it only administers the policy in England (Hogwood, 1982).

3.7 'Non-internalizable' issues and the role of Parliament

Internalized processing, whether within departments or within broader policy communities, does not apply to all issues. First, some issues such as value-laden issues like abortion or some constitutional issues which split the governing party are seen as *inappropriate* for handling within departments. Government is normally happy to leave these for consideration by Parliament (see also 5.7). On issues which involve both commercial interests and value issues, such as Sunday trading, the government can face difficulties in trying to force its legislation through Parliament.

Other issues may not be capable of being processed through discussion in departments, communities, or Parliament. All governments except the 1979 Thatcher government have tried to get the agreement of the TUC and the CBI to incomes policies and are often prepared to make substantial concessions. However, this often fails and the issue becomes one of government imposition and union resistance.

Political parties, particularly in opposition, perform important roles in analysing issues when preparing their programme. This can be seen as the partial *pre-processing* of issues. However, this does not normally eliminate the usual consultative procedures *once in office*. Policies are rarely worked out in detail in opposition or in the manifesto. The exception which proves the rule was the Industrial Relations Act of 1971, which was effectively rendered inoperable at the implementation stage by union opposition. That is, the party role, including the role of party leaders in Parliament, is at least as much an agenda-setting as a processing role.

The limited direct participation of Parliament does not necessarily mean that its role at agenda-processing stage is trivial. As noted in 3.1, debates and questions can help to ensure that an issue is not pushed off the agenda. Further, Parliament is an important channel for pressure to expedite the processing of issues; the columns of *Hansard* are full of questions about when ministers will be able to make a statement on a particular issue.

Even on issues processed largely through consultation between departments and groups Parliament may perform a subsidiary role as a *sounding board*. Views expressed in debates and questions are not necessarily ignored. Strongly expressed feeling, particularly by government backbenchers, may effectively act as a veto over a particular option the government is considering: for example, the government could not have decided simply to ignore the Argentinian invasion of the Falkland Islands in 1982. Reflecting both the increased assertiveness of backbenchers and her perception of the deficiencies of Edward Heath's leadership, Mrs Thatcher has attempted to maintain close contact with the executive of the backbench Conservative 1922 Committee and ministers have been encouraged to put policy proposals before the relevant backbench policy committees (Burch, 1983, 409). These arrangements did not prevent a series of breakdowns in communication and ministerial *faux pas* from the end of 1984 onwards. It should be stressed that Conservative backbenchers have not been involved in actual decision-making. The concern has been to sound out opinion in advance so that party reaction, among a number of other considerations, can be taken into account by the participants who actually take the decisions. Ministers are not in any case always accurate in assessing in advance which are the issues on which backbench and wider party opinion is likely to be sensitive.

The Commons as a whole may express a view while an issue is still being considered. In January 1985 the Commons voted against placing the third London airport at Stansted. In June 1985 the government announced that the third London airport would nevertheless be at Stansted. This underlines that the views of members of Parliament are at best only one of the considerations which the government weighs when considering the options.

Not surprisingly, many MPs feel left out in the cold by the sometimes cosy arrangement between departments and interests. They would like to be involved at the issue-processing stage rather than be presented with an accomplished decision. The House of Commons has sometimes played a more formal role on appraisal of options, for example, through select committees on corporation tax and wealth tax in the 1970s. The select committees set up in 1979 are seen by some as having this role (their potential role in evaluating government policies once they have been put into effect is considered in 9.4). All major departments are covered by one of these committees. Although seen by some as new, in many ways they represented a development of the subcommittees of the Expenditure Committee, which were wound up as the new committees were established. The party composition of the committees reflects that of the Commons as a whole.

Any impact which the committees have on the shaping of policy will normally have to be through reports or the actual process of collecting evidence and examining witnesses, since only about 10 per cent of reports are debated directly or indirectly on the floor of the Commons (Lock, 1985). Many of the reports have been extended investigations whose reports were not timed to feed into government decisions. Others, like the investigations into the Westland affair, have been set up in reaction to government decisions, though the knowledge that the background to a decision may be retrospectively examined may itself influence the way the issue is processed or even the decision arrived at.

However, a number of reports, particularly of short investigations conducted for the purpose, have been timed to be of possible influence in government decisions (see Giddings, 1985, 370). Certainly a number of committees have pointed to examples of what they feel has been of influence on subsequent government decisions (Downs, 1985, 66). Equally though, one can point to a number of examples where committee recommendations have been rejected or ignored by government (Giddings, 1985, 375). The government response to recommendations (many of them concerned with reviewing existing policies rather than those currently under consideration by government) made by two committees in the 1979–83 period was that 30.3 per cent of recommendations from the Social Services Committee were accepted, 54.5 per cent were 'to be kept under review', and 15.2 per cent were rejected, while for the Education, Science, and Arts Committee, 28.5 per cent of recommendations were accepted, 43.8 per cent kept under review, and 27.7 per cent rejected (Lock, 1985, 344). Thus, under a third of recommendations were formally accepted by government. The difficulty is in assessing actual influence, since such reports are only one consideration which the government has to take into account: pressure exercised is not necessarily equivalent to influence felt.

However, making the policy process more public can be regarded as an objective in itself, and in this the committees have had some modest success, though interest has naturally been normally limited to those who already have a specialist interest in the subject under discussion (Rush, 1985, 101). An overall assessment is that 'The effect of these committees on ministeral and departmental policy-making has been indirect and marginal, contextual rather than substantive' (Giddings, 1985, 376). The committees have done little to broaden participation in decision-making beyond established interest groups: 'There has been no significant widening of the policy community as a result of the committees' calls for evidence' (Giddings, 1985, 378).

The relatively peripheral role of Parliament, both committees and the floor of the Commons, at the agenda-processing stage on most issues can be underlined by asking what is in it for departments and interest groups if Parliament became a major participant at this stage. While interest groups may find Parliament a useful supplementary line of communication and pressure, those with a close relationship with their departments will be unlikely to welcome public scrutiny of the process of consultation. However, this arrangement, particularly where a consultation amounts to negotiation, is dependent on the government's ability to deliver on its side of a bargain. A period of minority or loose coalition government might remove that assumption and open up the potential for an increased role for Parliament in exploring policy options.

Chapter 4

Making Authoritative Choices

4.1 Is decision-making a myth?

While it is often meaningful in the context of British public policy
to think in terms of key decisions taken by central government,
decisions which shape public policy are taken at all stages of the
policy process and in a range of different types of public and
private bodies. Where key decisions in central government can be
identified, they may be taken in a variety of different arenas, with
the location varying according to type of issue and across time.

Decision and decision-making have been key concepts in the
study of British government. The implication is of climactic
decision events at the centre of government. A 'rational' model of
decision-making would stress the importance of a key decision
taken by a single decision-making body. By contrast a 'partisan
mutual adjustment' model would stress that not only are there a
number of relevant actors but that policies are the outcomes of
their interaction rather than a single decision moment. (For a
discussion of different decision-making models, see Hogwood and
Gunn, 1984, ch. 4.).

The approach adopted in this book is that decisions are choices
between alternatives and that the policy process can be seen as a
flow of such decisions. Decisions at one stage become the basis for
further choices at later ones; they will vary considerably in the
extent to which they can be considered to be definitive. 'Decisions'
taken by a body like the Cabinet may be altered or abandoned
before or during legislative stage (see chapter 5). Decisions about
implementation may be crucial in giving substance to what were
only vague formulations at the 'decision-making' stage.

That having been said, in contrast to some other political
systems Britain does have a high degree of centralized decision-
making at options selection stage. Decisions taken in the name of
the government are almost always important in strongly shaping

policy. To some extent the integration which is achieved by some of the mechanisms described in this chapter is weak; decisions may be taken within single government departments, and even inter-departmental mechanisms such as cabinet committees may simply be the institutionalization of policy communities or sectors which cross-cut departmental boundaries. However, on some issues ministers, especially the prime minister, who are not full members of the relevant policy community, may be involved in decision-making. Thus, there is a degree of integration within the British executive which does provide some counterbalance to the view of the policy process as being totally segmented into sectors.

The concepts of individual and collective ministerial responsibility can be seen as 'Myths of the British Constitution', rather than as accurate descriptions of how decisions within the executive are actually taken. Under the myth of individual ministerial responsibility the minister is answerable to (and by implication punishable by) the House of Commons for all the decisions of his department and for the operation of agencies ('quangos') sponsored by his department. The myth of individual ministerial responsibility has gradually dissolved in face of the fact that ministers are not even aware of most of the decisions taken in their name. Except for Lord Carrington and other ministers in the Foreign Office who resigned over the Falklands invasion in 1982, no minister had resigned since the early 1950s because of an error made by his department. Mr Brittan's resignation in January 1986 over the leaking by his department of a letter from the Solicitor-General in the Westland affair might be argued to be of this kind, but since he had obtained the approval of the prime minister's private office for the leak it is rather different in nature.

Under the myth of collective responsibility all ministers have the opportunity to comment on government proposals and once decisions are taken on them all ministers have to support those decisions publicly, even if they disagreed with them in Cabinet. Even the public face of collective responsibility sometimes cracks: there was partial agreement to disagree within the Labour Cabinet in the mid-1970s over the European Communities. More frequently, by judicious leaking, ministers who disagree with an important decision can publicly disassociate themselves from it. Prior to his resignation at the beginning of 1986, Michael Heseltine, the Secretary of State for Defence, made quite public his disagreement with the Secretary of State for Trade and Industry's view, endorsed by the prime minister, about how the rescue of the Westland helicopter company should be handled.

Cynics will have observed that whichever myth is most convenient politically will be the one that is invoked. Thus when Mr Benn made a statement on Court Line in 1974 to the House of Commons which misled many holiday-makers into thinking that their holidays were secure, the myth of collective responsibility was invoked by the government to protect Mr Benn as an individual minister.

More importantly, the myth of collective responsibility does not represent reality in that few decisions taken in the name of government are in fact taken collectively by the Cabinet. Decisions are variously taken by individual ministers, by departmental–Treasury deals, by cabinet committees and, only occasionally on important matters, particularly involving conflict between departments, by the full Cabinet. The effective decision-making arena is rarely identified. Indeed, the confidential document *Questions of Procedure for Ministers* specifically forbids the public identification of the arena in which the decision was taken:

Decisions reached by the Cabinet or Cabinet committee are normally announced and defended by the minister concerned as his own decisions . . . The growth of any general practice whereby decisions of the Cabinet or of Cabinet committee were announced as such would lead to the embarrassing result that some decisions of government would be regarded as less authoritative than others. Critics of a decision reached by a particular committee could press for its review by some other committee or by the Cabinet, and the constitutional right of individual ministers to speak in the name of the government as a whole would be impaired. (Quoted in Hennessy, 1986.)

We would expect policy areas to vary in the extent to which decisions about them are taken in particular arenas; for example, the locations of decision-making about foreign policy are likely to differ from those affecting, say, energy policy. These various decision-making arenas are now examined in turn.

4.2 Decisions within departments

Most government decisions are made within the confines of single government departments. Most of these are, of course, detailed decisions about the implementation of agreed government policy. Such decisions can, however, be quite important individually.

The extent to which important decisions, including policy decisions, can be made within individual departments will vary according to a number of factors, including the way in which portfolios were initially divided up and intrinsic characteristics of the functions of the department which will determine the extent to which they interact with the functions of other departments. A number of former education ministers have commented on how most of the decisions relating to education (other than negotiations with the Treasury about finance) were taken within the education department (see Kogan, 1971; Butler and Crowther-Hunt, 1965). For example, Anthony Crosland, who served both as trade minister and education minister in the Labour government of 1964–70, pointed out that in the trade ministry almost every issue that came up involved other departments—the Treasury, the Department of Economic Affairs, Housing and Local Government, Scotland and Wales, but that education was a particularly independent department. In the 1980s, with the overlap between training and education, the education department appears to have become less self-contained.

Another minister in the 1964–70 Labour government, Roy Jenkins (1971), who served as Home Secretary and Chancellor of the Exchequer, commented on how few of the decisions involving the Home Secretary involved collective ministerial discussion, but that the work of the Treasury was intrinsically interdepartmental:

Many of the Home Secretary's most important decisions are exclusively reserved for his individual judgement. They need not be taken to Cabinet and they ought not to be so taken.

Crosland also drew attention to another factor which leads to a large number of issues being taken within departments:

The other thing is that if you're carrying out agreed Party policy, and seem to be doing it reasonably successfully and without frightful rows breaking out, your colleagues won't particularly want to interfere. They are all exceedingly busy men in their own jobs, and I think they were prepared to trust my judgement. (Kogan, 1971, 160–1.)

In contrast to the education department, the work of the Treasury is intrinsically interdepartmental, with the Treasury having both to bargain bilaterally about departmental allocations and seek collective agreement to overall ceilings (see chapter 6).

Decision-making is often less than strictly unilateral: as was discussed extensively in chapter 3, it is often the product of negotiation between a department and relevant groups, with only limited scope for the Cabinet to undo bargains struck between them. Lord Butler, the minister responsible for the 1944 Education Act, claimed in an interview with Lord Crowther-Hunt that 'it was only at the later stages, when we wanted authority, that we went to a government committee to get authority for it'.

Hunt: And was the Lord President's Committee able to alter your policy at all?
Lord Butler: No, I think they mostly endorsed what we had been doing: it was the result of a big piece of legislation and therefore it would not have been sensible at that stage to alter it much.
Hunt: Would it be true to say that increasingly major measures are often the product of a department and the minister in consultation with outside bodies, and that, once they have agreed, it is then really very difficult for even a Cabinet committee, let alone the Cabinet, to alter them in any substantial way?
Lord Butler: Yes, and there I get back to what I said at the beginning, that it is when political issues arise that the Cabinet really comes in. The Cabinet does not alter the structure of the hard work done by a department in framing a measure, say a transport act or something of that sort. (Butler and Crowther-Hunt, 1965.)

4.3 Co-ordinating ministers

Occasionally, prime ministers have attempted to introduce in-dividual ministers as co-ordinators over departments headed by other ministers. One such attempt was the introduction by Churchill of 'overlords' responsible for co-ordinating a number of related departments. This experiment is generally considered to have failed since it blurred ministerial responsibility for depart-ments, and it was abandoned in 1953 (see Walker, 1972; Jones, 1975). These 'overlords' were appointed on top of the existing departmental ministers rather than being heads of departments themselves. An interesting exception is the Minister of Defence after the Second World War, who did have his own department while the War Office, Admiralty, and Air Ministry continued. The three service departments were merged into the Ministry of Defence in the early 1960s.

86   MAKING AUTHORITATIVE CHOICES

Other ministers with 'co-ordinating' functions may be appointed. For example, Britain normally has a minister responsible for co-ordinating government information services. Ministers without departmental responsibilities may be given broader responsibility for assisting the co-ordination of numbers of sets of related functions, as was Shirley Williams as Paymaster General in Britain in the 1974–9 Labour government. However, this role is exercised not at an individual or simply at an interdepartmental level, but by giving such ministers the chairmanship of cabinet committees, and is thus part of the process of resolving issues in such committees (Jones, 1975, 42).

4.4 Bilateral

Many of the key decisions affecting a department, namely those concerning programme finance, are the subject of bilateral negotiation between the spending department and the Treasury; this is discussed in chapter 6. Another important set of bilateral links within the cabinet framework is between the prime minister and a few key ministers, particularly the Chancellor of the Exchequer and the Foreign Secretary. Prime ministers tend to devote a much larger proportion of their time to foreign affairs than to the work of other departments and many issues may be discussed between the prime minister and the Foreign Secretary without ever being brought to the attention of other ministers (see e.g. Rose, 1980, 335–8; Walker, 1972, 88, 116). On the annual Budget (which in Britain deals only with taxation), the Chancellor of the Exchequer closely consults the prime minister, but other ministers normally have to accept a *fait accompli* (see 6.5).

Even when a decision is formally within the competence of a single minister, the prime minister may intervene, as she did in 1985 over a proposal by Peter Palumbo to build a skyscraper near the Bank of England. Even though the prime minister stressed that the decision was one for the minister alone, it would be surprising if the minister took no notice at all of the prime minister's views on such an issue. More generally, all prime ministers become interested in particular issues which would otherwise be handled solely within a single government department, though to do so on the whole range of decisions would be impossible. The criteria for choosing on which decisions to intervene will be a mixture of perceived importance and individual idiosyncrasy. Hennessy (1985b) argues that Mrs Thatcher has made particular use of the practice of asking an individual minister to prepare a paper on a particular topic for her rather than the Cabinet, then summoning the minister to 10 Downing Street before making her decision.

4.5 Multilateral

There is a complex network of interdepartmental committees outside the cabinet committee structure, mainly interdepartmental committees of officials rather than ministers (see 3.6), but this is only the most formal aspect of multilateral contacts. All prime ministers make use of informal groups of ministers to advise them or to reach decisions, but Mrs Thatcher seems to be particularly fond of using them, both to deal with continuing issues and on a one-off basis to resolve political problems (Hennessy, 1985b). For example, the decision partially to reverse cuts in student grants in 1984 was taken at a ten-minute meeting at 10 Downing Street of ministers and advisers presided over by the prime minister. During the summer of 1985 Mrs Thatcher became interested in the problem of football hooliganism, following the disaster at the Hysel stadium in Belgium in which British supporters were involved. She held a number of 'summits' involving ministers and civil servants and representatives of the Football Association and the Football League.

Theakston (1984) found that junior ministers attend many interdepartmental meetings outside the formal cabinet committee structure. These meetings might consist of two or three junior ministers accompanied by civil service advisers, meeting for a short session on a particular problem. If agreement cannot be reached in this way, the matter may go before a cabinet committee. If the matter is important or controversial, it is likely to be channelled into the formal committee structure, in part because of civil service distaste for 'casual and haphazard deals between small groups of junior ministers' (Theakston, 1984, 307).

Communication involving a number of ministers is not necessarily on a face-to-face basis. Noting that the multiplicity of policy decisions requiring interdepartmental clearance is far greater than could be handled in Cabinet or even cabinet committee meetings in Britain, Pliatzky (1982, 36–7) states that:

A great deal of business is therefore carried out by inter-Ministerial correspondence: it is in fact rather exceptional for one individual Minister to write to another individual Minister and almost always his letter is copied to, say, half a dozen other Ministers, or to the rather large number of Ministers who make up a Cabinet committee, or to all the members of Cabinet. The photocopier is nowadays both literally and figuratively an essential element in the machinery of government. Even so the system could not work without the technocratic back-up, whether working through official committees run by the Cabinet Office or other inter-Departmental committees, or the network of informal contacts between officials.

4.6 Cabinet committees

The various co-ordinating and decision-making mechanisms described in the previous sections are insufficient to reduce the burden on full Cabinet. Thus a formal system of cabinet committees is required. Since 1979 the existence of four standing committees and their chairmanship has been officially published. Following the 1983 general election, it was announced in a Commons written answer that the cabinet committees were Home and Social Affairs (chaired by Lord Whitelaw, the deputy prime minister), Economic Strategy (chaired by Mrs Thatcher), Overseas and Defence Policy (chaired by Mrs Thatcher), and Legislation (chaired by John Biffen, Leader of the House of Commons). An important feature of the chairmanship of these standing committees, apart from the fact that Mrs Thatcher herself chairs two of them, is that none of them are chaired by departmental ministers.

However, this revealed information does not divulge the important role played by *ad hoc* cabinet committees, to say nothing of the small, informal groups of ministers which appear to have played such an important role in decision-making under Mrs Thatcher. The existence of a committee on intelligence and security is also not mentioned. Both standing committees and *ad hoc* committees may have subcommittees, which usually report to the parent committee, although they may report direct to the Cabinet (Theakston, 1984, 307).

Although the system has varied under each prime minister,

since Atlee's government of 1945–51 all British Cabinets have had highly ramified sytems of subcommittees and *ad hoc* committees. These *ad hoc* committees are alternatively labelled MISC and GEN under succeeding governments and are numbered in a continuous series which includes both ministerial and civil service committees. Hennessy (1985b) estimated that Mrs Thatcher had established about 30 standing committees and about 115 *ad hoc* committees in just over six years, including committees of officials which shadow the ministerial committees. Mrs Thatcher's total is relatively modest compared to previous administrations, though large compared to her apparent original intention to avoid having cabinet committees at all (Hennessy, 1984). Attlee established 148 standing committees and 313 *ad hoc* committees between 1945 and 1951, and Churchill set up 137 standing committees and 109 *ad hoc* committees in three and a half years in his final period as prime minister (Hennessy, 1985b). Figures for more recent administrations are patchy, but after four and a quarter years in 1969 Harold Wilson had set up 236 *ad hoc* committees; in his second period as prime minister he set up around 120 *ad hoc* committees in two years between 1974 and 1976. Callaghan set up about 160 *ad hoc* committees in three years between 1976 and 1979. However, in comparing the figures of different governments it is important to bear in mind the use of other devices, such as Mrs Thatcher's greater use of informal groups of ministers, which might under other administrations have constituted formal cabinet committees (see 4.5).

At any given time, only a few of these committees will be meeting regularly, and it is sometimes difficult to distinguish between the functions of a subcommittee of a standing committee and an *ad hoc* committee which deals with an issue which continues to attract the attention of government. For example, the so-called War Cabinet on the Falklands War was a subcommittee (OD(SA)) of the Overseas and Defence Committee though its work was temporary. Similarly, H(HL) met only a few times to discuss the reform of the House of Lords before deciding that nothing should be done (Hennessy, 1984). On the other hand, the so-called 'Star Chamber' under Lord Whitelaw, which met each year from 1982 to try to reconcile public expenditure bids which had not been resolved in bilateral discussions between departments and the Treasury, was an *ad hoc* committee (MISC 62) (see 6.3).

Formally, ministerial cabinet committees are made up of cabinet ministers, and junior ministers attend only as representatives of a cabinet minister. In practice, some committees are composed only of cabinet ministers (the main standing committees, with occasional substitute appearances by junior ministers), most others of cabinet and junior ministers, and some only of junior ministers (Theakston, 1984, 308). Normally ministerial *ad hoc* committees or subcommittees are chaired by a full cabinet minister, though they may be chaired by a junior minister.

Departments are involved to varying extents in cabinet committee work. Because the Foreign Office and the Ministry of Defence are only occasionally involved in legislation and do not overlap much with other departments (except for the Foreign Office in European Community matters) they are represented on only a few committees, and their secretaries of state normally attend where they are represented (Theakston, 1984, 309). By contrast, the Treasury is represented on almost every committee, so that Treasury ministers, especially junior ministers, have an especially heavy load.

The level of ministerial participation in cabinet committees is a subtle indicator of personal and departmental interest. Ministers have many demands on their time (Headey, 1974), and may not give priority to cabinet committees. By sending a junior minister to a committee a minister may seek to stall a decision (Theakston, 1984, 310). Naturally, for subjects which the department considers of crucial importance the secretary of state will attend; issues perceived as peripheral are more likely to have a junior minister from the department attending. Naturally, the status of other ministers likely to be present, especially in the chair, will influence attendance. One minister interviewed by Theakston (1984) said 'The status of the Minister likely to be defeated is important: the Chancellor cannot lose to the parliamentary secretary to the Post Office', thus implying that winning and losing are not simply related to the status of attenders, though they are related to the possible loss of face. A cabinet minister who is outvoiced in committee by a junior minister (rather than outvoted, since formal votes are never taken) is likely to reserve his position so that the committee is unable to carry out its task of taking decisions and saving the Cabinet from having to consider an issue. Conversely, junior ministers are in difficulty if they try to reserve their superior's position on a matter they know he will oppose. Often junior ministers have to attend as substitutes for their ministerial head of department or other junior ministers at short notice. A junior minister who is known to carry the political backing of his minister is more likely to carry weight; this is particularly likely to be the case with Treasury ministers. The relative status of ministers attending committees is likely to be important only on major issues (Theakston, 1984, 315).

Secretarial support for the Cabinet and cabinet committees is provided through the Cabinet Office, with a secretariat of about 100 civil servants headed by the Secretary of the Cabinet. In 1985 the Secretary oversaw six secretariats, each headed by an under-secretary; they were responsible for overseas and defence matters, economic affairs, home and parliamentary affairs, European affairs, science and technology and, finally, security and intelligence. Each secretariat services several cabinet committees.

It is important to note that these committees comprise not only committees of ministers, but also committees of civil servants which shadow the ministerial committees. The official committees are chaired either by Cabinet Office officials or by officials from the 'lead' department (Theakston, 1984, 307). In addition to servicing ministerial committees by preparing papers and briefs and clearing away minor points, these official committees consider matters delegated to them by the ministerial committee. These committees are a part of the cabinet *system* in so far as they are serviced by the Cabinet Office, but it is important to note that there are also interdepartmental committees which are not part of the formal Cabinet Office network but which nevertheless play an important role in decision-making; for example, the interdepartmental committee of civil servants which conducted a major review of regional policy prior to the White Paper on regional policy in 1983 was chaired by a Treasury official. As was noted in 3.6, the role of such interdepartmental committees in shaping or foreclosing options is disputed.

The Cabinet Secretary, in addition to acting as secretary to the full Cabinet and to cabinet committees chaired by the prime minister, frequently exercises a more personal influence on the prime minister as a result of the often close personal links which have developed between the prime minister and his or her civil servants (Seldon, 1981; Crossman, 1976, 296; Campbell, 1983; Hennessy, 1980).

Despite the importance placed in British constitutional doctrine on ministerial responsibility and accountability, all British governments have made use of mixed committees of ministers and civil servants. The Conservative government of 1970–4 was led by Edward Heath, who felt that the cabinet committee system had got out of hand and made extensive use of mixed committees of ministers and civil servants (Hennessy, 1983a; Fay and Young, 1976, 8–9). A problem with such committees was the unwillingness of civil servants to disagree with their ministers. The use of such mixed committees was cut back under the subsequent Labour government of Harold Wilson. The Callaghan government of 1976–9, after extensive discussion of economic strategy in full Cabinet at the time of the IMF loan in 1976, made use of a mixed group of ministers (Dennis Healey, Chancellor of the Exchequer, Harold Lever, Chancellor of the Duchy of Lancaster) and officials (the prime minister's Principal Private Secretary and the heads of the Treasury, Bank of England, the Cabinet Office, and the Central Policy Review Staff) (Hennessy, 1983a).

Cabinet committees could in practice perform a variety of different roles, with the same committee performing different roles in relation to different decisions. First, discussions between departments in preparation for cabinet committees may lead to consensus so that the committee meeting itself may merely endorse the decision. Such decisions would invariably not be discussed by full Cabinet, so here it is effectively the cabinet committee which is performing the 'legitimating' role.

Cabinet committees may fail to agree sufficiently to arrive at a final decision; however, even here the cabinet committee will have played an important role in defining the issues and narrowing the options for the full Cabinet. It will rarely be the argument in the cabinet committee itself that will determine how ministers line up on an issue; the ministers in dispute (if any) will already have evolved their views and ministers not directly involved tend to follow the line of their briefs (see e.g. Barnett, 1982; Kaufman, 1980).

Cabinet committees may arrive at agreement but these decisions may be subject to review by full Cabinet. Cabinet cannot possibly give full consideration to all issues already considered in a large number of cabinet committees, and in consequence most decisions, even under a system where all committee decisions are in principle reviewable, will in practice be 'nodded through' the full Cabinet.

Constitutionally the most significant role for cabinet committees is where their decisions are treated as final without any reference to Cabinet and where these decisions are given equal authority with full Cabinet decisions. When prime ministers operate this approach, only those decisions where agreement cannot be reached are discussed in full Cabinet.

The roles which cabinet committees perform will in part depend on the extent of interdepartmental and party disagreements within the government and on informal procedures which have grown up over the years. In Britain each prime minister may lay down his or her own (unpublished) rules, but the practice in most recent governments appears to be encapsulated by the ruling in 1967 by the then prime minister, Harold Wilson, that a matter could be taken to the Cabinet from a committee only with the agreement of the committee chairman (who is appointed by the prime minister). In theory, ministers still had the constitutional right to bring any matter to the Cabinet, including a question settled in a committee, but 'in practice this right was greatly attenuated' (Walker, 1972, 44; see also Kaufman, 1980, 69).

In exercising discretion, a committee chairman was expected to consider the degree of disagreement in the committee or the intrinsic importance of the issue or its political overtones. A dispute between an aggrieved minister and the chairman of the committee over referring an issue to full Cabinet would be resolved by the prime minister. Based on his own experience, Patrick Gordon Walker (1972, 119), emphasized that 'It is the chairman's duty to try and settle things in committee and as far as possible save the time of the Cabinet'. Even where there is disagreement, the committee chairman may refer the matter back for reconsideration by individual ministers and only refer it to Cabinet if disagreement persists.

One of the potential dangers with a system of permitting cabinet committees to make final decisions is that a minority in the committee might be overruled yet be potentially capable of mobilizing a majority in the full Cabinet. In chapter 6 the special arrangements which have been devised to prevent the Treasury being overruled on expenditure matters are discussed.

The appointment of the committee chairman is particularly important given the lack of formal votes and the key role of the chairman in summing up the decision of the committee (see Walker, 1972, 119–20; Kaufman, 1980, 72). For example, in 1978 the cabinet committee on energy (ENM) was chaired not by the left-wing energy minister, Tony Benn, but by the more right-wing industry minister, Eric Varley. More generally, Page (1978, 74) alleges:

given Benn's following, there could be no question of his exclusion from the publicly-appointed Cabinet, but within the secret system of committees the Premier can register disfavour by excluding Benn from chairmanships, which are reserved for trusties like Varley and Rees.

The prime minister herself chairs a number of key committees.

A former permanent secretary has argued that the allocation of departmental and cabinet committee responsibilities enabled the 'monetarists' to dominate the 1979 Thatcher government on economic matters:

The monetarist minority nevertheless prevailed in economic and industrial policy because they had strategic control of the key Departments and *Cabinet committees*; as in previous administrations, only the Prime Minister and Treasury Ministers were effectively involved in taxation policy and, in conjunction with the Bank of England, in interest rates and exchange policy. *The doubters and dissenters were either given no opportunity to mount a challenge in full Cabinet or were unable to do so effectively.* (Pliatzky, 1982, 178; emphasis added.)

Although each new government can define its own rules for cabinet committee procedure, and the 'Wilson ruling' was not continued by the incoming Conservative government in 1970, the ruling appears to encapsulate the reality of practice under most recent British governments. For example, under the 1974–9 Labour government the prime minister would rarely allow ministers to bring matters settled in committee to full Cabinet; even in the case of an exceptionally influential minister this had to be on a matter of major importance. Under the Heath government of 1970–4, however, it appears that 'all Cabinet committee decisions, even non-controversial ones, were reported to the Cabinet, giving ministers who had not been closely involved the opportunity to have their say' (*The Times*, 7 February 1984), though it is not clear how often ministers availed themselves of this opportunity. In December 1985 Mrs Thatcher refused the request of Michael Heseltine, the Secretary of State for Defence, to discuss the rescue of the Westland helicopter firm in full Cabinet.

The issue had until then been handled in cabinet committee and it is worth noting that Mr Heseltine only attempted to raise the issue in full Cabinet because he contended that a cabinet committee meeting to discuss the matter further had been cancelled on the prime minister's orders.

The status of cabinet committee decisions which are not discussed in full Cabinet in Britain seems quite clear:

Cabinet committees are parallel and equal to the Cabinet itself. In matters within their terms of reference, committees can come to a decision that has the same authority as a Conclusion of the Cabinet: it will be accepted and acted upon as if it were a Cabinet decision. (Walker, 1972, 119.)

Other former British cabinet ministers have also confirmed that 'a lot is settled at Cabinet Committees without having to go to the Cabinet' and that 'A lot of the big defence issues will be decided by the Chiefs of Staff, and by the Defence Committee, and they would not themselves come to the Cabinet except for confirmation' (Butler and Crowther-Hunt, 1965, 194; see also Kaufman, 1980, 69, 72).

It should not be assumed that cabinet committees will deal with low-level issues and that all important decisions will be dealt with in full Cabinet. There can be few more important decisions than whether and how to launch or curtail major military operations, yet in Britain these are more likely to be handled by a cabinet committee than by full Cabinet. The handling of the war between Britain and Argentina over the Falkland Islands in 1982 was supervised by a committee variously referred to as the Inner Cabinet, the War Cabinet, and the Falklands groups of ministers, consisting of the prime minister, the Home Secretary, the Foreign Secretary, the Defence Secretary, and the chairman of the Conservative Party in his guise as the Paymaster General, a sinecure post. The relationship between this cabinet committee and the full Cabinet is well brought out in the following report from *The Times* of 24 April 1982, clearly based on an unattributable official briefing (almost certainly from the prime minister's press secretary):

Yesterday's Cabinet meeting [i.e. on 28 April 1982, four weeks after Argentina had invaded the Falkland Islands], which followed a meeting of the Falklands group of senior ministers, lasted one and a quarter hours. It was described as stocktaking.

In fact, the chief of the Defence Staff, Admiral of the Fleet, Sir Terence Lewin, was present and *the full Cabinet were for the first time given a briefing on the military policies and difficulties.*

They appear to have been told only in outline what the military options are, but they were not asked for their opinions and there was no detailed discussion [emphasis added].

A similar cabinet committee performed a similar role in the Suez Crisis of 1956, with the prime minister and the Foreign Secretary making arrangements on some key matters (Seymour-Ure, 1984; Walker, 1972, 90; Mackintosh, 1977, 24–5).

One of the most momentous sets of decisions taken by British cabinet committees rather than full Cabinet was that concerned with the development of the British nuclear deterrent. Particularly notable about this set of decisions was the way in which Cabinet was not merely almost completely excluded from all the major discussions on atomic policy in 1945–51 but was not even kept informed of decisions taken in cabinet committees. Gowing (1974, 20) in her history of British atomic energy, spells out the extent to which decisions were taken in committee rather than Cabinet:

It [the Cabinet] took no part in the decisions to establish a research establishment, to build piles to produce plutonium, or, later, to build gaseous diffusion plants to separate uranium-235; no part in the decisions to make and then test an atomic bomb, and about the planned place of atomic bombs in British strategy; in the decisions about priorities; in the decisions concerning atomic relations with other countries, including the important atomic negotiations with America after 1945 . . . It was usual, during and after the Second World War, for many other policy questions to be formulated and settled within cabinet committees and small groups of Ministers. The difference in the case of atomic energy was that major decisions were not reported to the full cabinet but were, even at that level, shrouded in secrecy.

Gowing (1974, 21) also notes that it is possible that ministers not attending one of the relevant *ad hoc* committees (GEN 75) may not even have known of its existence. Attlee even replaced GEN 75 by GEN 163, which excluded Dalton and Cripps, who had expressed misgivings about developing the bomb (Hennessy, 1982). This again illustrates the ability of the prime minister to skew membership of cabinet committees.

In contrast, the subsequent Churchill Cabinet did have an opportunity to discuss the development of the hydrogen bomb

(*The Times*, 3 January 1985). However, the decision in 1980 to replace the Polaris strategic nuclear force with Trident was effectively taken in a cabinet committee (MISC 7). The full Cabinet was informed but not consulted a few hours before the decision was announced and there was no discussion on Trident at that cabinet meeting (Hennessy, 1985b).

Cabinet committees, then, perform the decisive role in the process of arriving at many government decisions. They can, to use Gordon Walker's (1972, 87–91) term, be seen as 'partial cabinets'.

4.7 Cabinet

In practice Cabinets rarely take on the role of setting strategic guidelines for government policy in explicit form. There have, however, been occasions when full Cabinet in Britain has participated in extensive discussion of strategic policy-making. In its first few years the Heath government of 1970–4 held six-monthly meetings with members of the Central Policy Review Staff, the government's think-tank based in the Cabinet Office, to review the extent to which the government was keeping to its originally stated strategy. However, this did not prevent the government's economic policies from undergoing dramatic changes. Mrs Thatcher called a meeting of the full Cabinet at Chequers in June 1985 to take 'a long-term strategic look at public expenditure in all its aspects' (*Financial Times*, 17 June 1985). No decisions were taken at the meeting.

An exceptional case was the extensive discussion under the Callaghan government in 1976 of the government's application for an IMF loan (see Hennessy, 1983a; Granada, 1977). A total of twenty-six meetings of the full Cabinet discussed the implications. However, the Cabinet had to rely extensively on reports of the prime minister and the Chancellor of the Exchequer on their discussions with the IMF and foreign governments—the full Cabinet did not and could not have conducted the negotiations with the IMF *en masse*. The views of the prime minister and the Chancellor about what would be acceptable to the IMF and foreign governments and the prime minister's personal interest in securing a sterling 'safety net' were crucial in winning the support of otherwise reluctant cabinet ministers. Further, once the Cabinet had approved the principle of the loan and the accompanying economic policy approach, the details were worked out outside the full Cabinet. Subsequent strategic economic policy discussions under the Callaghan government were undertaken by a mixed group of ministers and officials (see 4.5 above).

One of the potential roles of full Cabinets is the selective review of decisions of cabinet committees. Jones (1975, 49) argues that this is important because:

a Cabinet committee realizes that its decisions will be acceptable only if it has the support of the Cabinet which can reject or refer back or amend them. The authority of a Cabinet committee comes from the fact that its members might be able to influence the Cabinet on a particular item.

However, matters resolved in cabinet committees cannot normally be reopened in full Cabinet, though the practice has varied under recent British governments. Matters may not even be placed on the Cabinet agenda. The full Cabinet may simply not have the opportunity to 'reject or refer back or amend' such decisions.

Nevertheless, commentators, ministers, and civil servants may believe in the importance of 'anticipated reactions' and this belief may itself give the idea some practical force. Hennessy (1983b) reports one cabinet minister who was not on the cabinet committee managing the Falklands War in 1982 as claiming that the prime minster had to carry all cabinet ministers on all major decisions and that the naval task force would never have sailed without Cabinet approval, and another 'Whitehall figure' claiming that the reason why there was no cabinet committee of just Mrs Thatcher and her sympathizers on trade-union reform was that what they produced would not have got past the Cabinet.

In Britain the major decision-making role of Cabinet is as resolver of controversial issues that cabinet committees have been unable to resolve, or which go straight to Cabinet. Jones (1975, 31) argues that 'for the most politically important issues the cabinet is the effective decision-making body' and the fact that non-controversial points are cleared away strengthens the role of Cabinet because it can then concentrate on the undetermined items. However, the significance of this in policy-making terms depends on the definitions of 'political importance' and 'non-controversial'. Jones makes it clear that 'politically important issues . . . may not be the most "objectively" or "intrinsically" important, particularly in terms of their long-run implications, but they are the most contentious at the time'. Other commentators and former cabinet ministers have similarly distinguished between 'politically significant' and 'objectively significant' decisions, with the Cabinet taking decisions on the former but not necessarily on the latter. Anthony Crosland, a former cabinet minister in the 1964–70 Labour government, noted:

There isn't much correlation between how important an issue is and how much time is spent on it in Cabinet. This may sound odd but in practice it is inevitable. The issues that take up Cabinet time are those which are controversial within the government. It's not their intrinsic importance, but their political content, that puts them on the Cabinet agenda. (Kogan, 1971, 161.)

Similarly, Seymour-Ure (1971, 202) noted that the cabinet agenda 'may bear no relation to the "objective" importance of an issue in terms of social or economic policy but may refer simply to some contentious and perhaps symbolic issue'.

It is by no means apparent that the British cabinet system is in any case very effective at ensuring that politically sensitive issues are filtered up to the full Cabinet. A number of examples from 1983–4 confirm this. For two years running, the annual expenditure review as announced in the autumn included decisions not considered by the full Cabinet (housing benefits in 1983 and student grants in 1984) which proved to be so politically sensitive that the government (unusually for a British government with a large overall majority in the House of Commons) had to announce partial reversals of the policy soon thereafter. That the failure to discuss politically sensitive issues was not confined to the overload associated with reviewing all public expenditure was confirmed by the decision taken in early 1984 to ban trade unions from the government's intelligence communications headquarters in Cheltenham. This decision was taken initially by Mrs Thatcher (prime minister), Sir Geoffrey Howe (Foreign Secretary), and Michael Heseltine (Secretary of State for Defence) (*The Times*, 7 February 1984). Lord Whitelaw, in charge of presentation of government policies, and Tom King, the Secretary of State for Employment, were involved later. The lack of discussion in Cabinet was confirmed by Sir Geoffrey Howe:

It was discussed, as almost every government decision is discussed, by the group of ministers most directly involved . . . There are very few discussions of government decisions by full cabinet. (*The Times*, 7 February 1984, citing the *Daily Mail*, 6 February 1984.)

A further indication that the full Cabinet is not regarded as the appropriate place under Mrs Thatcher to deal with politically important issues came with the appointment of Mr Tebbit as party chairman in September 1985, with one of his main tasks apparently being to defuse difficult issues *before* they reached full Cabinet. As section 6.3 points out, allocations of public expenditure between departments are not settled in full Cabinet and senior ministers were reported in 1985 to feel that if public spending had to be discussed by the full Cabinet there might have been an appearance of public disunity and disagreement (*Financial Times*, 8 November 1985).

Even the prime minister may not be aware of what subsequently transpire to be politically sensitive issues, as the former Labour prime minister, James Callaghan, discovered to his embarrassment in April 1984 when he challenged a Conservative government decision that the Metropolitan Police should be allowed to buy sub-machine-guns. It transpired that the original decision had been taken under his own administration in August 1976, and that the decision had been taken by the Home Secretary of the time without being considered in Cabinet or cabinet committee or being referred to the prime minister.

Given that the cabinet system is designed to avoid overloading the full Cabinet, some issues which it is difficult to classify as scoring high on either 'objective' or 'politically sensitive' factors do nevertheless appear to take up the time of full Cabinet. The Churchill Cabinet in 1955 discussed the date of the St Leger horse-race meeting at Doncaster; the Cabinet was concerned about possible effects on production in the neighbouring Yorkshire coalfield (*The Times*, 3 January 1986). The prime minister found time in 1955 to look at American children's comics, which were causing concern because of their violent nature, and to ask for a report on flying saucers from the Air Ministry.

While the full Cabinet does not normally consider non-politically sensitive issues, it is not the case that as a result politically sensitive issues are inevitably channelled up to full Cabinet for discussion. Indeed, some issues, such as the decision to ban trade unions from the communications headquarters at Cheltenham, may be considered *too sensitive* for discussion in full Cabinet. There may even be explicit attempts to push responsibility for sensitive issues back to other decision arenas, as in the November 1984 public expenditure review at a time when the Ethiopian famine was attracting public attention, when the Treasury claimed that decisions on the total size of the overseas aid budget were a matter for the Foreign Secretary within the total amount allocated to him.

When issues do go to full Cabinet it tends to be individual issues and not consideration of policy areas. For example, Cabinet may be asked to take a decision about the closure of an individual industrial plant rather than to reappraise all aspects of regional policy. In dealing with politically important issues, cabinet members inevitably have a fragmentary picture of the broader policy context in which the issues have arisen.

Both the contents and the position of an item on the cabinet agenda are strongly influenced by the prime minister. For example, if an item comes up a few minutes before the end of a cabinet meeting a matter can be dealt with very speedily in the way the prime minister wants. The prime minister's refusal in December 1985 to allow the Westland affair to be discussed in full Cabinet illustrates both the extent and the limits of the prime minister's power to keep matters off the agenda. The willingness of Mr Heseltine, the Defence Secretary, to go public about his dispute with the Department of Trade and Industry and his subsequent resignation were clearly conditioned by Mrs Thatcher's refusal to allow him to raise the issue in full Cabinet after it became clear that a cabinet committee meeting which Mr Heseltine had expected to discuss the matter further did not take place.

4.8 Conclusion

Since the Second World War the British government has always had a highly ramified system of standing cabinet committees, subcommittees, and *ad hoc* committees, though the bulk of government decisions are made in individual departments or through interdepartmental negotiations outside the cabinet structure. The use which is made of the full Cabinet, cabinet committees, and more informal groupings of ministers and political advisers has varied between governments, reflecting largely the decision-making style of individual prime ministers. These individual differences appear to have been more important than differences between the two parties which have held office since 1945.

The full Cabinet does not necessarily consider all issues which are important on 'objective' indicators such as financial cost or number of persons affected. Supposedly, this leaves the Cabinet free to consider the most politically sensitive issues. However, this chapter has suggested that the British cabinet system is poor at filtering up to the Cabinet issues which are potentially very politically sensitive but which are not structured in terms of conflict between two or more departments. Where the sponsoring department is satisfied in its own mind (or has done a deal with the Treasury if it is an issue involving expenditure), then the Cabinet may only consider the issue *after* the political alarm bells have started ringing and may not be involved in taking the actual decision to resolve the problem.

A simple hierarchical model of executive decision-making is inappropriate to describe decision-making in British central government. First of all, the idea of a hierarchical pyramid of individual ministers topped by cabinet committees, topped by Cabinet, topped by the prime minister, with implied delegation downwards and upwards referral of all strategic or important decisions is not accurate. We find individual ministers exercising a wide power of decision-making about their departments, with *the minister* exercising much discretion about which issues should be referred to colleagues. Where an issue is of such a nature that it does not just affect his own department, it is more likely to be resolved by interministerial negotiation or cabinet committee decision than by full Cabinet. A number of decisions will be taken in full Cabinet, but these will not necessarily include all the most important ones, unless one accepts the circular definition that politically important decisions are those which are taken in Cabinet.

The prime minister will rarely be directly involved in issues, though he or she will be able to select a very limited number of issues for personal intervention and that intervention will normally be decisive. The prime minister will often be unaware of decisions taken in the name of his or her government, even decisions taken in the name of cabinet committees (though the Cabinet Office would draw his or her attention to anything considered to be of importance). The prime minister's main methods of shaping policy lie in the control of the cabinet agenda and in deciding on the number, coverage, composition, and chairmanship of committees as well as which ones to chair personally.

Thus in examining how decision-making takes place within British government it is essential that we do not confine analysis to the process by which individual decisions are made (whether case studies or a broad sample of decisions) since the interplay of power and personalities takes place in a context which has itself been structured in a way which will shape the range of likely outcomes even if the prime minister or other key actors do not necessarily intervene in the discussion of an issue.

The model of cabinet structure which best describes British government is one of interrelated but fragmented decision arenas derived from membership of a Cabinet which gives the system a focus but which itself takes only a small proportion of decisions in full session. This is not inconsistent with the fact that Cabinets normally have a full agenda of issues for decision; it is to prevent overcrowding of the cabinet agenda that mechanisms for taking decisions elsewhere are established.

Policy areas (and individual issues) vary in the extent to which they are distinct, and in the extent to which they are subject to decisions taken in departmental, multilateral, cabinet committee, full Cabinet, or other arenas. Some policy communities or sectors will largely involve discussion between interest groups and individual departments, while others, because of intrinsic characteristics, the allocation of functions between departments, or current political interest, will involve a number of departments in formal or informal discussions and will more frequently be the subject of consideration by a full Cabinet.

Chapter 5

The Legislative Process: Executive Power and Legislative Legitimation

5.1 The concept of the legislative process

This chapter examines the process by which those policies which are the subject of legislation are shaped at that stage. For most legislation the executive dominates *all* phases of the legislative process, including the parliamentary ones. Not all government decisions or policies have to be the subject of legislation; for example, the Anglo-Irish Agreement of 1985 did not have to be the subject of legislation. Treaties are an alternative form of legitimating instrument.

It is important to distinguish between the legislative process on the one hand and the role of the legislature and the legislative procedure on the other. The role of the legislature is concerned with what goes on in Parliament and amongst other things with the procedures through which legislation has to go to become law. The concept of legislative process is concerned with the various steps by which proposals are transformed into legal language, receive parliamentary authorization, and are brought into practice. This distinction can be brought out clearly by the following quotation from Drewry (1981, 90):

The House of Commons spends at least half its time talking about matters which may give rise to legislation and matters arising, directly or indirectly, from past legislation. Yet it is a common place that Parliament is not a law-making body, save in the important but formal senses recognised by the courts and by constitutional theory.

The legislative process in Britain can be divided into pre-parliamentary, parliamentary, and administrative phases. In each of those stages the influence of the executive is predominant. In what is still the best book on this subject even though it was written in the late 1960s, *The Legislative Process in Great Britain* (1968), Walkland went so far as to argue that 'Legislation is now an almost exclusively executive function, modified, sometimes heavily, by practices of group and Parliamentary consultations'. This assessment is as valid now as it was then, qualified only by the need to take account of the government's somewhat reduced control of the parliamentary stage of the legislative process when it is in a minority or has a very small majority (5.3), by a greater tendency towards backbench revolts in the 1970s (5.3–5.5) and by an increased assertiveness on the part of the House of Lords since the mid-1970s (5.6).

5.2 Government control as the norm

The pre-parliamentary phase of the legislative process is 'legislative' because considerable shaping takes place at this stage, and 'pre-parliamentary' because the legislature is not actively involved at this stage. The actual drawing up of bills is done within departments in most cases. These will often reflect the outcome of discussions with groups as described in chapter 3. At this stage civil servants 'will be taking into account possible problems when the Bill is introduced into Parliament' as one of a number of political considerations (Englefield, 1985, 62).

The legislative role of the House of Commons is often considered under the heading of 'Parliamentary Scrutiny of Government Bills', which is the title of Griffith's 1974 book on the subject. However, for the bulk of the post-war period a far more relevant heading would be the title of a chapter in Walkland's book on the legislative process headed 'Government control of stages of parliamentary scrutiny and criticism'. This gets the emphasis right by stressing the government's domination of the legislative process and parliamentary procedure—when it has a clear overall majority at least.

This state of affairs did not, of course, arise suddenly. Increasingly since the end of the nineteenth century the way the House of Commons operated recognized that government in Britain had become party government. The dominant party in becoming the government would not only control the workings of the *executive*, but also the *discussion*, and more importantly the *outcomes* of those discussions in Parliament. Thus Walkland (1968) argues that:

Parliamentary procedure is best seen not as a set of impartial rules designed to facilitate the transaction of public and private business, but as a political instrument largely designed to help the governing party to govern.

Thus there has been a move amongst writers on Parliament away from constitutional theories of the role of Parliament in legislating and controlling finance to more realistic assessments of the political control of Parliament by the executive as outlined in Walkland's book.

When a government has a clear overall majority in the Commons we would not expect that parliamentary influence over the programme of bills introduced each session by the government will amount to very much. It is only rarely that a bill will be withdrawn as a result of parliamentary pressure. This does happen occasionally—the Conservative government withdrew four bills in the 1950s. The Labour government was forced to abandon its industrial relations proposals in 1969 before they even reached the stage of a bill, though it is worth noting that this was achieved by a combination of trade-union and backbench pressure rather than *within* the House of Commons itself, where only a combination of opposition and government backbenchers could lead to the government's defeat if it had an overall majority. Such pressure may, however, lead to the abandonment of a bill—the Labour government was forced to abandon its proposals to reform the House of Lords in 1969 as a result of the activities of both Labour and Conservative backbenchers. The difficulties faced by the majority Conservative government from 1979 are discussed in more detail in 5.4.

When the government is not itself wholeheartedly behind its own proposals then opposition to legislation from Parliament may lead to postponement. For example, it took over a decade before legislation on seat-belt wearing was finally passed in 1982, and that for only an initial trial period of three years (Irwin, 1985, ch. 7).

In general, however, if a government with an overall majority fails to achieve its programme, the bills which are not passed will usually have failed because of defects in the government's planning of the legislative timetable for the session. This planning is undertaken by the legislation (QL) standing committee of Cabinet under the chairmanship of the Leader of the House of Commons. Table 5.1 confirms that the government does get most of its bills through Parliament, in contrast to the success rate of private members' bills.

Table 5.1 Public Bills and Acts 1968–83

Session	Government Acts			Backbench Acts	
	Total Acts	Consolid. Acts	% failure of Bills	Acts	% failure of Bills
1968–9	51	4	7.2	12	88.6
1969–70*	38	3	39.7	15	83.1
1970–1	76	11	1.3	13	83.1
1971–2	59	9	3.3	17	78.8
1972–3	57	7	0	15	83.3
1973–4*	15	2	60.5	0	100
1974*	35	5	18.6	7	85.4
1974–5	73	18	11.0	10	89.5
1975–6	72	13	6.5	16	82.4
1976–7	42	6	16.0	11	88.9
1977–8	49	10	3.9	11	87.9
1978–9*	44	14	19.0	3	95.2
1979–80	71	17	4.1	10	93.0
1980–1	56	13	1.8	15	86.0
1981–2	46	7	2.1	10	91.5
1982–3*	42	5	16.0	11	89.1

* Session brought to an early end by General Election.

Sources: Drewry (1981, 96, 113) and updated by calculations on data in Burton and Drewry (1985).

The first reading of a bill in the Commons is simply the formal tabling of the bill. Given our interest in how policies are shaped, it is not worth spending much time examining second reading debates, since at this stage no alterations are possible—the bill can only be passed or defeated—and the government's majority when it has one will ensure that it is passed. The opposition may put down a 'reasoned amendment', but this is an amendment to the government's motion to give the bill a second reading and not to the bill. Other amendments may be put down, but they will not be called. They provide advance notice of points which will be raised and concessions which will be demanded from the government at committee stage.

Thus while the second reading debate receives considerable media attention, it is largely an exercise between the government and opposition front benches. Far less public attention is normally given to the *committee stage*, which is arguably the main parliamentary stage of bills. The distinction is sometimes made between the second reading which is to consider the principle of a bill and the committee stage which is to consider the details. However, for politically controversial bills the distinction is rather unreal, since the party political battle is extended into the consideration of individual clauses.

For almost all bills their committee stage is taken in a standing committee. As we have already seen, most legislation has already gone through a fairly extensive process of consideration before it is even introduced in the Commons. However, it may well be incomplete in the sense that many representations on the details of the bill may remain to be made, together with a number of last-minute drafting amendments. Much of the committee stage is therefore what Walkland calls a 'Ministerial' stage, where refinements are added and administrative oversights corrected on the basis of the printed and published bill. Ministers are often accommodating even to hostile elements during the parliamentary stages of a bill. This reflects the belief that special interests should be listened to and that their concern with public policy which affects them is legitimate. No minister wants to alienate opinion if he can help it and if concessions can be given without too much compromise of principle, the chances are that they will be. Thus the kind of intransigence which the Conservative government showed over the Industrial Relations Bill in the early 1970s is the exception rather than the rule.

It is important to emphasize that government–group consultations may continue while a bill is being considered at committee stage. For example, the CBI (but not apparently the Consumer Association) continued discussions with the Department of Trade and Industry over the Fair Trading Bill 1973 (see Granada, 1973). At times, the relative importance of these discussions compared to the role of MPs in 'scrutinizing' the bill can reach ludicrous proportions, as when the minister at first refused to let MPs in the committee considering the Water Bill in 1973 see copies of an agreement he had drawn up with local authority associations about the operation of sewage functions after the bill would have come into force since he did not have the consent of the associations to let MPs see it (Richardson and Jordan, 1979, 128–34). However, within five minutes the minister had obtained that consent, obviously conducting negotiations with the associations while the committee was actually meeting. Finally, it transpired that the agreement had already been published in full by the journal, *The Surveyor*, without MPs even having been aware of the agreement or the negotiations leading up to it.

In extreme cases, consultations with relevant groups may lead to the temporary withdrawal of a bill or major clauses of it even after it has been published. For example, the Social Security (Contributions) Bill introduced in November 1980 originally contained provisions for employers to take on responsibility for sick pay during the first eight weeks of an employee's sickness, in return for reductions in their National Insurance contributions. Despite last-minute concessions by the government, the CBI and other bodies continued to express dissatisfaction with the proposals, particularly as they affected small firms and parts of the engineering sector, and the relevant clauses were dropped from the bill to enable further consultation (Burton and Drewry, 1983). A system of Statutory Sick Pay was eventually introduced by the Social Security and Housing Benefits Act 1982 and came into effect in April 1983.

Opposition or backbench MPs may also move amendments of a fairly technical nature, and some of these may be quite acceptable to the government. In addition to seeking to influence the minister during the committee stage, affected interests may try to get amendments moved by sympathetic opposition MPs or government backbenchers, some of whom may be associated with the interest group through being an honorary officer or by being sponsored. Groups may do this as a 'belt and braces' operation, continuing to carry on consultations with the government without informing the MPs whom they have asked to put down amendments on their behalf. For 'outsider' groups or those with unfavourably skewed influence, this may be the only avenue open to them. However, where the government has an overall majority such amendments have little chance of success if they are unacceptable to the government, except for relatively rare occasions when government backbenchers combine with opposition MPs to defeat the government. Even then a defeat in committee may be overruled at report stage. On the other hand, the government itself sometimes moves amendments at report stage as a result of giving an undertaking in committee to the opposition to look at the issue raised by an opposition amendment, which is then withdrawn. These two points illustrate the fact that the report stage is best regarded as an extension of the committee stage.

It can be seen that the committee stage is important not just for what goes on actually in the committee proceedings, but for discussions outside the committee. There are obviously discussions between interest groups and the government and between interest groups and the opposition, but there are also discussions between government backbenchers unhappy with aspects of the bill and the minister concerned, and even between opposition MPs and the minister.

These general comments can be illustrated by looking at figures compiled by Griffith (1974) as a result of his examination of all legislation in sessions 1967–8, 1968–9, and 1970–1 (see Table 5.2). These figures obviously require some interpretation, quite apart from the possibility, considered in the next section, that developments since 1971 may have altered their significance. The obvious and overwhelming impression is the high success rate of government amendments and the low success rate of those moved by others, resulting in the overwhelming mass of changes to bills being made by the government to its own legislation. Looking first at the committee stage, the government figure may exaggerate the nature of the changes brought about by governments; many are technical in nature. However, similar considerations also apply to the figures for government backbench and opposition amendments: of the 171 successfully moved at committee stage, Griffith estimates that only nine could be said to have changed in some part the principle of the bill. These 171 successful amendments did not all represent defeats for the government. Only 8 of the 40 backbench successes and 12 of the 131 opposition successes represented government defeats.

Before drawing conclusions about the overall impact of the House of Commons we have to examine the report stage. We

Table 5.2 Success rate of amendments at committee and report stages 1967–8, 1968–9, 1970–1

Moved by	Total moved	Agreed to	%
Committee stage			
Ministers	2700	2699	99.9
Government backbenchers	436	40	9.2
Opposition	3074	131	4.3
Report stage			
Ministers	2414*	2413	99.9
Government backbenchers	89	10	11.2
Opposition	599	29	4.8

* 365 amendments moved as a result of undertakings in committee.

Source: Griffith (1974).

should, however, note that during the years covered by Griffith the government was forced to withdraw the Parliament No. 2 Bill to reform the House of Lords in the 1968–9 session. So while MPs make little impact on most bills under governments with overall majorities they may score the occasional spectacular success.

Turning now to the report stage, which is normally taken on the floor of the House, the general pattern of government domination is repeated, with fewer opposition amendments getting selected in the first place than in committee. Again, most amendments were drafting or consequential. Griffith estimates that of the 39 amendments successfully moved by opposition and government backbenchers only 9 were of some importance. None represented government defeats. Of the 26 defeats of various kinds inflicted on the government in committee during the three sessions, the government reversed 14 of those on report, modified its position on 3, and accepted the change in only 9 cases. On the other side of the coin, there was a sizeable indirect impact by the positive response of the government to points made in committee. Griffith estimates that there were 365 occasions during the three sessions when government amendments moved on report which were traceable to points made in committee by government back-benchers and opposition members. Of these about 125 were important in varying degrees.

Table 5.3 confirms that before 1970 it was very rare indeed for the government to be defeated on the floor of the House of Commons. Defeats in standing committee were also rare, though the last two sessions of the 1964–70 Labour government did show a substantial increase on the previous selected years shown. This suggests that the years analysed by Griffith were years of larger numbers of defeats than the pattern for the period of majority governments from 1945 to the late 1960s, and were similar for standing committees though not for the floor of the House of Commons for the 1970–4 Conservative government.

Table 5.3 Defeats of the government in the House of Commons (selected years)

Session	Defeats	
	Floor	Standing committee
1947–8	0	1
1953–4	1	2
1962–3	0	3
1964–5	3	1
1968–9	0	10
1969–70	0	10
1971–2	2	6
1972–3	3	12
1974	16	10
1974–5	6	18
1975–6	5	27
1976–7	4	20
1977–8*	8*	9*

* incomplete year, up to 15 April 1978 only.

Source: Schwartz (1980, 28).

The evidence reported so far suggests that the Commons does have a modest role in shaping the details of legislation when the government has an overall majority, but it is overwhelmingly through persuading the government to accept amendments which it might not otherwise have made rather than forcing those changes on government. The vast bulk of shaping results from the government itself, with changes made to accommodate groups being a major source of proposed changes. What is difficult to assess is how government would behave in dealing with its legislation if it did not have to present and if necessary justify in public the details of its bills.

5.3 Developments in the 1970s: mould-breaking, deviant or contingent?

This section examines whether developments since the early 1970s have led to a change in the government's ability to control the parliamentary stages of the legislative process, in the Commons at least. There were a number of developments which have to be untangled if we are to be able to assess whether there has been a long-run trend, a temporary deviation, or a set of circumstances which might recur to have a more profound impact on shaping public policy at the legislative and perhaps even other stages. These developments include the increase in backbench dissent from the early 1970s, the existence of governments with a minority in the Commons in the 1974 Parliament and for much of the 1974–9 Parliament, and the extent to which the devolution issue dominated the parliamentary timetable for much of the 1974–9 session.

Prior to 1970 there was very little backbench dissent from the party line, but as Table 5.4 shows, there was a relative increase from 1970 onwards. Our concern is with the extent to which such changes in behaviour led to a change in the way in which policy was shaped by the legislative process. Most episodes of dissent do not alter the result of votes on the floor of the House. As Table 5.4 shows, dissent led to only six defeats for the government on the floor of the Commons in the 1970–4 session, of which only three were on three-line whips. The most important of these was on immigration rules in 1972. Norton's (1980) own conclusion was that 'Conservative intra-party dissent within the 1970 Parliament may not have had much effect on the particular measures involved, but its effect in terms of parliamentary behaviour may yet prove to be lasting'. Given the emphasis placed on the committee stage in the last section, it is perhaps of more significance that the 1970–4 government suffered twenty-four defeats in standing committee (Norton, 1985, 27).

Table 5.4 Divisions in Commons witnessing dissenting votes

Parliament	Divisions with dissenting votes			
	Total*	Lab	Con	% of all divisions
1945–50	87	79	27	7
1950–1	6	5	2	2.5
1951–5	25	17	11	3
1955–9	19	10	12	2
1959–64	137	26	120	13.5
1964–6	2	1	1	0.5
1966–70	124	109	41	9.5
1970–4	221	34†	204	20
1974	25	8	21	23
1974–9	423	309	240	28

* As one division may involve dissenting votes by both Labour and Conservative MPs, the Labour and Conservative figures do not necessarily add up to the total.

† excluding the Labour 'ginger group' of votes of February–March 1971.

Source: Norton (1980, 284).

As can be seen from Table 5.5, all seventeen defeats of the Labour government in the short 1974 Parliament were due to its minority status. The government also suffered ten defeats in standing committee (see Table 5.3). However, it is worth remarking from 1974 that even in a short session when it was in a minority the government did get most of its bills through more or less intact (see Table 5.1).

The Labour government started the 1974–9 session with a small overall majority, which it had lost by 1976. During 1977–8, it was sustained in office by the Lib–Lab pact, though the Liberal party did not form part of the government. The government suffered 39 defeats on the floor of the Commons; 22 were due to dissent; of these 20 related to legislation (calculated from Norton, 1980, appendix). The other two defeats were in two successive years on the government's public expenditure White Paper, a gesture which made no difference whatever to the implementation of the government's expenditure plans (see 6.3). Of the 20 defeats on legislation arising from backbench dissent, 12 related to devolution bills. The question therefore arises of how much the scale of the defeats related to the special characteristics of the devolution issue and the minority status of government for part of the Parliament rather than a general upsurge in dissent. If defeats on devolution, a constitutional issue on which some Labour MPs felt very strongly, are excluded, then the number of defeats arising from dissent was comparable to the 1970–4 session. On this basis there is little evidence of a secular upward trend in dissent.

Turning to standing committees, the government suffered 74 defeats in the period from October 1974 to April 1978 (see Table 5.3). Even more significantly, most of these defeats were accepted, wholly or in part, by the government (Schwartz, 1980, 28). These included the Rooker–Wise amendment (both Rooker and Wise being Labour MPs), which raised income tax allowances and provided for their indexation against inflation (see 6.4 where it is argued that the role of the House of Commons in considering taxation is more meaningful than its (non)role over expenditure decisions). These are much higher figures for defeats than revealed by Griffith's survey in Table 5.2, but they are still tiny relative to the total volume of amending activity on bills.

In dealing with the House of Commons when it has only a small majority or is actually in minority, the government has benefited

Table 5.5 Government defeats on floor of Commons 1970 to summer recess 1984

Parliament	Caused by		Total
	Dissent by government backbenchers	Opposition parties combining against minority government	
1970–4	6	0	6
1974	0	17	17
1974–9	23	19	42
1979–83	1	0	1
1983–4	1*	0	1
Total	31	36	67

* The vote went against government advice, though not a formally whipped vote.

Source: Norton (1985, 14, 27).

considerably from the operation of House of Commons procedures largely designed to assist governments with overall majorities in a House of Commons with effectively only two main parties. The procedures cannot guarantee government victories, but they are generally geared to getting government legislation through. Further, the government still controls the pre-parliamentary stages of the legislative process and the bulk of executive activity does not require new legislation.

Obviously, minority and slim majority governments are much more likely to suffer defeats than are those with adequate overall majorities, either because all or most of the opposition parties vote together or because even as few as one or two government backbenchers abstain or vote against the government. However, even on a defeat on a major issue the government is unlikely to resign or call a general election unless it is defeated on an explicit vote of no confidence. On matters of less importance, the government may simply have to accept being overruled. When it is in a minority the government is likely to find both that it will suffer more defeats in committee and that it will be more difficult to reverse those defeats at report stage. Similar considerations may apply when the government tries to reverse House of Lords amendments; it was defeated over the Dock Work Regulation Bill and the exclusion of ship-repairing from the nationalization of the aircraft and shipbuilding industries (see 5.6).

However, it is important to get into perspective the greater frequency of reverses faced by minority governments and governments with small majorities. Even the 1974–9 Labour government managed to get through most of its politically controversial measures relatively intact though it had to spend a lot of time getting its devolution legislation even in modified form. Thus governments in such situations still dominate the House of Commons rather than the other way round. The big difference between such governments and those with adequate majorities is that they no longer have a *virtually automatic* majority.

The government can still expect to win most votes, but the real prospects of defeat impose a much greater strain on the Commons (see Table 5.1). In the 1976–7 session, when the Labour government was in a minority, 42 out of 49 government bills were passed and in the 1977–8 session 49 out of 51 were passed—no worse in 1977–8 than a 'normal' government. However, this picture is to some extent misleading because of the much greater chance of substantial amendments being made under minority governments, for example to the Dock Work Regulation Bill, which was effectively emasculated, and the Aircraft and Shipbuilding Industries Bill.

However, this situation of business more or less as usual is contingent on minority government being seen as deviant from a norm of majority government. A greater frequency or a longer run of minority government may lead to changes in the procedures of the House of Commons which favour government. More importantly, the 'internalized processing' or processing in policy communities in the pre-parliamentary stages for many issues as described in chapter 3 depends on the ability of government to deliver its side of the bargain.

5.4 Majority government since 1979: reversion to the 'norm'?

The existence of a majority Conservative government since 1979—from 1983 with a huge Commons majority—does enable us to assess whether the surge in government defeats in the 1970s and the factors leading to them continued or developed further. Data is not available for all divisions in the 1979–83 Parliament, but there were 18 'main occasions' of dissent, some of them involving more than one division, with the number of Conservative dissenters ranging from 6 to 52 (Norton, 1985, 30). The only actual defeat was, ironically, on immigration regulations in 1982.

However, even when dissent did not lead to defeat, the government did make changes on a number of occasions. For example, the March 1981 Budget provoked a fairly substantial revolt by Conservative backbenchers, mainly from rural constituencies, against a proposal to increase hydrocarbon (i.e. petrol and diesel) duties by 20p. Nine Conservatives voted against the government on this point and there were an estimated 25 abstentions, bringing the government's potential overall majority down from 40 to 14 (see Burton and Drewry, 1983). Although the government won the vote, it was clearly concerned about the scale of the dissent and at the committee stage of the Finance Bill the Chancellor accepted an amendment from a Conservative backbencher that the increase in duty on derv should be halved while retaining the 20p increase for petrol. This left a shortfall of £85m, which the Chancellor later announced would be made up by further increases in tobacco and gaming duties. A change of this kind in a Budget when the government had an overall majority is very unusual.

The government was forced in 1981 to drop its proposals for rates referenda as a result of pressure inside and outside Parliament. It abandoned its Local Government Finance Bill, its only 'failure' for the 1981–2 session (see Table 5.1), and replaced it by a bill which did not contain the rates referendum provision, and which was in its turn modified to meet backbench objections (see Burton and Drewry, 1985, 226). Note, however, that the government did subsequently force through legislation imposing rate-capping, arguably a more dramatic imposition of controls on local authorities. This leads one to speculate about the usefulness of a 'pinball' theory of government: when government hits a problem it bounces away from it, but if this pushes government in a direction which subsequently causes continuing problems which the original proposal was designed to resolve, then the government may use its flipper to propel the ball more firmly in the desired direction than had been envisaged in the original proposal which was withdrawn because of opposition.

Norton (1985, 33) analysed dissent from June 1983 to the summer recess in 1984. He found 62 divisions which had Conservative backbenchers dissenting from the party line, slightly above the annual average for Conservatives in the 1970s; dissent has not therefore disappeared, nor does it appear to have escalated dramatically. From a perspective on shaping policy, the interesting point is that only one of those 62 divisions witnessing dissent resulted in a government defeat, and that was on a vote which was not formally whipped, though it did go against government advice.

Signs of dissatisfaction among Conservative backbenchers received a lot of attention towards the end of 1984 and the beginning of 1985. However, it is worth noting that these revolts did not tend to result in the government actually being defeated, since the government's majority was so large. Some of the government's political setbacks did not occur from defeats or from legislation; this was true of the partial reversal of cuts in public expenditure on student grants following the Chancellor of the Exchequer's 1984 Autumn Statement. An important development in the 1984–5 session was that the government was forced in December 1984 to shelve its Civil Aviation Bill as a result of rebel Conservative backbenchers voting with the opposition to block discussion of the bill in standing committee. The rebels were concerned that passage of the bill might pre-empt a government decision on the future of Stansted airport as London's third airport. The government abandoned the bill in May 1985 following the publication of the report on the third London airport, claiming that the bill's contents were no longer required as a result of the report.

In the following session the government was defeated in April 1986 on the second reading in the Commons of the Shops Bill on Sunday trading as a result of the rebellion of 68 Conservative backbenchers on a three-line whip. This was an unprecedented reverse for a government with an overall majority. However, the bill had special features in terms of its moral and religious connotations and should not be assumed to be the start of a series of similar defeats.

From the 1980–1 session there has been a modest experiment of a different form of committee consideration of legislation by a special standing committee which can hold three one-and-a-half hour public sessions at which it can examine witnesses before reverting to traditional standing committee format (see Norton, 1985, 164–5). The new procedure can be used for bills which do raise substantial issues but are not of acute party political controversy. In the remainder of the 1979–83 Parliament the procedure was used for four bills. In the first session of the 1983 Parliament a further bill went through this procedure and it was used for the Armed Forces Bill in the 1985–6 session. In the Criminal Attempts Bill in the 1980–1 session four substantive amendments to the bill were made as a result of representations made during the hearings. The hearings are unlikely to have involved witnesses making any representations which they would not otherwise (or as well) have made in private to government departments or opposition spokesmen on the committee, but they do give a greater degree of openness as well as scope for the public airing of the views of groups which may not have been involved at the earlier stages of consideration of the issue by government. Traditional standing committee 'scrutiny' remains the norm.

The departmental select committees set up in 1979 have had only a limited direct impact on legislation, reflecting the fact that they have no part in parliamentary procedure for considering legislation. (The role of the committees in dealing with issues at agenda-processing stage was considered in 3.7.) The two main exceptions in the 1979–83 Parliament were reports from the Home Affairs committee on the repeal of the 'sus' law, which was instrumental in the government bringing forward legislation, and from the Foreign Affairs committee on the patriation of the Canadian constitution, which influenced the Canadians and was much referred to in Commons debate (Giddings, 1985).

5.5 Assessing the impact of developments since 1970

There is a problem in assessing the impact of dissent on policy: how many things are changed by government or not put forward as a result of dissent? We can distinguish between specific dissent and the general possibility of dissent. On specific dissent, a majority government can assess what dissent it can expect on a specific proposal and judge whether to adapt its proposals to forestall expressed dissent or calculate that it is better to suffer the political embarrassment of a 'revolt', secure nevertheless in its majority. If the government gets its calculations wrong it may actually suffer a defeat as it did on the Shops Bill in April 1986. The past pattern of dissent also introduces a generalized uncertainty. The government still dominates, but to a certain extent it must now also anticipate.

One countervailing development tending to limit the scope for effective dissent on the government backbenches is the growth of the so-called 'payroll vote', that is ministers plus whips plus Parliamentary Private Secretaries. The total number of MPs involved in the government in this way rose from 115 in 1970 to 136 in 1985, largely as a result of the growth in the number of Parliamentary Private Secretaries (Butler and Sloman, 1980, 78; Riddell, 1985). In the context of 397 Conservative MPs elected at the 1983 General Election and a majority over all other parties of around 140, it can be seen that a very high proportion of backbench Conservative MPs would have to vote against the government to have a chance of defeating it.

The main consequence for the policy process of increased backbench dissent since the 1960s is not the defeats actually inflicted on the government but a greater degree of uncertainty about whether the Commons will approve a proposal. This puts a greater premium on the assessment by whips of the likely reaction of backbenchers. Although backbenchers are still not involved in the direct formulation of proposals, their approval of government proposals is rather less likely to be taken completely for granted.

The impact of backbench dissent on shaping legislation is not a trend which continues to increase steadily after the initial 1970–4 manifestation, but dissent has introduced a new note of uncertainty into the government's orchestration of the legislative process. The major government reverses of the late 1970s are considered here to be the result of contingent but recurrable factors: the devolution issue and minority status. Of these, minority status is the one of more interesting long-term significance, since if it were to recur frequently or for a sustained period of time, many of the political assumptions underpinning the government's domination of the legislative process—and of the pre-legislative stages of the policy process—would be undermined.

5.6 Shaping legislation in the Lords

Although the Lords can always be overruled by the Commons, the Lords can make an impact on the shape of legislation by making amendments which the government is unwilling or unable to reverse in the Commons. The government may be unwilling to try to reverse a Lords amendment where that amendment has a great deal of appeal to its own MPs. For example, on the British Nationality Bill 1981 the government did not seek to reverse a Lords amendment which entitled citizens of Gibraltar to register as British citizens. Ironically, in view of later developments, a vote in the Lords to give similar rights to the Falklands was tied and declared lost. The floor of the House of Commons may not previously have had the opportunity of discussing the aspects of a bill which come before it for consideration of Lords amendments, or rebels may be encouraged (or perceived by the government whips to be encouraged) by support in the Lords. Governments with only a small majority or actually in a minority may be unable to muster the votes to reverse the amendment. The other weapon available to the Lords is the delay it could cause to the government's parliamentary timetable, even if the Lords were overruled in the same session, or, if the Lords insisted on its amendment the next session.

As a comparison between Table 5.6 and Table 5.5 shows, the Lords have inflicted more defeats on the government than has the Commons, a pattern which was most obvious under the minority Labour government in the 1974–9 session, with its devolution legislation, but which has subsequently continued under the Conservative government, with the government suffering a high annual rate of defeats in the Lords in the 1983–4 and 1984–5 sessions. At first sight, Table 5.6 appears to confirm that the Lords is far more likely to defeat or amend Labour government legislation. However, as Shell (1985, 19) points out, these are only 'defeats in the first instance'. In the vast majority of cases the Lords gives way when the Labour government reverses defeats in the Commons, which it has difficulty in doing only if it is in a minority or very small majority. Where a Conservative government is defeated in the Lords there is a much greater chance of the defeat being allowed to stand. Taking this into account, Shell (1985) concludes that there is in practice a rough parity of impact by the Lords on governments of either party. The clear trend which emerges is of the Lords being more 'awkward' for both Labour and Conservative governments in the 1970s and 1980s than in the 1940s and 1950s, or even the 1960s. It is worth noting that defeats of the Conservative government in the Lords since 1979 are not simply the result of Conservative or cross-bench peers supporting opposition amendments. Of the 45 defeats in the 1979–83 Parliament, 18 were on amendments moved by Conservative backbench peers, 14 by Labour peers, 7 by Liberals, and 6 by cross-benchers (Shell, 1985, 21).

There are two main reasons for the growing assertiveness of the

Table 5.6 Government defeats in the House of Lords

Parliament	Total divisions	Government defeats	Defeats as % of divisions
1959–64	299	11	3.7
1964–70	273	116	42.5
1970–4	459	26	5.7
1974–9	445	355	79.8
1979–83	725	45	6.2

Source: Shell (1985, 18).

Lords (see Baldwin, 1985; Shell, 1985). The first is the changing composition of the Lords, with 'working' life peers becoming an increasingly large proportion of those active in the chamber. The second is the removal of the immediate likelihood of reform, so that peers have concentrated on a practical continuing role for the chamber. Contrary to popular wisdom, the Conservatives do not have a reliable overall majority in the House of Lords, though they are in a happier position than the Labour party, particularly since the defection of the SDP. The introduction on an experimental basis of the televising of the Lords from the beginning of 1985 gave increased prominence to its activities, but the change in its behaviour had clearly preceded this innovation.

Some bills are introduced in the Lords and they and others introduced in the Commons may receive most of their effective scrutiny and shaping in the Lords. An example of this was the Wildlife and Countryside Bill 1981, which was substantially reworked by the Lords, with the government being defeated on seven occasions and being forced to make other significant concessions. In the 1983–4 session the Lords forced the government to accept a number of amendments to its Housing and Building Control Bill to exempt accommodation for the elderly and the disabled from the 'right to buy' provisions. In the same session the Lords prevented the appointment of an interim administration for the Greater London Council in what was known as the 'paving bill' and the government, while cancelling the 1985 elections, was compelled to keep the Labour administration in the GLC in office for a further year. In the following session the Lords passed 98 amendments to the bill abolishing the Greater London Council and the metropolitan counties, of which only two were subsequently reversed by the government.

In July 1985 the government was forced to abandon the Education (Corporal Punishment) Bill. This had been introduced reluctantly by the government to comply with a ruling by the European Court of Human Rights that a parent's objections to corporal punishment must be respected (see 8.4). Rather than abolish corporal punishment, the bill would have allowed parents in state schools to opt out of corporal punishment for their children. This proposed solution had been criticized by the opposition and teachers and a number of Conservatives in the House of Commons had refused to support it. When a Lords amendment to abolish corporal punishment was passed by four votes, the government abandoned the bill, which left it still to find a means of implementing the ruling of the European Court of Human Rights.

The overall assessment has to be that the Lords, through the amendments it forces on government, makes more of a substantive contribution to shaping policy at the legislative stages than does the Commons in its votes.

5.7 Shaping policy through non-government bills

In one area, non-government MPs do retain influence over the preparatory stages of bills, and that is obviously over private members' bills. Many of these deal with issues, such as divorce and abortion, which are of profound importance to the lives of individual citizens. However, in contrast to government bills, virtually all of which receive the Royal Assent, most private members' bills never pass into law (see Table 5.1). Where the government has an overall majority a private members' bill to which the government is opposed will be unlikely to get through. However, where there is a strong groundswell of parliamentary support for a bill, as there was for the Disabled Persons (Services, Consultation and Representation) Bill in the 1985–6 session, the government may have to back away from trying to dilute it.

Successful private members' bills may also require the government to be prepared to find time for bills to complete their closing stages. Thus the string of famous bills in the late 1960s leading to legislation such as the Abortion Act and divorce reform in England and Wales depended on government support in the sense of ensuring adequate time outside the normal allocation for private members' bills. The subsequent Conservative government proved much less willing to provide time in this way, though it did so on a number of occasions. The 1979 Conservative government has given positive support to a number of private members' bills, for example, the Indecent Displays (Control) Bill in the 1980–1 session, and more recently with the so-called 'video nasties Bill'. Indeed, private members' bills can from the point of view of the government provide a means for passing legislation which they cannot fit into their own crowded timetable, as when the government tried to find a backbencher in 1985 who would introduce a bill which would implement the Conservative's pledge on civil defence.

Occasionally a bill which is important in redefining the relationship between Parliament and the executive can pass, even against government opposition. The National Audit Act 1983 reduced the control of the Treasury and increased that of Parliament over the appointment and tasks of the Comptroller and Auditor General and changed his office into the National Audit Office. The Treasury was initially opposed, but the government did not oppose the bill on second reading because of the strength of backbench feeling, though the bill was substantially modified during its passage.

Most private members' bills still have no chance of success, and their introduction would perhaps best be seen not as a legislative one but as a debating or agenda-setting one, providing MPs with an opportunity to air a cause or grievance in a similar way as at adjournment debates. This is particularly true of ten-minute rule bills. Section 2.6 gave illustrations of the way in which private members' bills, though not themselves becoming law, resulted in the government introducing its own legislation. The actual legislating role is confined largely to issues which cannot be processed by consultation between the executive and groups.

5.8 Secondary legislation

The term 'delegated' legislation is inappropriate, since it implies that the minister in his role as legislator delegates to himself as minister as executive. Secondary legislation can be considered to be the 'administrative stage' of the legislative process in the sense used by Walkland (1968). This subordinate legislation is overwhelmingly a departmental rather than a collective Cabinet function; even where other departments are affected, clearances will normally be obtained on a department to department basis. Statutory instruments are relatively rarely in any way controversial.

Consultation plays an even greater role in the preparation of statutory instruments than in the preparation of bills. This consultation is again sometimes formalized (e.g. through advisory committees), but also informal. In some cases subordinate legislation actually has to be approved by a statutory body before it is laid before Parliament. In case of disagreement the minister would have to defend his position before Parliament.

It is worth noting the sheer scale of secondary legislation. The number of statutory instruments each year is well over 2,000, and the number of pages fluctuates between 6,200 and 8,600, compared to between 1,800 and 2,700 pages of Acts. Obviously, many are technical, but some deal with matters which in the past would have been the subject of Acts.

In the face of this flood of legislation, the role of Parliament in even looking at or discussing statutory instruments at this stage of the legislative process is minimal, especially since there is no procedure for amending them (see Harlow and Rawlings, 1984, 119–30). Since March 1973 it has been possible for the House of Commons to discuss the merits of statutory instruments as well as their technical correctness. Only a few are ever debated.

The involvement of Parliament does prevent occasional 'defects' as on the Immigration Rules in 1982, resulting in the government's first and only defeat on the floor of the House of Commons in the 1979–83 Parliament. However, a ruling by the Joint Committee of both Houses of Parliament which examines all statutory instruments may be sufficient to persuade the government to withdraw proposed regulations. In October 1985 the committee ruled that regulations which Mr Norman Fowler, the Secretary of State for Social Services, had introduced on time limits for board and lodging payments to young people to replace a set ruled illegal by the High Court were themselves of doubtful legality (see 8.2). As a consequence, ministers decided to withdraw the revised regulations.

5.9 Assessment of the impact of the legislature

Enacted legislation continues to be overwhelmingly dominated by government. An assessment of the impact of Parliament on legislation depends on:

1. The significance attached to the occasions when the opposition or government backbenchers have been successful.
2. An assessment of the extent to which the government adjusts legislative proposals which it would otherwise prefer because of the fear that these might get defeated.
3. The extent to which proposals fail to get past the stage of processing within a government department because of the prospect of having

to justify an unpopular policy in public (even if defeat in either chamber was not expected). This is not a trivial point—Parliament may be important not for what it does to legislation but because it is there.

While backbenchers have shown themselves more prepared to vote against their party over the last twenty years, their revolts have relatively rarely led to the actual defeat of the government. An assessment of any trend over time is muddied by the minority status of the 1970s Labour governments and the devolution issue. In section 5.6 it was shown that the House of Lords has been playing an increasingly important role in shaping legislation since the mid-1970s. However, when a government has an overall majority the picture continues to be one of government domination of the parliamentary stages of the legislative process, with only occasional exceptions.

Parliament still largely legitimates rather than legislates. This legitimation is of decisions in the formulation of most of which Parliament has not participated. However, it is arguable that legitimation is an essential function in any ordered society. As Drewry (1981, 91) points out, we should not dismiss an arena for public discussion of policy issues simply because it falls a long way short of some ideals about representation and democracy.

This legitimating role of Parliament has come under pressure in recent years from a number of directions. Perhaps most importantly, government itself has not always felt it necessary to obtain formal authorization from Parliament before implementing important decisions. A particularly significant example was the black list operated by the 1974–9 Labour government of firms which did not comply with the government's proclaimed pay targets. Firms on their black list might be subject to penalties such as being refused Export Credit Guarantees. The government operated this black list without parliamentary approval for the pay policy or the black list. However, when the opposition forced a vote on the black list at the end of 1978 and the government was defeated, the government abandoned the operation of the black list. Thus, legitimation still seems to have some significance. Secondly, the legitimation role of Parliament has come under challenge from some trade unionists who urge that certain kinds of legal restrictions on trade unions are inherently illegitimate whatever Parliament says. Thirdly, as was illustrated at the 1984 Labour

Party Conference, there are a number of party activists who do not consider what they call 'class laws' legitimate; that is, certain perceived rights, for example, of trade unions, are seen as having greater legitimacy than formal authorization by Parliament. More generally, there is an often supported view that policies are only fully legitimate if relevant interests are consulted in advance. Thus the legitimacy of a policy is seen as adhering to the process by which it was arrived at rather than parliamentary authorization.

Chapter 6

Allocating Resources to Policies

6.1 Making and remaking policies through budgeting

Virtually all forms of public policy, with the possible exception of simple exhortation, require the allocation of public expenditure, either directly as expenditure or as 'tax expenditures' in the form of tax reliefs. Even policy instruments, such as regulation, which are not directly concerned with distributing cash or applying resources require expenditure on their administrative apparatus. Given that expenditure is a depletable resource (see Hood, 1983, 143–4), expenditure allocation for anything except short-term policies will be a recurring rather than merely a one-off stage in the policy process. Targeted taxes are also a budgetary aspect of policy-making. Taxes vary in the extent to which they are self-adjusting to inflation and economic trends and therefore in the extent to which explicit changes have to be made to maintain the original policy or to which lack of explicit change results in unannounced changes in policy priorities.

Budgeting is more than merely the automatic translation of government decisions or legislation into resource allocation. Public expenditure decision-making is highly politicized. Budgeting decisions can determine the time profile of a new programme coming on stream (if at all) or the level at which a programme is delivered over a period of years. Because budgeting entails review at least annually (though most programmes are certainly not reviewed explicitly in policy terms every year) programmes can be continuously remade in terms of the resources devoted to them and the priority accorded to them without there necessarily being any explicit change in government statements or legislation.

Although the conventional wisdom on the budgetary process in Britain and elsewhere is correct in arguing that the consideration of individual programmes is often highly particularistic and incremental in relation to existing allocations (Wildavsky, 1975), the arguments about these individual allocations do take place in the context of economic policy and policy about public expenditure decision-making. This emphasizes that public policy-making does have an aggregate and to a certain extent 'integrative' dimension, as well as a sectoral one. Public expenditure constraints also form part of the background and sometimes foreground consideration of options at the agenda-processing and government decision-making stages of the process.

Thus, the study of budgeting gives us some idea of the changing priorities of government. In the short term, changes in priority will be reflected in marginal changes in the total allocated to a particular activity, since it is difficult to make large changes in the short term and impossible to consider a programme from scratch. Governments (both central and local) have legal obligations to provide certain services. The statute book cannot be completely reworked on an annual basis. Contracts or other commitments will have been entered into for some projects, and others will be in the process of being completed. The large scale dismissal of the staff providing a particular service would have profound economic and political implications. Over the longer term, however, substantial changes are possible; for example, the share of housing in public expenditure fell from 7.6 per cent in 1978–9 to 4 per cent in 1985–6, while the share of employment and training rose from 1.6 per cent in 1978–9 to 2.4 per cent in 1985–6 (see Table 6.1). The party complexion of the government, though only one factor affecting expenditure, does appear to make some difference to the relative priority accorded to different programmes, with the share of both law and order and defence increasing, and that on housing and industry decreasing since 1979 (see also Pliatzky, 1985, 2–6). The study of budgeting involves looking at how price tags are attached to policies and how the conflicts arising from policies competing for the same resources are resolved.

Budgeting in Britain is not something which just takes place at the very top—among permanent secretaries and the Treasury and in the Cabinet. Budgeting is a pervasive activity throughout organizations in the public sector. Budgeting is *interorganizational* both collectively (for example, through local authority associations) and individually. Budgeting also involves aggregation and allocation within organizations.

This chapter examines the development of the public expenditure

Table 6.1 Percentage shares of public expenditure by function

Function	1978–9	1985–6
Employment and training	1.6	2.4
Health & personal social services	13.9	15.0
Law & order	3.7	4.6
Defence	11.3	13.1
Agriculture, fisheries, and food	1.5	2.1
Transport	4.9	4.0
Industry, trade, and energy	5.1	2.9
Housing	7.6	4.0
Education & science	14.3	12.7
Social security	25.6	30.7
Other	10.5	8.5

Source: Cmnd. 9702–I, 1986, Chart 1.11.

decision-making system in 6.2 and the process by which tax reforms are considered in 6.3 before looking at the annual cycle of budgeting on the expenditure (6.4) and taxation sides (6.5). Central–local finance and budgeting within local authorities are then examined in 6.6.

6.2 The development of the British public expenditure system

The development of the system of public expenditure decision-making reveals the tension between budgeting as controlling cash and budgeting as delivering the public policy goods. Following the Plowden Report of 1961, the focus of public expenditure decision-making moved away from annual Estimates for central government in cash for only one year ahead to a focus on expenditure of the public sector as a whole over a period of five years ahead in relation to prospective resources in the economy as a whole (see Pollitt, 1977). The emphasis on resources (such as number of teachers or the resources involved in building new schools) rather than finance was important both in attempting to link public expenditure to economic planning and in insulating public expenditure decision-making from consideration of its cash cost. In addition to analysis by responsible department and by economic category, expenditure was presented by programme, that is by policy area. Thus where a policy area was affected by expenditure by a number of departments, this expenditure could be pulled together for examination. However, in control terms, the central government could not determine the detailed allocation of local government spending, particularly following the introduction of a block grant system in 1958 (see 6.5).

The most important result of the Plowden Report was the introduction of the Public Expenditure Survey (PES) system. This involved the creation in 1961 of the Public Expenditure Survey Committee (PESC), a committee of civil servants composed mainly of senior departmental officials and chaired by a senior Treasury official. PESC, as such, does not try to agree on any particular level of government expenditure to be recommended to ministers or upon its allocation. It confines itself to agreeing on a factual report showing where present policies are likely to lead over the next three (originally five) years. Why should this be considered such an achievement? Because it is not always clear what is meant by 'existing policy', 'cost', and 'projection' (Heclo and Wildavsky, 1981, 216–26).

The PES process never lived up to the Plowden Report's hope of strengthening the collective responsibility of the Cabinet. The PES process does not in practice force ministers collectively to weigh proposals against each other. Big expenditure proposals still get taken up by the Cabinet often on an *ad hoc* basis. However, PES did make it more difficult to consider proposals in isolation from their implications for total public expenditure in the long term.

The development of the system of public expenditure decision-making and control cannot be considered in isolation from political and economic events. Both the Conservative government in 1963 and the Labour government in 1966 linked public expenditure plans to economic growth targets. However, despite the effective abandonment of Labour's National Plan later in 1966, public expenditure plans were not cut back. As the balance-of-payments crisis deepened in 1966–7 it became obvious that cutbacks in public expenditure plans were necessary and a series of *ad hoc* expenditure cuts took place outside the annual PES timetable.

However, the failure to control public spending was taken to constitute evidence not that the PES system should be discontinued, but that it was more essential than ever. The most important change in PES after 1967 was not so much in the way the survey was carried out as in the way it was seen by others in government. That is, there was a reduction in political wishful thinking rather than improvement in techniques. After devaluation of the pound in November 1967 the government cut back on public spending plans for the coming year and future years. To make control easier, costs were also to be projected for second, third, and fourth years as well as the first and fifth years of a programme. In the words of the government's 1968 Public Expenditure White Paper, there was to be 'planning the path as well as the whole'. From 1969 plans were published as open commitments in annual Public Expenditure White Papers.

Just as the system had reached this stage of development there was a change of government. The Conservatives were committed to bringing about changes in the system by which public expenditure decisions were made, but they were intended to build on and expand the existing system rather than replace it. Most of the proposed changes were developed by the Conservatives in opposition, though they coincided with the way some senior civil servants wanted to see the system developed.

One of the recurring criticisms of public expenditure decision-making was that existing policies did not receive the scrutiny reserved for proposed new expenditure. The reforms announced in 1970 included the introduction of a team of businessmen to introduce 'programme analysis and review' (PAR). Although there had been previous special studies and reviews, the special aspect of PAR was supposed to be that these features would be applied systematically and regularly across the whole field of government. There was to be closer consideration of the objectives of programmes, more attention to the relationship between expenditure incurred and returns obtained, and a wider review of alternative ways of achieving the objectives. In practice, those PARs which were carried out varied very widely in quality, with some largely defensive of a department's interest, while others brought attention to problems of existing policy for the first time. However, a variety of reasons, including the lack of a supportive organizational and political base for PAR and a lack of identifiable mileage for the departments whose activities were being examined, led to the atrophying of PAR, and its eventual formal abolition in 1979 (see Gray and Jenkins, 1982). PARs failed to become integrated with the PES decision-making cycle: the vision of a small Cabinet collectively reviewing existing public expenditure programmes together with PAR analyses and tax changes remained a vision (see Clarke, 1971).

As became clear following the return of a Labour government in 1974, problems had been developing with the PES system as a mechanism of public expenditure decision-making and *control*. July 1975 saw the introduction of a new incomes policy following the failure of the original 'Social Contract' to contain inflation. In 1975 and 1976 there were a number of mini-budgets, culminating with the one in December 1976 associated with the granting of the IMF loan (see Pliatzky, 1982, ch. 5; Barnett, 1982, ch. 10; Granada, 1977, 49–61). The political debate about the control of public expenditure came to a head in December 1975, with the publication of a critical report from the House of Commons Expenditure Committee (HC 69, 1975–6). This pointed out that on the information available to them at the time, expenditure at 1974–5 prices was about £5.8bn more than it had been planned to be in the Public Expenditure White Paper of November 1971. Of the £5.8bn, £1.8bn was due to announced policy changes. However, £4bn—amounting to 5 per cent of the UK GDP—was not the result of announced policy changes. In fact, the situation was even worse than the committee thought, since subsequent revisions revealed the addition of a further £0.7bn overspend.

These 'missing billions' were the extra *before* including the general rate of inflation and errors in forecasting the rate at which prices of public sector inputs would go up faster than general inflation (the relative price effect). With a rate of inflation of around 25 per cent in 1975 the cash cost was increasing even faster. The expenditure plans at that time were presented in 'volume terms', that is in terms of the cost of a given level of resource inputs in a given year. But while measurement on a cònstant price basis in this way enabled resources to be allocated in 'real terms' over the plan period, PES could not be used to control the cash cost of using those resources. Until 1976 this meant that if the cash cost increased faster than expected, Supplementary Estimates were automatically given.

Even before the Expenditure Committee Report, the Treasury

had been attempting to get better control over the cash cost of public expenditure, including plans to introduce 'cash limits' from April 1976. Under cash limits the level of provision of services and goods was still determined annually in real resources (i.e. volume terms). However, the figures for about two-thirds of public spending were to be converted into cash figures which represented 'limits' or 'planned ceilings' for blocks of expenditure. The intention was that the cash cost of financing a programme in the year ahead should not exceed the prescribed level. The areas which did not (and still do not) have cash limits are those which are 'demand determined', e.g. social security payments. Where the cash cost of one aspect of a block of expenditure looked like exceeding the limit, the additional cash cost could normally be met only by (a) a reduction in the volume of the service or (b) by making compensating savings elsewhere. Where the allowance for inflation built into the cash limit was lower than the actual rate, as it was during the 1976–7 financial year, cutbacks would be necessary in volume terms.

In their first two years of operation cash limits and other devices were successful in preventing overshoots of the 'missing billions' type. However, there were cash undershoots of around £1bn in each year. Another measure of deviation from the government's budgetary plans was that the final Public Sector Borrowing Requirement (PSBR) for 1977–8 was £5.5bn, which, allowing for interim budgetary changes, was £4.2bn less than forecast at the beginning of the financial year, and substantially less than the £11bn being talked about at the time of the IMF loan discussions in December 1976.

In 1978–9 under Labour and in subsequent years under the Conservatives large wage claims, and more accurately uncertainty about wage settlements, caused severe problems for the government's budgetary plans. If cash limits were set lower than the eventual level of wage settlement there was a squeeze on the volume of public expenditure and a danger of cash limits being breached. If cash limits were abandoned or set high enough to finance all settlements the government would have to find the cash cost. For 1979–80 the Labour government appeared to be setting an unrealistic initial figure for cash limits which implied from the start an expenditure pattern which contradicted the volume plans announced at the same time. This implied that the government was planning to use cash limits as an arbitrary way of cutting back public expenditure relative to the rest of the economy. At the same time, the government partially relaxed the original cash limits when it failed to keep pay settlements within the guidelines, thus undermining the credibility of initial cash limits.

Control of public expenditure was important for the incoming Conservative government in 1979 both as an end in itself and because of the perceived link between the Public Sector Borrowing Requirement and the money supply and between the money supply and the rate of inflation. In practice, as Table 6.2 shows, public expenditure continued to rise under the Conservatives. 1981 saw the phasing in of 'cash planning': decisions were now to be made in cash terms rather than volume ones: under cash limits decisions had been made in volume terms and then translated into cash. This change represented a major reversal of the resource-based approach which had developed in the 1960s and emphasized the extent to which the government was concerned about financial restraint rather than planning the resources for policy programmes.

The distinction between cash-limited programmes and others remained, with cash planning representing ceilings for cash-limited programmes and forecasts for demand-led programmes. Difficulties in forecasting inflation and unemployment led to overshoots in some programmes. Lack of central government control over local government expenditure despite an increasingly complex set of restrictions was emphasized by continuing overshoots of local government actual expenditure against central government plans

Table 6.2 Growth of public expenditure in real (cost terms)

	1978–9	1979–80	1980–1	1981–2	1982–3	1983–4	1984–5	1985–6
Planning total (£bn)	117.4	118.5	119.2	121.5	123.8	125.7	129.6	127.8
% change on previous year	—	1.0	0.6	1.9	1.9	1.6	3.1	−1.4
Expenditure (£bn)*	117.4	119.1	119.7	122.0	124.3	126.9	131.7	130.3

* Calculated by adding back in central privatization proceeds to planning total.

Source: Derived from Cmnd. 9702—II, 1986, Table 2.2.

Table 6.3 Public expenditure (planning total) plans and out-turns (£bn cash)

White Paper	1980–1	1981–2	1982–3	1983–4	1984–5	1985–6
March 1980	91.2	101.0	106.3	112.4		
March 1981	92.8	104.4	109.9	113.6		
March 1982	93.0	105.7	114.6	120.7	127.7	
Feb. 1983	92.7	104.7	113.0	119.6	126.5	132.3
Feb. 1984	92.7	104.7	113.4	120.4	126.5	132.1
Jan. 1985	92.7	104.6	113.4	120.3	128.2	132.1
March 1985 (Budget)	92.7	104.6	113.4	120.3	129.7	134.2
Jan. 1986	92.6	104.0	113.3	120.3	129.6	134.2

Note: Figures above the stepped line are plans, those below are out-turn or estimated out-turn.

Source: Cmnd. 9702—I, 1986, Table 1.9.

for local government (see 6.5). However, central government had little more success in meeting its targets for its own expenditure and for public expenditure as a whole (see Table 6.3). Further the government's attempts to link its public expenditure decision-making to economic policy through a 'Medium Term Financial Strategy' can be regarded as a failure, or as at best a learning process for government (see Thain, 1985). Ironically, inflation fell, even though this should not have occurred under the assumptions underlying the government's original reasoning.

The Conservative government launched a number of procedural initiatives related to public expenditure. These included the so-called Rayner exercises, named after Lord Rayner, who headed an Efficiency Unit in the Cabinet Office. The exercises were largely concerned with carrying out existing activities more effectively rather than reviewing policies. In its first five years, the Rayner exercises identified about £560 million of potential savings, of which £330 million were accepted and £240 million actually achieved (compared to £120bn total expenditure in 1983–4). As Pliatzky (1985, 70–1) points out, 'the great bulk of the civil service cuts were made by Departments through measures other than the Rayner scrutinies, in response to the blunt instruments of cash limits and manpower targets'. Another major initiative was the

Financial Management Initiative (FMI) which was mainly concerned with clarification of objectives and accountability at senior
management level rather than with the policy implications of
public expenditure (though see 9.5).

A third development, unheralded unlike the other two, was
much more directly concerned with the policy aspects of public
expenditure choices. When an issue arises between the Treasury
and a spending department which cannot be resolved in the course
of the annual expenditure cycle a review may be set up with the
intention of feeding its results into the next year's Public
Expenditure Survey (see Pliatzky, 1985, 42). As with PAR (see
above) not all the reviews are announced, though the social
security reviews resulting in the 1985 Green Papers and White
Paper were publicly announced. Unlike PAR, there is no formal
set of procedures, nor is there an aspiration towards eventual
systematic coverage.

The continuing difficulties the government faced in constraining
the total of public expenditure were emphasized when in the
March 1985 Budget, only two months after the publication of the
annual Public Expenditure White Paper, the Chancellor announced
the adding of £2bn to the contingency reserve for the new financial
year and for the two subsequent years. This was an increase in
public expenditure and a substantial increase in the amount of
public expenditure not allocated to programmes. The amount
allocated for debt interest was also increased. According to the
Chancellor's Budget speech, this raised the planning totals for the
next three years by about 1.5 per cent.

Cash planning from 1982 onwards might appear to have an
inbuilt bias to understate future inflation (as with cash limits) and
therefore an incentive to cut future expenditure in real terms
(Ward, 1985). There has been a blurring of changes due to price
increases and real increases. Only if the government correctly
anticipated inflation would its plans in real terms be achieved. We
might have expected that there would have been underprediction of
inflation. In practice over 1982–5 the government *over*predicted
inflation. Compared to 1982–3 plans for 1984–5 there was an
overexpenditure in cash of £5.5bn (out of £135bn), of which about
£2.5bn was due to the miners' strike. Because the general rate of
inflation had been overpredicted by over 5 per cent for the period,
the out-turn in cost terms (i.e. after allowing for the general rate of

inflation) was an overspend of £12.5bn, close to 10 per cent of expenditure as projected in the 1982–3 plans.

This experience raises a question mark about planning ahead in cash terms, with cash plans being held to be sacrosanct and price and real changes being blurred. The cash figures lose their meaning if underlying economic conditions change. The available finance may also change. Control has been relatively ineffective in terms of cash anyway. Cash planning also diverts attention away from provision of public services *per se*.

The January 1986 Public Expenditure White Paper (Cmnd. 9702) was the first to set out the spending plans mainly by department rather than by programme (i.e. policy area). The justification offered for doing so was that 'This reflects the way decisions are taken' (Cmnd. 9702–I, 1986, 4). As a result of mergers, departments in the mid-1980s more closely conformed to broad policy areas than they had in the early 1960s when the PES system was first set up, and the focus on policy area had already been eroded by the establishment of separate programmes for Scottish and Welsh Office matters. Also, some information about spending by policy area continued to be provided. However, to use the White Paper's words, the emphasis in public expenditure decision-making was now even more on 'Who plans it' rather than 'Where it goes'.

Developments over the decade from 1975 led to a redefinition of what is meant by relating public expenditure to resources and by control. There has been a shift away from economic resource management to how much money is made available in cash terms. 'Control' now means keeping below the cash ceiling rather than ensuring that a certain volume of inputs into public policy is made available.

6.3 Tax policy-making

Most taxes have in principle greater flexibility than expenditure. Though the introduction of a new tax may involve upheaval (see Johnstone, 1975), this is less than the upheaval which would be associated with the introduction of a new expenditure programme of the same scale. A much greater proportion of taxation than expenditure is in central government hands. These features should in principle provide the central government with a greater capacity for strategic decision-making on taxation. However, there is no Tax Survey system or interdepartmental Tax Survey Committee corresponding to the Public Expenditure Survey and PESC.

A distinction can be made between fundamental tax decisions, such as the abolition of a tax or the introduction of a new one, and routine annual adjustments, such as changes in income tax allowances or excise duties as announced in the annual budget. However, the distinction is not a hard and fast one; for example, the Conservative government's increase in the VAT rate in 1979 to 15 per cent was part of a restructuring of the tax system. Robinson and Sandford (1983, ix) point out that changes in tax rates may have more social and economic significance than changes in the tax structure. Fundamental changes in the tax structure can occur by default through failure to index tax thresholds for inflation. Similarly, the inflation of house prices has led to the tax forgone as a result of relief on mortgage interest to increase dramatically to £4.75bn in 1985–6. The tax structure can itself alter behaviour in a way which in turn feeds back into the tax collected: mortgage interest relief has led to the purchase of more and larger houses than would otherwise have been the case, and may well have contributed to the inflation in house prices.

As noted in 2.6, almost all new taxes were placed on the government agenda through party determination of the objectives of the proposed new tax (Robinson and Sandford, 1983, 220). However,

the parties showed only limited capacity for rational considertion of their chosen objectives. They did not examine them in sufficient detail, nor did they fully explore the consequences of their chosen actions. For successful policy-making it is not enough for parties simply to state broad and general aims.

For example, Robinson and Sandford (1983, 222) suggest that the failure of the Labour Party to clarify and refine its objective of redistribution lay at the heart of the failure of the taxes that it introduced to meet that objective. The proposal to abolish rates in the 1974 Conservative manifesto (modified to give it lower priority than cutting income tax in the 1979 manifesto) and the floating of the idea of introducing a poll tax are examples of Conservative lack of following through thinking about tax proposals, at least as far as proposals for abolition and replacement are concerned. For both the wealth tax and (up to early 1986) the abolition of rates the lack of thinking through meant that the proposal was never taken to the legislative stage. However, lack of thinking through may not prevent the tax proposal reaching the legislative stage but may result in it being ineffective in meeting its (perhaps not very well articulated) objectives or being riddled with loopholes and anomalies which reduce its tax-raising capacity. Overall, tax policy-making in the early stages operates in the reverse of what might be considered the most rational manner; instead of first determining and refining objectives and then selecting the means of achieving them, parties have tended to put forward a tax proposal and only then try to refine their objectives.

The next stage in the policy process would appear to be the detailed design of policy instruments and the selection of the best one for meeting the stated purposes of the proposed tax or tax reform. This might appear to be where the traditional model of the role of government departments and of civil servants comes in: the civil servants, having carefully read the party's manifesto will present the minister with a briefing paper on the advantages and disadvantages of different methods of implementing the proposal.

In fact, the relevant government departments appear to lack the capacity to do this. The Treasury itself is mainly concerned with macroeconomic policy, expenditure control, and budgetary policy in the sense of striking the preferred balance between public expenditure, taxation, and borrowing. Tax collection is not the direct responsibility of the Treasury, but of the Inland Revenue for direct taxation (e.g. income tax) and of the Customs and Excise for indirect taxation (e.g. VAT). However, the main function of these revenue departments is the administration and collection of *existing* taxes, and they do not have a detailed research capacity. Thus, they can monitor the effects of *current* tax policy and provide ministers with feedback on problems encountered in the administration of taxes. Because they can only build on what they already know and have directly experienced, they tend to exhibit an incremental approach to tax policy-making. For example, in the reform of death duties the Inland Revenue undoubtedly favoured continuing a donor-based death duty along the lines of the previous estate duty, and this was indeed reflected in the design of the capital transfer tax which was introduced by the Labour government. Robinson and Sandford (1983, 227) found that there did not appear to be either great enthusiasm, or powerful machinery, in the revenue departments for turning over to them a new function as tax designer. Nor is this gap filled by the Treasury, which does not appear to have a strong tax design capacity, as opposed to its capacity for analysing budgetary and macroeconomic impact.

The parties themselves do not have the large, well staffed party machines which would enable them to do the detailed analysis of alternative policy instruments. The Labour party in particular is poorly funded. At the same time, Britain has lacked the wide range of large, independently funded institutes with some tax analysis capacity which exist in the United States, such as the Brookings Institute, though the establishment of the Institute for Fiscal Studies and the Policy Studies Institute in London does provide independent sources of advice. Parties have also been haphazard in their use of academics as a source of advice. 'As a result there is something of a policy vacuum between the articulation of broad and general goals and the establishment of well worked out schemes by which those goals can be attained' (Robinson and Sandford, 1983, 224). One consequence of this failure by parties to explore alternatives before making a commitment to tax reform is that ideological stances in favour of different forms of taxation may not be reflected in empirical evidence. For example, Whittington (1974) concluded that the empirical evidence offered no grounds for strongly held views on different forms of corporation tax.

Given the lack of detailed working through of proposals by parties with ideas for tax changes and the incremental bias in the bureaucracy, it is not surprising that even apparently radical proposals are either diverted (wealth tax, abolition of rates) or come into effect in a form which resembles the tax they were designed to replace (e.g. capital transfer tax compared to estate duty).

Interest groups are active at all stages of tax policy-making, but are particularly involved after parties have set out their broad objectives (Robinson and Sandford, 1983, 228). Their involvement may occur after the government has decided in principle to introduce legislation but wishes to engage in wider consultation, including the publication of a Green Paper, or even the involvement of a parliamentary select committee. Interest groups may also play a considerable part while legislation is being processed through Parliament. The number of groups active at every stage of tax policy-making has increased since the early 1960s and many of them have developed machinery for responding to government tax proposals. By the 1970s a more open approach to tax policy-making was adopted and this brought the claims of interest groups under the light of publicity as well as drawing them more closely into the policy-making process.

In addition to making use of an extension of consultation with departments and ministers, changes in the procedure of the House of Commons have provided new routes for interest group involvement. One is the use of select committees to examine tax reforms in the case of corporation tax, wealth tax, and personal tax reform (see Robinson, 1985a). Another is the use of standing committees rather than the floor of the House to examine parts of the Finance Bills which put tax changes into legislative form. Interest groups, with their specialist knowledge of the details of taxation, were able to assist MPs by the provision of information. In contrast to the 1950s, by the 1970s new tax legislation tended to be substantially altered by its passage through Parliament. However, nearly all these changes were proposed or accepted by government. The changes say more about the success of increased interest group involvement than a dramatically increased role for Parliament *per se*. Pressure from interest groups or the media has led to important changes in the details of taxation. This had been true both for business groups and for groups without obvious direct power, such as the Child Poverty Action Group. However, Robinson and Sandford (1983, 230–1) argue that:

Concessions to pressure groups, whilst they may show political wisdom or good judgement . . . are almost always contrary to rational policy-making. Thus the zero-rating of children's clothes created anomalies; large children fail to benefit and small adults can benefit. If the object had been to give more support to parents, the rational choice would have been to increase child allowances rather than to complicate VAT with this additional zero-rating and awkward borderline. Similarly, the concessions under CTT [capital transfer tax] for farmers are of doubtful benefit to the industry . . .

Such tax reliefs . . . are all in the nature of tax expenditures . . . In their costs to the Exchequer they are the equivalent of outright subsidies, and the benefits frequently go to the better off. They complicate taxes and create anomalies, and make further reform more remote by introducing 'losers'.

This involvement of interest groups does in part reflect the general pattern of interest group involvement in the policy process which has been reflected throughout this book, but a special feature of much tax policy-making is that the lack of clearly thought out proposals creates opportunities for interest group shaping of the finally legislated form which would not be so great if better researched and more detailed proposals had been developed in the first place.

Overall, the limited changes and limited success resulting from many tax reforms suggest that all the effort and partial analysis which went into them was often disproportionate to the outcome actually achieved (Robinson and Sandford, 1983, 231). This is true both of broader social objectives and (with the exceptions of selective employment tax and VAT) in terms of raising substantial new revenue.

6.4 The annual budgetary cycle: public expenditure

In Britain there is not a single cycle of budgetary decision-making but two separate but occasionally interacting cycles, namely the expenditure cycle and the Budget (taxation) cycle. The Treasury is at the centre of both; the central Treasury is a very small department indeed, with only around 1,300 civil servants to cover public expenditure, taxation, and economic policy-making. However, the Treasury has a very high proportion of senior policy-level civil servants and senior ministers: in addition to the Chancellor there are the Chief Secretary (who handles public expenditure and who is normally in the Cabinet), the Financial Secretary, the Economic Secretary, and a Minister of State. The work of the Treasury varies very considerably in the extent to which it is a matter for internal consideration within the Treasury or for negotiation or implementation through other bodies. Control and allocation of public expenditure involves the Treasury with the Cabinet collectively in determining the overall level of public expenditure, and with individual departments in bargaining or conflict over their allocations. By contrast, the preparation of tax changes is a much more internalized affair within the Treasury.

The expenditure cycle can be divided into six parts: (1) the PESC exercise and dialogue between Treasury and departmental officials; (2) political bargaining about changes in policy; (3)

publication and debate on Public Expenditure White Papers; (4) translation of public expenditure decisions into Estimates and formal parliamentary approval of the Estimates; (5) expenditure and monitoring; (6) preparation of Appropriation Accounts and any subsequent scrutiny. The stages in the expenditure cycle are summarized in Table 6.4. This section examines stages (1) to (4), while the subsequent scrutiny of expenditure is considered in 9.4.

In order to carry out its work the Treasury has to maintain a dialogue with the spending departments individually on the size, composition, objectives, and management of their programmes of expenditure and on the policies which underlie them. This means developing a pattern of relationships with departments suited to the type of spending for which they are responsible, and special

Table 6.4 The annual expenditure cycle

Year −1	April	Treasury issues guidelines on survey
	May/June	Treasury agrees new survey baseline with departments based on latest White Paper updated by Budget
	July	PESC Report to Cabinet. Cabinet sets ceiling
	Summer	Bilaterals between Treasury and departments
	Autumn	Unresolved issues to 'Star Chamber' and prime minister
	November	Autumn Statement. Outline plans by department for three years ahead
	December	Rate Support Grant for local authorities announced
	January	Public Expenditure White Paper: detailed plans for three years ahead
	March	Estimates for year ahead presented
Year 1	March/April	Any adjustments in Budget Statement
	April–July	Passage of Appropriation Act (no debate)
	April–March	Expenditure of funds; monitoring; decisions on use of Contingency Reserve
Year 2		Auditing by National Audit Office and possible consideration by Public Accounts Committee

machinery for general consultation and discussion. Fierce battles do take place between departments and the Treasury on individual issues, but there is recognition of a shared interest in keeping the procedures manageable even if there is not shared commitment to policy objectives. The task of maintaining manageable procedures is more difficult in an era of restraint.

Collective discussion is conducted primarily through the Public Expenditure Survey Committee, whose role was referred to in section 6.2. The growth of confidence from collective discussion in this way has led to the emergence of what has been called the 'PESC Club', that is, the body of officials with major responsibility within departments for programme planning and financial control and their opposite numbers in the Treasury who sit with them in PESC.

In terms of dialogue with individual departments, a crucial feature is the trust which Heclo and Wildavsky (1981) describe as necessary between civil servants in the spending departments and the Treasury expenditure divisions. Inevitably, departments are selective in the information they volunteer to the Treasury, but, as the Principal Finance Officer at the DHSS has put it,

I would have said that we, and indeed other departments, attempt to play this straight with the Treasury, just as we would expect them to play straight with us. We would not make statements that could not be fully substantiated or that were not in fact fair statements or reasonable judgements of the case and in a sense one is in a position perhaps of the advocate, but we are not wanting, as it were, to mislead the court. (Young and Sloman, 1984, 49.)

This relative straightforwardness is seen as being in the long-run interests of the department, since, as the Permanent Secretary to the Department of Health and Social Security put it: 'sooner or later something would go wrong as a result of having only a partial awareness in the Treasury of what it is that we're doing' (Young and Sloman, 1984, 51). In return the Treasury does not take advantage of frankness by cutting back on a department unduly.

This trust—and the Treasury civil servants' understanding of a department and when to ask probing questions (see Young and Sloman, 1984, 46–7)—is built up because dialogue between the departments and the Treasury is conducted on a continuous basis rather than only at certain times of the year. For example, the Treasury is likely to be consulted by a department's civil servants about an idea which is being developed even before the proposal is put to the department's minister—a procedure which might be interpreted by some as going behind the minister's back, but, depending on how it is done, is really a manifestation of political common sense, if opposition from the Treasury is to be anticipated.

Treasury dialogue is not, of course, confined to such initial stages of policy-making. It keeps a watch on policies to see whether original expectations are being fulfilled and to take action if they are not. The Treasury is obviously directly concerned in ensuring that departments are able to carry out effectively all the tasks involved in public expenditure decision-making, for example, that the figures embodied in the PESC report are accurate and that departments have good internal monitoring systems. Much of Treasury concern is to ensure that departments themselves have adequate internal systems for appraisal and monitoring and that these are relatively transparent and comparable with the systems used in other departments, rather than trying to second guess all the original decisions made by the departments.

Each year in July the Cabinet considers the PESC Report and the bids for extra resources which have been made by ministers. Until 1986 spending ministers were able to submit claims routinely to be included in the Public Expenditure Survey report considered by Cabinet. Ministers were also supposed to suggest offsetting cuts in spending, but in practice that requirement was often ignored. From 1986, the automatic right to bid for extra cash was removed, and no new bids were to be included in the Public Expenditure Survey. Any minister wanting to bid for extra finance had to write to the Chief Secretary to the Treasury with a detailed justification for the claim and options for offsetting cuts. A copy of the request would have to be forwarded to the prime minister.

The July Cabinet meeting sets a ceiling for total public expenditure and may set some broad guidelines. However, the detailed discussions about departmental allocations take place not in full Cabinet or even in cabinet committee but in 'bilaterals' during the summer and early autumn between each department individually and the Treasury. At ministerial level this involves the minister concerned and the Chief Secretary to the Treasury. Most allocations to departments are settled at this stage, but mechanisms have had to be developed to deal with the remaining 'hard cases'. From 1981 there has been a cabinet committee (MISC 62), commonly referred to as the 'Star Chamber'. The committee is chaired by Lord Whitelaw, the deputy prime minister, and is unusual among cabinet committees in excluding ministers from large spending departments. However, even the Star Chamber mechanism has been unsuccessful in resolving all outstanding disagreements between spending ministers and the departments, and remaining disputes have to be resolved by the prime minister and endorsed by full Cabinet. The full Cabinet, however, never considers those departmental allocations which have been settled between the Treasury and the spending department and there is no collective overall view of the relative merits of the various departmental programmes. The effect of the changes in procedure introduced in 1986 will be to shift much of the political haggling over expenditure to earlier in the year.

Expenditure decisions do not invariably have to go through a traumatic resolution in cabinet committee, as in 1984. In 1982 resolution was achieved without any decision having to be referred to a cabinet committee (see Young and Sloman, 1984, 59). However, it is worth noting that this was the cycle immediately before the 1983 general election.

Many decisions about expenditure are made on an *ad hoc* basis throughout the year rather than all coming up for decision at this stage in the cycle. It is an especial danger that in any conflict involving a dispute about public expenditure the Treasury will be outvoted in cabinet committee by a coalition of spending ministers, whereas in full Cabinet it may be able to rely on the support of the prime minister and other non-spending ministers. An important change in the mechanisms for resolving this problem took place in 1976 (see Pliatzky, 1982, 140–1; Barnett, 1982, 18). Before 1976 Treasury ministers had a long-standing right to reserve their position in cabinet committees on financial matters and take them to full Cabinet. Treasury ministers had to be selective in choosing which issues to take to full Cabinet, since, as a former Treasury minister put it, 'taking issues to Cabinet all the time would not endear me to the Prime Minister' (Barnett, 1982, 27). However, from 1976 the rule was that Treasury ministers could not be overruled in cabinet committees on financial matters. In other words, the Treasury no longer had to reserve its position, and the onus was shifted to the relevant spending minister to take his case to Cabinet.

The results of decisions on public expenditure are announced in stages. The first Autumn Statement was in 1982, following a report from the Treasury and Civil Service Committee of the Commons, which had called for a more thoroughgoing reform of the budget decision-making process. The Autumn Statement brings together announcements previously made at that time of year: the economic forecast required under the Industry Act 1975, outline public expenditure plans for the year ahead, and a summary of proposed changes in national insurance contributions. In addition, the Autumn Statement includes 'revalorization' projections, i.e. adjustments to tax rates or allowances which would be necessary to adjust for inflation, and tax 'ready reckoners' showing the revenue implications of illustrative changes to major taxes. The early statements also included an implied 'fiscal adjustment', i.e. the amount by which the Chancellor might be able or required to adjust revenue or expenditure based on assumptions about revenue, expenditure, and borrowing requirement. However, this was dropped from the Autumn Statement in 1985 because, the Chancellor claimed, he would not actually be taking his decisions until the spring.

Detailed allocations within departments still have to be determined, and as the student grant case illustrated (see 4.7), these can be at least as politically sensitive as the block allocations between departments. Individual ministerial announcements at this time may make these clearer. Also at about this time the various Secretaries of State announce the rate support grant for local authorities and external financing limits for the nationalized industries.

More detailed plans for the next three years are then published in the Public Expenditure White Paper at the beginning of the following year. Since annual publication of the White Papers on public expenditure from 1969 there has been debate on them in the House of Commons. Some of the early debates were flops: in 1971 opposition members refused to sit through the debate and it petered out without a vote. In 1976 and 1977 the debate was indeed vigorous, so vigorous that the government was defeated on both occasions—but this made no difference to the government's execution of its plans. There is, then, an air of unreality about the debates, both because of the huge range of often technical material in the White Paper and because the debate is not linked to formal authorization of expenditure.

Although the PES process is the effective decision-making process, there is a need to translate those decisions in terms of that part of the money which has to be voted by Parliament, including central government expenditure and grants paid by central government to other bodies, such as local government. One of the great myths of the British Constitution is that the power of Parliament stems from its ability to grant or deny Supply, that is, the right to incur expenditure, to the government. Until the 1982–3 session the House of Commons still formally devoted a lot of time to Supply (Treasury, 1983b). In practice, control of the twenty-nine Supply days had passed to the official opposition, which tended to use them for debates on matters of general political interest, subject only to the convention that some of the days were used for debates on specified topics—the armed forces, European Community affairs, Scottish affairs, and select committee reports. Similarly, debates on the Consolidated Fund Bills had little to do with the Supply Estimates to which they were related, and the second reading was used as an opportunity for back-benchers to raise virtually any issue. Thus, despite considerable nominal opportunities there was very little serious debate of the Estimates.

The fiction of 'Supply days' has been abolished. They have been replaced by (1) nineteen Opposition days available to the official opposition for debates of their own choosing; (2) regular topics previously discussed on Supply days are now taken in government time; (3) three 'Estimates days' specifically allocated to debates and votes on Supply Estimates, including Revised and Supplementary Estimates. Second reading debates on the Consolidated Fund Bills were abolished, with more time being allocated to private members in other ways in compensation; all stages of Consolidated Fund Bills are now taken formally, that is, without any debate. Thus, Parliament now has three days in which to debate all the Estimates, and this constitutes an improvement! The first Estimates day was held on 14 March 1983, when the House debated as issues with crucial expenditure implications the two estimates for parliamentary stationery and printing and for development in the Turks and Caicos Islands. Attendance was low and continued to be in subsequent debates on the Estimates (Norton, 1985b, 165).

The other main arena for scrutiny of government expenditure

plans are the specialist committees of the Commons. The Treasury and Civil Service Committee is the only one to look at expenditure as a whole (see Robinson, 1985a). Although it is within their terms of reference to examine the expenditure of government departments and other bodies, the other departmental committees do not undertake regular investigations into public expenditure (Robinson, 1985b). The committees have varied considerably in the extent to which they have looked at expenditure or Estimates, e.g. Welsh Affairs only once, Scottish Affairs frequently, though to little apparent effect. Even for those which do look at expenditure more frequently, it forms only a small part of their total activity. Each committee operates independently and there has been no attempt to co-ordinate the scrutiny of public expenditure or to link it to the work of the Treasury and Civil Service Committee.

6.5 The annual budgetary cycle: taxation

The annual tax decision cycle is not a process which involves all departments in the same way as public expenditure, but nor is it a matter for the Treasury alone. The revenue departments which actually collect the taxes are also involved, though with the Treasury playing the key role in relating tax changes to budgetary judgement (see Robinson and Sandford, 1983, 99–101). The Bank of England will also be involved in the general strategy and in many of the detailed proposals (Treasury, 1983a).

Another sense in which the consideration of Budget tax changes is not completely self-contained is that there is constant interest group pressure on the Treasury, not just during the peak period leading up to the Budget, but throughout the year (see Table 6.5 for a summary of the annual cycle of tax decision-making). The extent to which individual groups will be given serious consideration varies between governments. For example, under the 1979 Conservative government the CBI has very regular contact both through meetings and by telephone, both between the top officials and ministers and between CBI staff and civil servants. The TUC, on the other hand, has had very much less frequent contact, both compared to the previous Labour government and previous Conservative governments (Young and Sloman, 1984, 73). Because the Treasury is in regular contact with most of the relevant groups

Tale 6.5 Budget (revenue side) cycle

Year −1	September	Representations from groups to Treasury begin in earnest, though discussions with major groups go on year round
	November	Autumn Statement provides revenue projections, revalorization projections, and tax ready reckoner
	February	Drafting of Budget Speech begins about six weeks before Budget Day
Year 1	March/April	Saturday before Budget documents go for printing
		Tuesday morning: Cabinet given Budget details; afternoon: Budget Speech
		Budget resolutions tabled
		Finance Bill published
	April/July	Finance Bill considered partly on floor, partly in standing committee
	July	'July measures' (optional!)

it is normally aware of those groups' views and the representations made just before the Budget will not normally change the Treasury's mind. However, some groups, particularly those with specialist interests, do come up with new ideas or draw attention to changed circumstances, and the Treasury will consider such representations carefully.

In the run-up to the Budget, starting the previous September, the Treasury will receive two types of advice, one relating to views about how the government should run the economy, and the other relating to particular taxes, almost invariably suggesting a reduction rather than an increase (Young and Sloman, 1984, 75). The letters and papers received range from one side of manuscript to forty pages of analysis (Treasury, 1983a). MPs and even Treasury officials themselves are rather concerned at the unevenness of pressure which can result from this interest group activity. Treasury officials like to think of themselves as being able to correct for any bias in pressure exerted by interest groups (see Young and Sloman, 1984, 77).

At an early stage in the annual budget cycle, officials list every possible tax change, and this is constantly updated up to the time of the Budget. This list is divided into minor and major possible tax changes. Some of these are dropped at various stages, though some are in turn reinstated. All these proposals are put to ministers, and against most of the entries by the time of the run-up to the Budget is a note about what minister on what date had authorized the proposal to be dropped. To assist ministers in taking decisions, the effects of tax changes are summarized by economists from the Treasury and the revenue departments in a 'ready reckoner', which lists the forecast effect of the proposed change in the PSBR, the exchange rate, and other economic variables. This involves judgement as much as arithmetic calculation, since the underlying condition of the tax base may be changing and judgements also have to be made of likely reaction to tax changes, for example whether and by how much consumption of an item like beer might go down if the tax was increased by a certain amount. In arriving at such judgements, the Treasury relies on part on the advice of the revenue departments (Young and Sloman, 1984, 78–9; Robinson and Sandford, 1983).

It would be wrong to see a rigid separation between ministers and top civil servants in the Treasury, except in the final stages where decisions are a matter for the Chancellor together with his ministerial colleagues and the prime minister. As one Treasury civil servant put it:

in the build-up there is a very real and continuing dialogue. We are constantly in the Chancellor's room, throwing ideas around and looking at various mixes and packages. (Young and Sloman, 1984, 79.)

However, another civil servant stressed that although there was dialogue it was not a dialogue between equals:

Officials will present papers to ministers which will then be discussed, generally with the officials present. Ministers will listen to officials' views, but of course the decision on which options are going to be explored is one that ministers take, not officials. (Young and Sloman, 1984, 80.)

The Chancellor of the Exchequer closely consults the prime minister, but other ministers normally have to accept a *fait accompli*. Individual ministers may be consulted by the Chancellor about tax changes relating to their departmental concerns. For example, during the 1974–9 Labour government the Chancellor consulted Eric Varley, Secretary of State for Industry, about abolishing the annual car tax and replacing it with a substantial increase in petrol tax. The Industry Secretary opposed this because of concern that it would lead to increased imports of small cars. Unusually for a proposed tax change, the whole issue was eventually brought to full Cabinet as well as the economic cabinet committee. Under the 1979 Thatcher Conservative government in Britain, other ministers reacted strongly to their total exclusion in 1981 from tax decision-making, but while they were subsequently given an opportunity to state their view in general terms about economic strategy the process of tax decision-making has not been altered.

There is no collective determination of a tax ceiling within which ministers can undertake bilateral negotiations with the Treasury. If individual departments think in terms of public expenditure as being 'theirs' then all taxes are Treasury taxes. This tends to inhibit discussion of trade-offs between expenditure, taxation, and tax expenditures as alternatives within particular policy areas; there is no mechanism for appraising them in this way. The tax decisions to be announced in the Budget are taken by the Treasury ministers with the involvement of the prime minister. Cabinet is merely told for information the contents of the Budget on the morning before the Budget speech.

The Budget speech receives much more popular attention than the announcement of the government's public expenditure plans, even though those are for a longer period ahead. In part this is because it is often easier for individuals to identify the direct consequences for them of tax changes than changes in public expenditure, of whose costs of provision to them they may be unaware. In part the reason is that the Budget speech is 'so much more of an occasion than a boring old White Paper' (Young and Sloman, 1984, 81). The Budget is also sometimes used (as in 1985) as an occasion for announcing changes to the already announced public expenditure plans, thus confirming its status as the definitive statement of the budget for the year ahead—subject to the mini-budgets which were a prominent feature of budgeting in Britain in the late 1970s and early 1980s.

So far the annual tax side of the Budget has been described as an executive process, as indeed it largely is. However, Commons consideration of the annual tax Budget is not quite so unreal as its notional consideration of public expenditure. The Budget and the Finance Bill are still decided on an annual basis, and formal authorization is also related to debate on the government's effective proposals. Two factors inhibit House of Commons discussion of tax; one relating to the rules of the House of Commons, the other to political structure. The initiative for taxation has to come from the government. Not that MPs want to impose extra taxes, but the rule does inhibit the proposal of alternatives. Secondly, having two main parties with the government having a reliable majority implies a set piece confrontation. However, this point is contingent on there being that majority. If it is lacking, the government is forced to alter proposals; thus in 1977 the government was defeated on provisions relating to petrol tax, the size of income tax allowances, and indexation of tax allowances. The following year the government was defeated on a reduction of the rate of income tax. Even a government with an overall majority may feel obliged to alter tax proposals at the legislative stage as a result of backbench pressure, as with the halving of duty on diesel fuel in 1981 (see also 5.4). Note by contrast the failure of defeats on public expenditure to make any difference (see 6.4).

6.6 Local authority budgeting

Formal procedures for raising finance are common to all local authorities, but they do not determine how local authorities will actually behave. Local authorities have considerably less discretion than central government in changing the main features of their financial system. They are unable to introduce new taxes or alter laws which lay down statutory standards of provision. However, for many programmes there is a considerable degree of discretion available to local authorities in the standard and type of service they provide, as is evidenced by the wide variation between authorities, even when account is taken of different levels of potential demand (see also 9.3).

The only effective control over local taxation which a local authority has is over the rate in the pound which it raises. Since 1985 this power has been limited for a number of specified councils selected each year by central government which are 'rate-capped', but for other councils it remains an important power. The unpopularity of rates as a local tax led the Conservatives, after long and inconclusive discussions since 1979, to propose in a Green Paper in January 1986 that domestic rates should be phased out and replaced by a 'community charge' or poll tax, and that business rates should be charged at a uniform national figure and distributed to local authorities on a population basis. The main political problem in making any change to the local tax system, particularly for domestic rate-payers, is that any change would have adverse redistributive consequences for some types of household, as well as improvement for others.

Another important way in which local budgetary choice is shaped by central government is through the grants paid by central government. Since 1958 the bulk of grant has been paid in a block grant (that is, not allocated to specific services). New consultation procedures between central government and local authority associations were developed in the mid-1970s, and cash limits on grant were introduced in 1976. The operation and effects of the rate support grant had already come in for criticism before the return of a Conservative government in 1979, since the definition of 'need' used in calculating the needs element of the grant depended heavily on the pattern of past spending.

The Conservative government replaced the needs and resources elements of rate support grant by a unitary block grant based on needs (as defined by central government), resources, and the spending policy of authorities. The new block grant allowed for a greater degree of equalization among authorities with different resources. 'Overspending' authorities originally suffered a tapered reduction on extra grant and later became liable to having grant clawed back from them. 'Overspending' could be defined by central government on the basis of two contradictory criteria: reductions from previous spending and the grant formula's assessment of the local authority's needs. Considerable variations could occur in the amount of rate support grant an authority could receive, with some authorities receiving no block grant at all. Local authorities faced considerably greater uncertainty about the amount of grant they would actually receive in the current financial year. The government also cut the percentage of expenditure to be met by rate support grant, from 60 per cent in England and Wales in 1980–1 to 46 per cent for 1986–7.

These changes undoubtedly constrained the range of budgetary choices open to local authorities, though grant was still in block grant form, not directly tied to allocation between different policy areas. The failure of the grant mechanism to constrain local spending as the central government would have liked led to the introduction of the selective 'rate-capping' of authorities from 1985. A system of controls over total spending levels and rate levels had already been introduced in Scotland in 1982. Relationships between the Conservative central government and some Labour local authorities over central government support and local government spending became highly strained, resulting in a series of court cases (see 8.2).

In 1985 the central government announced that it was abandoning the use of targets based on previous expenditure and the associated system of penalties, thus turning the emphasis back to the grant distribution system. In its January 1986 Green Paper on local government finance, the government proposed a grant system consisting of (a) a needs element to compensate for differences in cost of providing a standard level of service to meet local needs; (b) a standard population-based grant. The total size of grant would be determined annually by the central government.

Although the bulk of central government grant to local authorities since 1958 has been in the form of a block grant, the role of specific grants (e.g. for the police) has been increasing since the early 1970s. Specific grants as a percentage of total central government grant dipped from 9.3 in 1967–8 to 7.9 in 1972–3 before rising to 14.2 in 1982–3 (Bennett, 1982, 77).

Central government had previously operated detailed controls on borrowing for local authority capital expenditure, but from 1980 these controls were directed at the expenditure itself, reducing the discretion of local authorities to fund capital expenditure from the rates. However, the controls are of a negative nature and the central government found itself in the embarrassing position of having in 1982 to appeal to local authorities to increase their capital spending. The new controls may have been less significant in reducing local authority capital spending than the squeeze on current spending and the high level of interest rates (Meadows, 1985). However, in subsequent years local authorities overshot their capital expenditure limit. Some councils proved ingenious in exploiting loopholes in the controls, such as the sale of mortgages to banks, and early in 1986 the government was contemplating the introduction of legislation which would impose a limit for each council for its gross capital expenditure each year, whether it was funded through borrowing, use of receipts, or creative accounting.

Individual local authorities are also affected by other constraints on their ability to make budgetary choices. Wage and salary levels are fixed nationally by joint negotiating bodies. The amount a local authority has to pay in loan charges reflects past commitments rather than current choices. More generally, there is the inertia of existing commitments. Once expenditure has been committed on a particular policy it tends to become more difficult to cut it than it would be to decide not to introduce it in the first place. Budgeting does not involve deciding afresh each year what items will go in, but what changes should be made. These expenditure commitments are sometimes referred to as 'the expenditure base'. Over an extended period of time substantial and variable rates of change in particular departments can occur. Sharpe and Newton (1984) argue that the extent of expenditure change for local budget items is a function of the proportionate share of the total budget absorbed by the item, that is, the smaller the item, the greater the scale of change. They also argue that incrementalism does not occur when there is a strong party system. Greenwood (1983) found some evidence that fiscal restraint from the 1980s had led to more local authorities scrutinizing the expenditure base of departments and taking a longer look ahead at budgetary implications.

Concentration on the formal procedures for budgeting in local government considerably overplays the role of council committees and particularly of the full council (see Danziger, 1978). It underplays the role of top officials, party groups, and majority leaders. The real argument about the budget may take place within the ruling party group. That is not to say that the full council never makes meaningful decisions—it may do so if there is a 'hung' council, that is one with no overall majority, or if there is a split in the ruling party. The point is that there are substantial variations between local authorities, and in the same authority across time, particularly after a change of party control.

One pattern of budget decision-making to have emerged in frequent use by the late 1970s was what Greenwood (1983) called the 'Spanish Inquisition', which makes considerable use of private meetings outside the formal committee system. When initial bids have been received by the treasurer, a series of meetings of the leading politicians and officers take place. These will normally involve only the leader of the majority party, the chief executive, and the treasurer, though in some authorities one or two other leading political figures in the authority may attend. Those attending these meetings act as links with the wider parts of the authority, both on the political and officer level, and each separately will engage in a series of soundings about likely reactions to the budget proposals when they emerge. A second series of meetings, similar to the 'bilaterals' in central government, take place between the leader, the chief executive, and the treasurer on the one side and the chairman and chief officer of each service in turn. While this system reflected the strengthening of the role of the chief executive and the treasurer on the officer side, there was considerable variation in the extent to which there was increased centralization on the political side.

The political complexion of councils has always been more complicated than the normal two-party picture in Westminster. Although there was a substantial increase in the role of parties following local government reorganization in 1974 and 1975, independents still play an important role in some councils. Following the May 1985 local government elections, a large number of councils were 'hung'. Most such authorities relied on the tacit agreement of a minority party to keep one of the larger parties in power. However, the agreements were unstable, and most likely to collapse when the council was trying to agree a budget.

Authorities vary in the extent to which the local party other than the councillors are likely to be involved in the budgetary process; this is most likely for Labour authorities, but there is considerable variation. Political complexion is important not just in terms of the party in power at any given time, but in the party system as it operates across time. Thus, some authorities are one-party dominant, with that party rarely if ever losing office, while others are alternating party systems. Clearly the budgetary options and style are likely to vary between such types of authority. There is, though, nothing deterministic about the impact of organizational and political factors on the budgetary process, as is evidenced by the way in which some Labour urban authorities in 1985 settled their budget and their rate with minimal publicity, while others attempted to engage in public confrontation with central government.

The individual characteristics of officials and politicians can also be important in affecting both the process and the outcome of budget-making, though by its very nature this is difficult to generalize about. Danziger (1978, 189–90) gives as an illustration on the officer side the Medical Officers of Health in Southend and Brighton: the Medical Officer in Southend took pride in the economical way that services were provided, whereas Brighton's Medical Officer was a vigorous proponent of extensive community care. Most officials may ask for more for their departments, but there are variations in their skill in asking for it and obtaining it. The personalities of politicians can be important, whether it is the flamboyant style of a Derek Hatton in Liverpool (technically only the deputy leader) or a Ken Livingstone in the Greater London Council or the greyer men who form the leadership of the Labour group on Strathclyde Regional Council.

Both central government and individual local authorities at times feel constrained and even helpless in their ability to shape local government finance. Yet the evidence suggests that a variety of processes continue to operate and that there is scope for variation in the choices actually made, even if these choices seem at times to be swamped by financial restraint or the seemingly arbitrary redistributions involved in the annual rate support grant settlement.

Chapter 7

Implementation

7.1 The significance of the implementation stage

This chapter analyses how policies are further shaped following government decisions and legislation. In analysing implementation we are not necessarily talking about administration in contrast to politics, since implementation may be highly political, both in party and other terms. Nor does the descriptive approach used here pose a contrast between 'policy' on the one hand and 'implementation' on the other. From a process perspective, the implementation stage can contribute to the shaping of policy. It will, however, be argued that it is often meaningful in the British context to talk in terms of a preceding decision or piece of legislation and the extent to which that is or is not implemented. 'Shaping' of policy at the implementation stage can occur both through failure and through creative filling in and application of a broad framework (compare Gunn, 1978, with Barrett and Fudge, 1981, and Ham and Hill, 1984, ch. 8). Clearly whether an activity involves 'policy-making' rather than implementation will depend on the organization's perspective. One man's implementation is another man's policy.

If we consider different types of programmes we can see that in some cases it is relevant to talk about a specified policy and 'success' or 'failure' to implement it, whereas in others reference to implementation failure or deficit is more or less irrelevant, since the key shaping of the policy takes place through implementation, that is the actual carrying out. Policy designs with different implications for delivery organizations and policy targets are set out in Table 7.1.

Mandatory programmes specify that certain actions must be undertaken or results achieved, and specify how they must be undertaken.

Flexible programmes specify in broad terms that certain results

Table 7.1 Types of programme and implemention implications

	Mandatory	Flexible	Promotional	Permissive	Regulatory/ Clearance	Proscriptive
Government organization						
Member of government organization						
Other organizations						
Individuals						

must be achieved or activities performed, but provide scope for variation by implementing organizations about the precise forms which the application of the policy will involve (e.g. comprehensive schools).

Promotional programmes provide a framework which enables the programme to be established but does not actually require specified activities. The government, however, actively seeks the application of the policy, either through exhortation or the provision of incentives. Clearly a degree of creativity is involved here, but particularly where the government has given an indication of expected level of activity, it may also be meaningful to talk in terms of success and failure.

Permissive programmes provide a legislative framework which enables government or other organizations to carry out an activity but does not actively require them to do so. The existence of such a framework is important in the British context where local authorities and government organizations other than central government departments exercising 'prerogative' powers are only permitted to carry out such activities as are specified by law.

Regulatory/clearance programmes cover cases where an organization or individual has to check with the central government first before carrying out an action (e.g. Scottish local authorities if they wish to engage in overseas industrial promotion).

Proscriptive programmes are those which specify that certain actions must not take place or take place only in certain conditions.

The row headings in Table 7.1 show how policy designs can vary in terms of how they are directed at different policy actors. The same programme may involve different approaches in terms of the role of different actors. In other words, different rows in Table 7.1 might have ticks under different columns because the programme was directed at different actors in different ways. (Not all rows will apply for every programme.) For example, the DHSS, as a government organization, may be *mandated* to provide certain cash benefits to applicants, but for the individual the programme may be *permissive*, or *promotional* if the government seems actively to seek applications.

Target organizations are worth separating from individuals, since policies directed at organizations may differ in their implications—it may be easier for an organization to displace the impact of a programme, for example by passing on the cost of a fine to customers (Hood, 1983). In some cases policies may be programmes mandated on organizations such as firms to provide facilities or protection for individuals, rather than directly targeted at the individuals themselves.

Law and order policy involves activities which are *flexible* for the government organizations involved (i.e. police forces are expected to enforce the law but have considerable flexibility in deciding how to go about it) but involve *proscriptions* directed at individual citizens; failure can be said to occur if the proscribed acts take place or the police forces fail to prevent or apprehend offenders.

The categories listed in the column headings in Table 7.1 emphasize that while some shaping of policy may occur for all types of programme, for some types such as flexible or permissive types such shaping makes a creative contribution, whereas in other cases such as mandatory programmes or proscribed activities it is fully meaningful to talk of success or failure from the perspective of the central government. In the case of flexible policies, 'failure' is meaningful but fuzzy if different (unspecified) activities could all be considered to be contributing to the stated desired state of affairs. For promotional policies, there may be ambiguity about whether failure can be said to have occurred, particularly where the government has not indicated an anticipated level of activity.

Even in the case of mandatory policies, there may have been pre-implementation bargaining or interaction; the initiative may even have come from the implementing organizations, for example, a particular professional group within local government. This does not alter the fact that if an activity is mandated it is meaningful to talk of failure rather than merely interaction at the implementation stage if the specified activity does not occur or the specified results are not attained.

Enforcement of mandatory or proscribed programmes depends not only on political pressures but also on the enforcement techniques available to the agency. Where such programmes mandate or proscribe activity by organizations or individuals, the question of compliance arises. Most people and organizations do comply with most laws of which they are aware. Among the reasons for this are respect for authority; reasoned acceptance— even where immediate self-interest conflicts with a policy, a person might be convinced that it is reasonable, necessary, or just; and self-interest, either because of the benefits to be obtained from compliance or the penalties for failure to comply (see Anderson, 1979, 113–24). Sanctions may be effective more because people desire to avoid being stigmatized as lawbreakers than because they fear the penalties involved; this will depend on the attitude to the relevant law of the group with which they identify and the community in which they live. Acceptance of most policies seems to increase with the length of time they are in effect.

Any failure to carry out implementation activities in the right order, in the right place, and at the right time will lead to non-implementation, either complete, or, more commonly, partial. However, even if all the activities in a programme are fully carried out, a programme may fail to have the effect intended—this would be *unsuccessful implementation* (see Hogwood, 1979b). Unsuccessful implementation may result from a poor understanding of societal processes embodied in the policy or from the failure to anticipate other effects. There may also be other influences on the target of the policy and it may be impossible for government to control these or even to predict them, a fate which has befallen much of British industrial policy.

There can be ambiguity in particular cases, particularly in promotional programmes, about whether there has been a failure of implementation or unsuccessful implementation, and this is illustrated by the Business Expansion Scheme set up by the government in 1983. The Scheme offered generous tax reliefs for investment in unquoted companies and was intended to encourage the start-up or expansion of small firms, which would in turn create job opportunities; the tax reliefs were designed to compensate for the high risk associated with such ventures. In practice, investors concentrated on low-risk, asset-backed investments rather than employment-generating ones. When the Treasury blocked off investment in agricultural land and in property, investors turned to vintage wine and antiques. The designers of the scheme had failed to notice one of the basic facts about tax reliefs and incentives offered by government: individuals will exploit them in a way that maximizes their own benefit rather than promote the policy purposes the government had in mind when establishing them.

Looking at 'failures of implementation' underlines the interaction between the implementation stage and the agenda-processing stage. Failures to carry out an activity or for it to have the expected effect may be due to culpable faults of the implementers. However, to the extent that some of these problems can be anticipated in advance but are simply assumed away, the fault can be seen to lie at the policy design stage.

7.2 Why implementation may fail

We have no systematic picture of the extent to which policies in Britain are successfully implemented. In part, this is because of the neglect until the mid-1970s of the implementation stage, but in part it is because of inherent difficulties in this type of analysis—in many cases it would be very difficult to assess what would count as a fully successful implementation because it is often unclear just what the policy is designed to achieve. Nevertheless, from the accumulation of *ad hoc* case studies and from our improving overall understanding of the role of the implementation process in shaping policy outputs it is possible to say that failure, particularly partial failure, of policies at the implementation stage is a widespread feature of British public policy. This can arise both from a failure to bring legal provisions into effect and from a failure to perform a legal duty or enforce the law.

Lack of available resources may be given as a reason for not bringing a legal provision into effect or not utilizing it fully. For example, the 1973 Employment of Children Act should have enabled the regulations currently made under local by-laws to be standardized across the country so that employers would be clear about the law. However, the law was not brought into effect because the local authorities argued in 1973 and 1977 that they did not have the resources to implement it (*The Economist*, 26 January 1985). Another example is the Legal Aid Act 1974, which contains an unimplemented provision for legal aid to be extended to representation at coroners' inquests. The cost of bringing the provision into legal effect had been estimated by the Home Office at £3m a year (*The Times*, 30 November 1985). The Lord Chancellor's Department argued that proceedings before a coroner were relatively informal and did not determine civil or criminal liability: 'In these circumstances and particularly in this time of economic constraint proceedings before a coroner are not considered to justify expenditure out of the limited resources available for legal aid.'

Even when a legal provision is brought into effect, resource constraints may limit its implementation. In particular, a new policy which requires resources may be given a low relative priority for implementation relative to existing activities, as happened with the Community Land Act 1975. Failure may result from lack of adequate time for administrative resources to be brought to bear, and for the right resources to be available at the right time and the right place. For example, industrial action by civil service unions in 1973 delayed the availability of the computer needed for the introduction of VAT.

Delays in bringing a law into effect may result from the self-interest of the implementing organization. The Control of Pollution Act 1974 provided for the keeping by water authorities of public registers. However, the bringing of the section of the Act into force was delayed when the water authorities and civil servants at the Departments of the Environment realized that the sewage works run by the water authorities were themselves the biggest polluters (*Observer*, 11 August 1985). One-third of the Thames Water Authority's largest sewage works did not meet the required standards and half the Anglian Water Authority's works also failed. The relevant provision of the Act was brought into effect in 1984, with the registers being opened for public inspection in 1985.

A law may not be implemented if it is widely ignored and few steps are taken to enforce it. This is particularly likely to be the case if the punishment is seen as disproportionate to the offence. A survey published by the Institute of Directors in August 1985 found that only 9 per cent of company reports complied fully with the Employment Act 1982 in terms of the information which employees must be given.

Implementation authorities may fail to ascertain whether the law is actually being obeyed. A report from the Hazardous Wastes Inspectorate in 1985 showed that the producers of waste, the waste disposal companies, and the local authorities responsible for supervising waste disposal were all failing to implement the Act properly. Controls on disposal were very unevenly supplied. Licence conditions were 'sometimes breached wilfully and with impunity'. Many licences placed too much reliance on the operator and local authorities often did not inspect sites frequently or rigorously enough. Even when non-compliance was found, the legal departments of many local authorities were reluctant to mount enforcement actions.

A law may not be implemented because the government does not have the powers to enforce it. Enforcement will be impracticable if the implementing organization has inadequate information about the target problem. Laws may go unimplemented for decades. For example, the 1930 Reservoirs (Safety Provisions) Act stipulated that all dams holding more than 5m gallons should be registered with local district councils and inspected every ten years. The Act was introduced after twenty people died as a result of two dam failures in Scotland and Wales, so the whole saga is a classic case of 'from crisis to complacency'. Because of the lack of enforcement powers, the owners of small dams in private hands could and did refuse to pay for the safety work that was ordered and the government could take no steps to force them to do so. In 1975 a new Reservoirs Act was introduced which made it a criminal offence to refuse to carry out repairs and set out a framework for establishing a comprehensive dams register. However, one of the preconditions for perfect implementation did not exist—perfect information (Hood, 1976; Gunn, 1978). Local authorities had lost track of who owned all the dams, and because private owners had to pay for the inspectors, there was a positive incentive for them not to co-operate. A spokesman for the Department of the Environment was quoted in 1985 as saying that 'It was thought that the legislation was working—but it wasn't' (*Sunday Times*, 28 July 1985). In April 1985 the Department of the Environment ordered county councils to begin a dams register and take responsibility for dams where the ownership is unclear. The cost of previous failures of implementation is high—estimated by a Department of the Environment study to total £200m, much of which will have to be borne by local authorities.

As will be considered in more detail in 7.4, *where more than one organization is involved, implementation may fail because of inadequate communication between them.* A whole series of reports on child abuse cases, from the Maria Colwell case in 1973 to the report on the death of Jasmine Beckford in 1985, confirm this. In the report of the inquiry into the death of Jasmine Beckford, *A Child in Trust*, it was found that the social worker had failed to inform the child's nursery school that the child was the subject of a care order; although the school authorities noted erratic attendances (which coincided with the periods of worst injuries to the child), the teachers were unable to appreciate the significance of the absences. Another example of inadequate communication is provided by the Popplewell inquiry into the Bradford City football stand fire disaster in 1985, in which fifty-six people died. An official of the Health and Safety Executive told the inquiry that they had not alerted the fire brigade to the risk of rubbish under the stand 'because it was their responsibility and I considered it inconceivable that there could be a ground the size of Bradford City in the middle of Bradford which the fire brigade did not know about' (*The Times*, 12 June 1985). However, the inquiry was told that apart from a visit to examine the clubhouse and administrative block the fire service had not made an inspection of the ground as part of any fire prevention programme.

A policy may fail or be only partly implemented because of political opposition to it, for example, from other political parties, or groups, or local authorities as the actual implementing bodies. Delays or partial failures of implementation occurred over the Community Land Act 1975, the Housing Homeless Persons Act, and over council house sales. This makes explicit that implementation is a political as well as an administrative process.

Although implementation failures are more likely to result from complex policies involving a number of organizations, *there can be difficulties in implementation even for relatively simple instruments delivered through single organizations.* The first annual report of the government's adjudication officer in 1985 found that 29.5 per cent of supplementary benefit decisions had errors or omissions;

half of these were attributable to insufficient information and a further 38 per cent were wrong decisions on available evidence. On non-supplementary benefits, 16.6 per cent of decisions contained errors or omissions. The adjudication officer said that a principle reason for errors was pressures on the system which resulted in priority being given to getting a payment, right or wrong, to a claimant, perhaps on the assumption that if dissatisfied a claimant would appeal.

Attempts to enforce a policy more rigorously may in fact lead to less rigorous enforcement. For example, concern over 'insider trading' in share deals led to responsibility being taken away from the self-regulatory Take-over Panel and insider trading was made a criminal offence. However, the burden of proof for criminal prosecution is higher than that for investigation by the Take-over Panel, so the more rigorous system is arguably more ineffective.

Implementation may be difficult because of unclear or incompatible objectives. It may not even be possible to determine after the event where there has been implementation if it is not clear what the programme was supposed to be or supposed to achieve.

One of the best ways of understanding what goes wrong with policies at the implementation stage is to turn the question on its head and ask what would be necessary for implementation of a policy to be completely successful. This is the approach adopted by Hood (1976) in his book on *The Limits of Administration* (see also Gunn, 1978). Effectively, the conditions necessary for 'perfect administration' are the absence of all the problems listed above. As Hood himself points out, no actual administrative system is likely to conform to all, or any, of these conditions. These conditions are those necessary for perfect implementation, but that does not mean that they are an ideal to be aimed at. Some of the costs of coming close to perfect administration—both resources required and reductions on freedom and diversity—are likely to be regarded as unacceptable in our society.

Despite the fact that the conditions for perfect implementation are unrealistic and unattainable, most of them are assumed either explicitly or implicitly by politicians launching new policies. They seem wilfully to ignore both the insights of this abstract approach and the lessons of history. Committees of inquiry seem particularly prone to assuming away problems of implementation when devising their neat packages, and thereby doom their proposals to problems at the implementation stage.

7.3 Organizing for implementation

Policies are not made and delivered by an abstract entity called 'the government' but by people in a number of different *organizations* which interact with each other to varying degrees. The actual operation of a government department or agency cannot be defined in detail in the statute establishing it or the tasks which have been set by those at the top of the organization. Large-scale projects may require firming up before actual implementation. The extent to which the activities can be defined in detail from above (both from outside the organization and by those at the top of the hierarchy within the organization) will depend on whether the tasks set are of a routine bureaucratic nature or require discretionary decisions, perhaps based on a professional assessment of individual cases. There are a range of public policies from routine administration of national insurance benefits, through some discretion in supplementary benefits, to more or less complete day-to-day discretion in the delivery of health care by doctors based on their professional judgement.

Except in the case of purely routine tasks, any attempt to prescribe in detail the day-to-day operation of an organization will result in the clumsy doubling-up of the bureaucracy and a danger of *over-conformity*; that is, activity may become focused on the detailed routines laid down rather than on the underlying purposes of the agency. Conformity with general purposes is to some extent secured through salary, status, and other prerequisites offered to staff, but, particularly in the case of senior officials with discretion in taking decisions, a greater degree of commitment to the purposes of the agency (which may in turn involve the shaping of those purposes) is required.

The smooth running of an organization is made easier if there is a set of ideas and purposes shared by organizational staff, which can be said to constitute an 'agency philosophy' or 'departmental view'. Where such a departmental view develops, the possibilities of delegation within the organization without injury to policy are considerably increased and the socialization of new members of the organization is made easier. The existence of a departmental view also assists co-ordination of the defence of the organization to the outside world, both in terms of its political acceptability and its acceptability to clients. Thus the existence of a departmental view is relevant at earlier stages of the policy process as well as at implementation

The extent to which an implicit departmental view is likely to develop in an organization responsible for an area of policy will depend on a number of factors, including (1) the internal coherence of the general purposes set for the organization, including the perceived possibility of carrying them out; (2) the extent to which the personal background of the officials is relevant to the broad purposes of the organization (for example, whether professional values coincide with general purpose); (3) the extent to which officials have a shared background; (4) the extent to which the organization is internally subdivided into units which may develop their own departmental view; and (5) the history of the organization, including its age and whether it has absorbed previous organizations. A new organization may take time to develop a common view.

This question of socialization in the organization—the extent to which newcomers to an organization are led to share its values—is often quite significant in public organizations. Civil servants in Britain actually talk about a departmental view. The classic case is the socialization of ministers newly appointed to head central government departments. It has often been remarked how quickly such ministers start to fight for the general values of their new departments, and indeed, that their reputation is partly judged on their ability to do so.

We should not assume that it is inevitable that a common departmental view exists—that would be as bad as assuming that organizations as such can have goals. There may be considerable differences in the values and perceptions of different groups within the organization, and officially stated objectives of the organization may reflect the views of a dominant group or coalition of groups within the organization rather than a universally accepted view. Because there may be a lack of consensus about goals, managerial techniques designed to make their implementation more effective may not attract the support they seem to deserve. The picture is further complicated when we realize that large public organizations such as government departments invariably have many different and sometimes conflicting goals, so there is plenty of room for differing interpretation of the relative priority which should be given to each. There may be problems of securing compliance at the lower levels of the organization, particularly where officials cannot feel any direct identification with the broad objectives set for them.

Clearly, the process of establishing a new organization, including the socialization of members, will take time to develop, but this is often overlooked by those advocating the establishment of new organizations to secure quick action. A period of at least a couple of years is likely to pass after the formal establishment of the organization before the process is routinized. There are also technical issues in the establishment of new organizations, such as the recruitment of staff and securing of office accommodation. Even changing the activities of an existing organization may take time.

Most new or replacement programmes in Britain are given not to completely new organizations to implement but to an existing organization, such as an existing government department or a local authority. Involvement at earlier stages of the policy process is likely to affect commitment at the implementation stage. If the initiative actually came from the delivery organization or if it was closely involved in shaping policy at earlier stages, then implementation is likely to be followed through actively; otherwise imposition may lead to recalcitrance. There can be opportunity costs to the organization in devoting attention to implementing a new programme. Thus, a new programme with few extra resources may get low priority, as with local authorities and the Community Land Act 1975. This is particularly likely to be the case if the new programme is peripheral to what the organization itself sees as its main objectives. Where extra resources are made available, organizational growth may be welcomed, but there may be concern with socializing new members, particularly if growth involves massive increases in the size of the organization, as when Customs and Excise had to expand by a third when Value Added Tax was introduced (Johnstone, 1975).

In Britain parliamentary approval is normally taken for granted. Therefore, implementation in the sense of starting any organizational arrangements typically takes place before the Royal Assent. However, this can lead to problems, as when extensive work to convert the Royal High School building in Edinburgh into an Assembly building was carried out on the assumption that the Scotland Act 1978 would both receive the Royal Assent and be approved in the subsequent referendum. The obvious advantage of 'building in' the assumption of parliamentary approval is that it does normally cut down on delay. Partly as a result, there is sometimes 'back-to-front' planning, for example, having to plan the extra number of civil servants to administer VAT before the coverage and number of rates were known (Johnstone, 1975).

The discussion so far in this section has concentrated on the implementation of new or changed policies. However, the bulk of policy delivery at any given time consists of the routine delivery of continuing programmes. Here there is a potential danger that implementation will concentrate on the continuing process of going through the routines of delivery without necessarily referring to the original objectives of the programme. Another potential danger is the potential 'capture' of the implementing organization by professionals involved in policy delivery or by the clientele at whom the programme is delivered. Policy delivery may become focused on activities which will promote a cosy relationship or trouble-free implementation, at the possible expense of the original intent of the policy. Finally, there is a danger with routinized activities that they continue to be performed when there have been changes in the circumstances which led to them being introduced in the first place (see also 9.5).

7.4 The multi-organizational setting of implementation

Some programmes are designed from the start to involve more than one level of government or more than one organization in their implementation. Other programmes may become mutually entangled because they come across each other at the point of delivery. Some such overlap and interaction is inevitable and sometimes desirable.

If we adopt a focus on individual projects, we may find the 'cocktail' phenomenon at work. In other words, a cocktail of funding and possibly legal authority from a number of different sources and sometimes different policy areas is put together in a single package to enable the project or scheme to take place. In such cases it is difficult to apply a single line policy–programme–implementation model. The cross-sectoral nature of some such projects, with funding, for example, of country parks from programmes for the countryside, for sport, for employment, for environmental improvement, and so on, does emphasize that we cannot necessarily characterize all stages of the policy process as falling neatly into self-contained sectors.

One major source of overlap between the concerns of different organizations arises from the way in which new policies and new organizations are developed in British government, and it may be said in all political systems. Typically, when some deficiency is identified in existing policy what happens is not a complete reappraisal of existing policy and existing organizations but the *addition* of further tasks to existing organizations or the establishment of an additional new organization. Thus in any given policy area we are dealing with a number of policy instruments administered by a number of different government departments and agencies. In a strict sense, Britain has no, say, industrial policy, only industrial *policies*, in the sense of programmes as outlined in 1.2. If this is true within a particular policy area, it is even more true that the consequences of new policies for other policy areas are rarely explored in full.

To some extent, then, this pattern of agencies with overlapping jurisdictions is a reflection of an 'incremental' rather than 'synoptic' form of policy initiatives. However, it is also partly an inherent consequence of the problem of relating agencies and instruments to their targets. However carefully the government attempts to define the demarcation of responsibilities there will inevitably be problems in specifying tasks unambiguously (see Hood, 1976, ch. 4). The problem is that both geographical and functional considerations of various kinds are used in administering policy. Public policies are not something tangible which can be neatly sliced into functional or territorial packages.

The existence of overlaps gives rise to what Hood (1976) calls 'multi-organizational sub-optimization'. That is, each organization separately pursuing its objectives can lead to an outcome which is not best overall, for example, where building urban motorways can have adverse effects on housing. Hood points to two main ways in which multi-organizational sub-optimization can come about. The first is a simple lack of co-ordination, that is, where the bodies concerned would be quite prepared to adjust their behaviour if they knew what everyone else was doing. The classic example of this is the 'holes in the road' problem. In one case a main road was dug up over 700 times in an eighteen-month period (Hood, 1976). At first sight, this appears as an amusing, if trivial, illustration. However, a report by the Department of Transport in November 1985, *Roads and Utilities*, calculated that gas, electricity, water, and telephone authorities dig about two million holes a year in Britain's roads at a cost of £1 billion. Apart from their direct financial cost, repairs were considered to leave an uneven and often dangerous surface. The report pointed to the particular irritation of the lack of co-ordination by the four utilities.

Sometimes two organizations with similar objectives may nevertheless feel unable to communicate or co-ordinate fully because of incompatible internal rules. In 1985 the Director of Public Prosecutions was investigating frauds in the Lloyd's insurance market. Lloyd's initially failed to disclose to the DPP transcripts of their own disciplinary proceedings, apparently because they considered that their own rules prevented them from handing over such evidence until charges were brought. The DPP, on the other hand, requires admissible evidence before he can bring charges.

The second way in which multi-organizational sub-optimization can arise is through conflicting objectives. This is illustrated by the government's attitude to Skoal Bandits, often referred to as 'tobacco teabags', consisting of finely chopped tobacco held in a tiny sachet between the cheek and the gum. In 1985 the government's chief medical officer warned doctors and health authorities that the habit 'significantly increases the risk of developing cancer of the mouth' (*The Times*, 3 December 1985). The government-funded Health Education Council wrote to student unions warning them of the dangers of using the product after the company was reported to be recruiting students to help promote the product and trying to persuade student union shops to stock it. The Independent Broadcasting Authority banned advertisements for the product on television and radio. Yet at the same time another department of the government approved grants of up to £1m to the American company concerned towards a factory built by the company in East Kilbride in Scotland to manufacture the product.

Multi-organizational sub-optimization arising from conflicting objectives is much more difficult to resolve than simple failures of communication or co-ordination. In effect, conflicts in objectives not resolved at the policy processing stage are left to 'fight it out' at the implementation stage. It may only be at the implementation stage in the application of programmes to particular cases that the latent conflict of objectives becomes apparent.

It should already be clear from some of the examples given that the multi-organizational aspects of implementation involve far more than central–local government relations. At the local level, two tiers of local government often have to work together, and relationships between them are frequently more fraught than those between local government and central government (see Alexander, 1982, chs. 2 and 3). The abolition of the Greater London Council and the metropolitan counties in 1986 will, if anything, make the picture even more complex, since there will be a whole range of indirectly elected and appointed bodies which will have to liaise with district councils and with each other.

Another complex area of intergovernmental relations involves non-departmental bodies, often referred to as 'quangos'. This is really a label for a diverse set of bodies with a diverse set of relationships with government ranging from those which are effectively an operating arm of government departments to those such as the BBC or the Arts Council which have deliberately been given a large degree of autonomy in deciding how to implement their broad remit (see Barker, 1982). Local authorities, too, frequently find themselves interacting with a wide range of such non-departmental bodies, from health authorities to the Scottish Development Agency.

Often such contacts are bilateral, such as those between two tiers of local government, but on many projects the links may be multilateral, involving a large set of public and sometimes private organizations. Glasgow's much hyped Eastern Area Renewal (GEAR) project, for example, involves the Scottish Development Department, the Scottish Development Agency, Strathclyde Regional Council, Glasgow District Council, the Scottish Special Housing Association, the Manpower Services Commission, and a large supporting cast. Booth, Pitt, and Money (1982) have described this arrangement as a 'mutually non-effective group of organizations' or MANGO.

Links between different government organizations can be formal, as in the establishment of liaison committees between two tiers of local government, while others may be much more informal, such as officials with similar responsibilities in different parts of the country checking with each other about how they have dealt with a matter, including their relationship with other organizations. Some links, such as those between local authorities and water authorities, will be recurring, whereas others will be *ad hoc* and relating to specific projects or problems. 'Links' may be lines of conflict rather than co-operation.

Even where one organization, such as a central government department, appears to have access to far more resources, organizations at the implementation stage are *interdependent* (Rhodes, 1981; 1985). In any given pair of organizations, each organization will need something from the other: for example, local authorities may need money, but central government may need information from local authorities. This relative dependence may vary from policy area to policy area. Organizations such as local authorities are complex and different departments of the authority may have different types of relationships with central government departments and other bodies. There are multiple bases of interdependence, not just law and finance, but also information, professional expertise, and political ability and skills, among others. Organizations, and different sections of organizations, can have differing goals, which may not coincide with those of the policies central government would like to see implemented.

Interaction takes place in the context of 'rules of the game' (see Rhodes, 1981). As we saw in chapter 3, 'consultation' was a key rule of the game at the agenda-processing stage, and this is true also at implementation stage in the relationship between different government organizations. Other rules include recognition of the ultimate right of the centre to put laws through Parliament, the need for trust and secrecy in negotiations, and non-intervention in other people's policy area. Central government has a special ability to change rules and even to change the other actors, for example by abolishing the Greater London Council and the metropolitan counties. However, making such changes to improve implementation (from central govenment's perspective) of a single programme would amount to 'overkill', so in any given round of the 'game' central government is mutually interdependent with other organizations.

In this process of interaction, organizations can adopt various strategies, which include trying to go it alone, bargaining, incorporation, competition, confrontation, persuasion, and the use of incentives (see Rhodes, 1985; Hogwood, 1979a). These strategies vary in the extent to which they require an organization to take the initiative in its relations with other organizations, the decision costs involved (e.g. in information collection and time spent negotiating), and in the type of resources needed to follow through the strategy successfully. One would expect organizations with different relative resources to tend to go for different strategies. Not all the strategies are mutually exclusive, especially when there are a number of different organizations involved, and several may be pursued simultaneously.

It will be noted that the strategies listed do not include 'co-ordination', since co-ordination is not a method but a desirable state of affairs. Co-ordination can arise through technical interdependence, coercion, common purpose, or political bargaining. In other words, co-ordination is not so much a method in itself of adjusting relationships between organizations as a possible outcome of a variety of methods. Normally when people demand greater co-ordination, they are either being naïve or they simply want the other organization to change its position.

The most extreme form of intergovernmental implementation is the implementation of international decisions, whether those of international organizations of which Britain is a member or specific bilateral or multilateral decisions in which Britain has participated. The blurring of the distinction between policy formulation and implementation is a particular feature of international policy-making (see also 3.5). The contrast with inter-organizational implementation within Britain is that international agreements cannot rely for their implementation on a similar set of formal or informal 'rules of the game', on authoritative political structures, or shared political values and assumptions (see Wallace, 1984).

The partial exception is the European Communities, which have developed political structures and policy processes similar to those of individual states, as well as having a higher degree of shared political values and concerns than most international organizations.

Since the European Commission has its own budget, it has a capacity for direct implementation of some aspects of Community policy, though for the most part implementation is through national governments or other public authorities within each mumber state. The impact on British public policy of a number of decisions of the European Court of Justice is examined in 8.4.

This contrast to implementation within the state means that international agreements will rarely be able to rely on mandatory programmes for their implementation, and will normally have to use flexible or promotional strategies (see 7.1). A number of international agreements do proscribe activities, so it would appear that international agreements are more likely to be implemented through requiring governments to ban activities than they are to mandate them to carry out programmes defined in great detail. We have already noted that policy-making within Britain often has vaguely specified objectives or ambiguity about what would be involved in implementing it. Internationally there is far less chance of a coherent policy emerging at the formulation stage, because bargaining and compromise are an even more pervasive feature of the policy process in arriving at international agreements. Consequently, there is more chance of divergent and contradictory patterns of implementation.

Because of the protracted nature of international decision-making, implementation of decisions may have to take place in a quite different set of circumstances than those that existed when the issue was placed on the international agenda. Although the original agreement will have been arrived at through negotiation, it may be difficult to reopen the original agreement to try to adapt its implementation to the circumstances which now prevail. However, to an even greater extent than for implementing authorities within states, international agreements have to rely on national governments for information about the extent to which the agreement has been implemented. By contrast, the protracted process of negotiation may mean that national governments begin to align their domestic policies to the emerging consensus even before the agreement is ratified.

Where a government anticipates problems in implementing an international proposal it will be unlikely to give its consent. Because the international 'rules of the game' are more fluid, individual governments do in practice have the opportunity to opt

out of implementing agreements which they dislike or would find a
nuisance to follow through.

Those engaged in negotiating international agreements are
likely to have some knowledge of and understanding for the
concerns of other participant countries and may have come to
know their fellow negotiators personally. Detailed implementation may depend on regional or local bodies where such
knowledge and sympathy may be missing and the obligation to
implement may be regarded as an external imposition. This is
much less likely to happen in policy areas, such as trade policy,
where the international dimension looms large, and in policy
sectors, such as agriculture within the European Communities,
which are 'functionally self-contained' but which straddle international boundaries (Wallace, 1984, 141).

7.5 Groups at the implementation stage

Groups concerned about the implementation of a policy will
realize that the best occasion to raise issues is not once the policy
has passed into legislation but while the government's response is
still being considered (see chapter 3). Groups which dislike a
policy will attempt to exercise a pre-implementation veto of a
policy or engage in 'policy erosion', whereby the most adverse
effects of the policy will be mitigated because of the details of the
legislation (Richardson and Jordan, 1979, ch. 7). Opponents
unable to block the enactment of a law may seek to blunt its
impact by handicapping its enforcement, for example on race
relations.

Groups which were unsuccessful in vetoing a policy or altering
its detailed content in such a way that its implementation affects
them less harshly may seek to prevent, delay, or weaken its
effective implementation. Failing to make enough finance available
is, as we saw in 7.2, one of the most effective forms of sabotaging
implementation. A group or its members may be able to thwart
the operation of a law by ignoring it or by exploiting its provisions
in an unanticipated way. For example, the trade unions were
unable to prevent the Industrial Relations Act 1971 becoming law
but they were effectively able to prevent its implementation. One
of their main tactics was to refuse to register; although this at first
sight meant that they did not benefit from privileges conferred by

the Act, it effectively undermined the whole operation of the Act. The Conservatives learned their lesson, and one of the reasons why the implementation of the 1980s industrial relations legislation was more effective was because no similar loophole was included.

A group may be in a strategic position where its refusal to co-operate can lead to the suspension or abandonment of a policy. For example, refusal of the National Union of Seamen to carry the waste effectively led to the suspension of the government's policy of dumping nuclear waste at sea.

Although the use of the courts as a delaying or vetoing tactic is less significant in Britain than in the United States, examples do occur. For example, seven months of legal action in 1985 forced the government to suspend work on a 35-mile extension of the M40 from Banbury to Warwick. The environmental campaigner who brought the case lost in the Court of Appeal as she had earlier in the High Court, and was ordered to pay the costs of the hearing and the appeal. However, even though the government 'won', it had still been forced to suspend work on the project for a while. Chapter 8 provides a number of examples where the government has been forced to delay or abandon actions as a result of court cases when the actions had already reached the implementation stage. Planning appeals are another tactic which groups or individuals can use to seek to prevent or delay particular projects (see also 3.4).

In contrast to cases where groups try to thwart the operation of policies, groups may be directly involved in the delivery or monitoring of a policy. For example, an effective prices and incomes policy depends not only on the co-operation of trade unions and employers but on the CBI to collect and provide information about price and wage changes. In 1980 the day-to-day management of herring quotas in the Clyde was delegated by the government to the Scottish Fishermen's Organisation. Civil legal aid is administered not by a government department, but by the Law Society, the solicitors' own organization. The Law Society was also given the job of drawing up the arrangements for a statutory duty solicitor scheme to provide suspects held in police stations with a statutory right to see a solicitor. The scheme came into effect on 1 January 1986, but the Law Society continued to press for changes up to the last moment against a background of threats that solicitors in some areas might boycott the scheme. The growth of employment and training programmes has depended crucially not just on the agreement of groups represented on the Manpower Services Commission when the proposals were made but their co-operation in the details of implementation. The CBI actively exhorted its members to participate in the two-year version of the Youth Training Scheme introduced in 1986. Some job creation programmes have run into problems at local level because trade unions in the public sector have refused to co-operate with them.

All this implies an important role for groups in 'clearances' for the implementation of policy (Pressman and Wildavsky, 1973). However, it is important to distinguish between group clearances and involvement in implementation and the continuing performance and actions taken by their members. Trade unions at national or firm level may agree to a policy, but the history of British industrial policy is littered with examples where the day-to-day actions of their members and of management led to performance not meeting the targets built into the policy (Hogwood, 1979b, 269–77).

7.6 Allocation to individual citizens

Where the actual or potential demand for public policy exceeds supply then there is the problem of how to bring supply and demand into balance. This demand may be *externally generated*, for example by individuals applying for national insurance benefits, or it may be *internally generated* by professionals on behalf of potential clients, for example, social workers contacting families in difficulty, general practitioners referring patients to a specialist in a hospital. Here we are concerned with policy delivery as allocation or rationing; that is, how fixed or limited resources are allocated to specific individuals and in what form. Since rationing arises as a result of a gap between potential demand and supply, the need for it would be reduced if a greater amount of resources could be devoted to the social services or if demand declined. However, greater resources would not eliminate the need for some kind of rationing, that is decisions about whether and how much of a service to provide to individual citizens.

This may seem to have little to do with politics or making policy. However, even if individual decisions about the provision of specific forms of service given to specific individuals are not political, then the overall system by which budgets are allocated and services rationed is a product of political decisions. For example, the reluctance of politicians to become involved in 'clinical' decisions involving the use of resources in the NHS is itself a political decision. The two key factors are the *degree of centralization* and the *degree of explicitness*. These questions of centrality and explicitness are crucial to whether the priorities are centrally determined or whether they are consciously determined at all. It could be claimed that there is an advantage in being conscious and explicit in setting priorities *before* the service is offered. Otherwise some forms of rationing will emerge by default through the manner in which the service is provided. Where priorities are not explicitly determined there is a danger that those who will suffer will be those least able to cope with finding their way through various rationing devies. On the other hand, centrally determined priorities or general rules might pose a threat to claims to professional or technical judgement in dealing with special individual needs.

In more detail, the relevant questions are:

1. *How far are decisions about resource allocation taken at the centre?* Resource decisions affecting the amount and quality of service range from decisions taken by the Cabinet about the allocation of funds between departments down to decisions taken by, for example, receptionists making appointments or social workers allocating their time.

2. *How far are priorities determined in an explicit way?* It is important to try to establish how far priorities are determined in an explicit way and how far they have emerged largely unrecognized. Explicit resource allocation decisions are those which are premeditated and planned in terms of what category of persons or problems is to receive what resources and the outcome of the plan is examined to see whether the priorities are being carried out. This, of course, assumes that priorities will actually be followed through: this has often not been true of health policy (Haywood and Elcock, 1982).

3. *How openly available is information about the allocation of resources?* The fact that resources are allocated in an explicit way does not necessarily mean that the knowledge on which decisions are taken is published or openly available. The greater the extent to which information on which decisions are based is published at an earlier stage, the greater the chances of open debate in advance of

the choice. The classic example of decision rules which were highly explicit but not open were the rules governing the discretionary awards to supplementary benefit recipients for special needs, which were highly detailed, but not generally publicly available; it is now possible to buy an officially published handbook.

4. *How far are decisions made on 'technical' or 'professional' rather than political grounds?* It is often held that politics should be kept out of clinical decisions made by doctors, for example, who should get what operation, stay in hospital for how long. However, it is often difficult to disentangle questions of fact or political judgement from values, for example, a hospital consultant making decisions about the priority use of a kidney machine or about queuing for operations in favour of young men with families rather than single old people. Such resource allocation decisions may be largely unrecognized—sometimes even by those taking them—but they are resource allocation decisions and value judgements nevertheless. Effectively such decisions reflect what can be called 'professional ideologies'.

There are many forms which allocation and rationing can take, and these vary considerably in their degree of explicitness (cf. Parker, 1967).

Eligibility requirements. The most straightforward of such rationing mechanisms is the setting of specific requirements about who is eligible to receive a service or benefit. They may be in the form of residence requirements or that only those with certain contributions records are eligible for full national insurance benefits, such as unemployment benefit.

Queuing, either in a literal or a metaphorical sense, is a common feature of many services provided by government: for example, waiting lists for council housing, waiting lists for entering hospital for certain forms of operation. One side-effect of waiting lists is that some people may drop out because of the delay; at its most dramatic this could be because they have died before being admitted to hospital or because the family has found housing accommodation elsewhere. In some cases those who have to queue longest or who drop out of a queue may be those least in need, for example, those not requiring urgent surgery, or those who, rather than wait for a council house, manage to get a mortgage and buy a house. However, in other cases the queuing priorities, perhaps in combination with eligibility requirements, may have the effect of making those most in need queue longest.

For example, there is some evidence that the 'points' system for allocating priority in council house waiting lists, particularly the local residence requirement, has operated against those in most immediate housing need. Similarly, in the 1960s waiting lists grew for nursery school places. Some headmistresses operated a first-come, first-served principle, which operated to the advantage of the most informed, active, and educated mothers, who were more likely to have heard of the system of allocation, rather than children in greatest social or educational need.

Ignorance. Many social benefits and entitlements are so complicated that it is sometimes difficult even for professional social workers to establish who is eligible for them. Many people may not know of the availability of the benefit or by how much they would benefit from it. It is particularly the case with social security benefits, particularly means-tested ones which require active applications, that the 'take-up' rate is low. A partial explanation for low take-up of some means-related tapering benefits is that the sums available to some potential applicants are very small and hardly worth applying for, but this is far from being a complete explanation. Whether intentional or not, the effect of this is to ration benefits. In some cases the effect is clearly unintentional: for example, the government has tried to improve the take-up of rate rebates and family income supplement by embarking on extensive advertising campaigns. In contrast, social security offices used to be secretive about what discretionary payments under supplementary benefit were available for special needs. Obviously, such withholding of information constitutes a fairly severe form of rationing. There may also be ignorance about the interaction between benefits, for example, which of alternatives is best to claim, whether claims will lead to loss of existing benefit.

Deterrence. Related to withholding information is providing the service in such an unappetizing form that demand for it is reduced. For example, housing accommodation provided for the homeless may be so unattractive that it will be sought only as an absolute last resort. Alternatively the conditions in which the benefit has to be applied for may be off-putting because of shabby offices, complex forms, or impatient officials. Again, such effects may not be intentional: the shabbiness may simply reflect a lack of money and the impatience of officials might reflect a heavy workload or a level of pay not much more than the benefits they are distributing.

Nevertheless, the effect may be to deter some potential bene-
ficiaries of a service. Another form of deterrence may arise from
deference to or a feeling of distance from professionals (for
example, teachers) which makes people think they are difficult to
approach.

Easement is a euphemism for a tactic used by overloaded
facilities. In 1985 local social security offices were reported to be
closing down parts of the offices' operations, for example, by
shutting the switchboard or closing the office to callers one day a
week (*The Economist*, 7 December 1985). Some offices had
stopped typing replies to written enquiries and some were not
answering written enquiries at all. Other offices were answering
only the specific questions that callers at the offices asked rather
than volunteering general information that might help them.

Dilution. Another form of rationing is to reduce the quantity or
quality of service provided to each individual. This is particularly a
temptation for those in health care and social work who have some
control over the organization of their work. They may attempt to
deal with all their clients and in consequence provide a curtailed
service, perhaps spending less time with each client than is
necessary to provide a minimum effective level of support.

Creaming. The apparent success of a programme is improved if
staff select for treatment only those potential clients from within a
large target group who will score highly on any measures of success
set for the programme. Indeed, such clients might well have been
successful even without the programme. Creaming may also result
deliberately or inadvertently from self-selection by clients, since
the very act of seeking help from a programme may indicate a
higher than average degree of personal initiative.

Gatekeeping is a form of rationing *within* the delivery system
rather than just at the initial point of contact with the citizen.
Professionals within the system may have considerable discretion
about whether to pass on a client to a specialist for further
consideration or may make suggestions about alternative treatment.
Even receptionists may act as gatekeepers. For example, in the
National Health Service patients do not normally turn up at a
doctor's surgery demanding specific operations and amounts of
health care. It is what happens to the patient once he or she is
within the system as opposed to simply turning up at the surgery
that has generated the extra demands for health care which are

reflected in the rising number of patients treated. It is not due to increasing numbers of patients turning up at doctors' surgeries in the first place. That is, demand is not something which is *external* to the NHS; rather it is largely the creation of professionals who take the decisions about treatment; they have considerable discretion in doing this, and this leads to variations between regions, hospitals, and doctors. This discretion extends to making suggestions about private treatment and about reference to specialists. This does not mean that this internally generated demand is unaffected by the free availability of hospital services; obviously the demand, particularly for the more expensive forms of treatment, would be reduced if payment were levied. However, it does indicate that charges *at the point of entry* to the system might by themselves have little impact on overall demand.

Deflection. Individual organizations can attempt to deflect demands made on them on to other organizations. For example, social work departments may try to deflect some of the demands made on them on to voluntary bodies. A recurring issue in British social policy has been the way in which council housing departments attempted to deflect demands made on them by the homeless on to social work departments, which are often the responsibility of a different tier of local authority. Legislation in the late 1970s attempted to deal with this by placing responsibility on housing departments. However, this has not prevented the problems recurring as a result of claims by housing departments that they are not responsible because of a lack of local residence requirements or that a would-be client is 'intentionally homeless'. Where this sort of buck-passing leads to an outcome which, it would be generally agreed, does not reflect overall social priorities, then it is an aspect of the 'multiorganizational suboptimization' referred to in 7.4.

Refusal. In extreme cases citizens may be refused outright access to public services. A patient who wishes to move from a doctor with whom she is dissatisfied may find herself 'blacklisted' by other doctors. A pupil regarded as badly behaved may be expelled from school: A patient regarded as troublesome may be taken off a kidney machine (*Sunday Times*, 13 January 1985).

The various forms of rationing are not mutually exclusive, and two or more may be in operation in any particular service. Thus rationing of supplementary benefits involves eligibility requirements, ignorance, and deterrence. Council house allocation involves eligibility requirements, queuing, and deterrence (some applicants may be shown undesirable council property). In other cases attempts to reduce the impact of one form of rationing which may be considered obnoxious may simply lead to the increased operation of another; for example, loosening of eligibility requirements may simply lead to dilution in the quality of the service available, reduced deterrence to longer waiting lists.

The National Health Service is an example of an organizational structure in which all the questions about criteria for allocation set out at the beginning of this section are muddled up in practice. Perhaps the easiest way to make this point is to argue that resource allocation in the NHS is something which takes place *at all levels* from front-line professional to the Cabinet. At the point of delivery, there is an almost infinite amount of further investigation and support which a GP could provide for his patients; he has to make rationing decisions about how he deploys his time. The distribution of hospital and other health staff within a district health authority will have been determined as part of a continuous process of interplay between the professionals, the administrators, and the appointed members of the authority. The district health authorities are in turn working with constraints imposed by the regional health authorities in England (Scottish Office in Scotland). These in their turn are constrained by resource priorities laid down by the DHSS and this too is constrained by Treasury and Cabinet decisions on public expenditure. Thus, there is a whole hierarchy of rationing and budgeting decisions which interact with each other. The allocation of funds is not made solely on the basis of central determination and distribution of funds, but on the basis of submissions originally made from the individual hospitals and other units. Once the allocation of funds is made there is still considerable scope for individual decisions within these allocations.

Attempts by the centre to allocate resources are not confined to the distribution of the funds. The central government also issues guidance to regional health authorities, for example, about raising the level of care in deprived areas, giving priority to geriatric care, mental illness, and the mentally handicapped. However, the figures given in the annual Public Expenditure White Paper do not give allocations between these priorities. Furthermore, some of these priorities are not so much priorities as generalized aspirations;

it is difficult to measure the extent of success in moving towards them. For those which it is possible to measure the evidence suggests that they are often ignored. Accordingly there is a great deal of scope left to professionals; for example, prescriptions written by doctors even after the drawing up of an approved list. In terms of allocation between geographical areas, rather than between programmes, the government is trying to allocate resources on the basis of need to a greater extent within the health services within England, but at a time of financial restraint has been able to do so only at the margin.

A focus on allocating resources to the individual citizen is concerned with the impact of public policy: it is concerned with how policies affect citizens in practice, and with possible disparities between general declarations of policy and priorities and how they appear to operate in practice. The problem of public policy is how to forge links between broad allocations, stated policy priorities, and actual decisions and allocations at intermediate stages and at point of final delivery of services—the sum of outputs may not equal the sum of intentions.

Chapter 8

Adjudication

8.1 The roles of adjudication

This chapter examines how the judicial system and other forms of
adjudication may shape public policy. Although this chapter
concentrates on formal mechanisms for adjudication, it is important to bear in mind that as far as the redress of the grievances of
individual citizens is concerned, 'the idea of "political" rather than
"legal" protection of citizens against administration is deeply
embedded in British political traditions and has imprinted itself on
British ways of thought' (Ridley, 1984, 4). Citizens are much more
likely to pursue informal, including political, methods of pursuing
their grievances. The relatively small part played by the courts also
meant that when the demand for citizen protection grew, less
formal techniques than the courts were developed.

The courts can shape public policy in three ways: (1) by
establishing or redefining common law; (2) by interpretation of
statutes passed by Parliament; (3) by judicial review of the actions
of ministers and government bodies. Each of these will be
examined briefly.

Opportunities for the courts to define or develop *common law*
are constantly occurring, and a number of illustrations from the
mid-1980s can serve to illustrate this point. In the case of *Furniss* v.
Dawson in 1984, the Law Lords ruled that any step inserted into a
pre-ordained composite transaction purely to avoid tax could be
disregarded for fiscal purposes. This decision was highly controversial and the Law Lords were attacked by the Law Society for
straying into areas which were a matter for legislation by
Parliament. The miners' strike of 1984–5 saw the courts establishing
a number of common law rulings affecting the right to picket and
the organization of pickets, the rights of union members against
their unions, and the powers and liability of union officers (see
Hughes, 1985a; Griffith, 1985, 80–2). A single obscure-sounding

case may provide an opportunity for laying down principles of broad application, as when the Court of Appeal's decision on *International Drilling Fluids Ltd* v. *Louisville Investments (Uxbridge) Ltd*. included laying down seven principles which would determine whether a landlord's refusal to assign a lease was unreasonable. The Gillick case, considered in 8.2, although a case of judicial review of the actions of government, did result in the judges laying out guidelines about a doctor's relationship with girl patients and their parents.

Virtually all statutes offer some scope for detailed *interpretation*, but in some policy areas, such as family law, restrictive practices, and consumer protection, governments have deliberately conferred on judges wide-ranging discretionary powers in applying the law to individual cases. Since the 1960s there has tended to be a more 'purposive' approach by the courts, involving the interpretation of the words of the statute in the light of the policy pursued by the statute, rather than simply the literal meaning of the words (Bell, 1983, 85–6). However, *Hansard* is still excluded in assessing parliamentary intention and judges adopt the view that the citizen ought to be able to plan his life on the basis of the wording of the statute rather than what the legislator was attempting to achieve.

Judicial review is the procedure whereby a citizen can challenge directly any act or decision of a minister, government official, or public body on the grounds that they have acted unlawfully or improperly. The present arrangements have been in effect for only a few years, having been adopted in 1977 (and modified in 1981) following a Law Commission Report in March 1976, which recommended a wholly new form of procedure entitled an 'application for judicial review' to replace the previous cumbersome procedure for challenging the actions of ministers and officials. The number of applications for judicial review rose from 375 in 1981 to about 700 in 1984 and more than 1,000 in 1985.

Unlike ordinary actions before the courts, an applicant for judicial review must first ask the court's permission to bring the proceedings. If the court refuses to grant that permission, the rule up to 1985 was that the applicant could go to the Court of Appeal and ask that court for leave. However, in the Administration of Justice Bill published at the end of 1984 the government sought to abolish the right of appeal when a judge initially refused permission to bring proceedings. The relevant clause appeared to have been introduced without prior consultation. The government claimed to be trying to save judicial time. In 1984 there were thirty appeals, of which two were successful, and in January 1985 there was a further successful appeal. The clause was rejected in the House of Lords in February 1985 without a division. The government introduced a compromise replacement clause whereby if a judge refuses leave to bring proceedings the individual could then go to a divisional court presided over by a Court of Appeal judge; where that court refuses leave, the individual could go as a final resort to the Court of Appeal provided he obtains leave to do so either from that court or the divisional court.

Britain lacks a systematic framework of constitutional principles, public law and administrative courts. However, this is far from saying that there is a lack of activity of the type which would be carried out within such a framework in countries, such as France, which do have a written constitution and a system of administrative courts. Rather, the pattern in Britain is haphazard and patchy, both between policy areas and across time (see Clutterbuck, 1985). For example, between the two world wars the courts had been willing to intervene in matters involving the exercise of ministerial discretion. During the 1940s and 1950s, including the period of the Labour government from 1945 to 1951, the courts were very reluctant to intervene. From the late 1960s onwards, however, the courts showed a greater willingness to intervene and, despite some reservations touched on in 8.3, this interventionist approach towards both central and local government matters has continued (see Griffith, 1985, ch. 5; Bell, 1983, 1).

Bell (1983) explored the question of whether the activity of judges could be divided off from that of legislators and administrators or whether they carried out a similar function in making rules. He pointed out that there are a number of situations in which judges may be required to create new rules or standards in order to resolve a particular case before them. These rules then applied to future disputes as well. After considering and rejecting the 'consensus' and 'rights' models, which gave a different policy-making role to judges compared to legislators, he concluded that it is the 'interstitial legislator' model which offers the best description of the judicial function in England. Judges, like others in government, have to balance a variety of social interests and arrive at decisions which they consider best within the discretion available to them. Statutes, precedents, and previously enunciated principles may shape the options, but in 'hard cases' the judge exercises genuine discretion. A particular parallel can be drawn between delegated legislation and discretionary decisions within the executive branch of government on the one hand and judges exercising discretion on the other. One difficulty which judges face in exercising this 'legislative' role is assessing whether the absence of statute reflects parliamentary neglect because of shortage of legislative time or an unwillingness by government to confront an issue or a deliberate desire to avoid laying down requirements or restrictions (Bell, 1983, 250). As noted in 2.8, a 'non-decision' can reflect policy as much as an explicit decision to take action, legislative or otherwise.

The material presented in this chapter, including the cases discussed in the next section, tends to support the argument that courts do at times play a similar role in laying down general rules to that played by statutes passed by Parliament or secondary legislation, and judicial discretion may be applied in cases which would otherwise be the subject of executive discretion. This point is even stronger when the European dimension of adjudication, considered in 8.4, is included.

8.2 Reviewing the actions of government

This section looks at a number of cases from the 1970s and the 1980s, that is, in the period of renewed court involvement in reviewing the activities of government. These cases, some of which are important in themselves, raise points of general interest in defining the powers and discretion of ministers and in regulating conflict between government bodies.

The courts have dealt with a number of cases which were concerned with defining the discretion of ministers or government officers. *Gouriet* v. *Union of Post Office Workers* dealt with the issue of under what circumstances an individual can take action when the government chooses not to enforce a law. The plaintiff sought an order from the court in 1977 to restrain the defendant trade union from breaking the law by refusing to handle mail to South Africa. (This was clearly illegal and its illegality was not the point at issue.) Usually an individual who suffers no special damage from a breach of the law in England must ask the

Attorney-General either to institute proceedings or give his consent (in what is called a relator action) to the plaintiff's proceeding. In this case, the Attorney-General refused to do either. One question that arose in the Court of Appeal was whether this decision was subject to judicial review. In the Court of Appeal Lord Denning held that, where the Attorney-General refuses his consent to a relator action to prevent a breach of the criminal law, the courts can override that refusal by allowing any citizen to apply for a declaration or an injunction. The other two appeal judges held, more narrowly, that in cases where there is no obvious ground for the Attorney-General refusing to intervene to prevent criminal actions then a citizen adversely affected could apply for a declaratory judgment and the courts could issue an intermediate injunction. The court also held that the plaintiff, in common with other members of the public, had a genuine interest in ensuring that postal and telephone services were maintained, and this gave the courts jurisdiction to grant him an interim injunction. However, the House of Lords unanimously reversed the decision of the Court of Appeal and held that when the Attorney-General has refused his consent to relator proceedings, a private citizen cannot seek a declaration or an injunction in the civil courts to protect the public interest against a threatened breach of the criminal law. (This was one of a series of 'Denning' judgments in the Court of Appeal which were subsequently reversed in the House of Lords.)

The courts have ruled that if ministers do have discretion, then they must place themselves in a position where they can exercise a meaningful choice rather than follow through a predetermined decision. On 12 December 1985 a High Court judge ruled that toll increases imposed on the Severn Bridge in June 1985 were invalidated. The inspector at a public inquiry who had reported to Mr Ridley had decided that he would consider only whether the planned rises were lawful under the Severn Bridge Tolls Act and how the rises should be split between cars and lorries and would not consider wider objections. The judge ruled that the inspector's failure to consider wider objections amounted to a 'procedural impropriety' which invalidated Mr Ridley's decision to raise tolls on the inspector's advice. The judge stated that 'The points would and should have assisted the Secretary of State in the exercise of his discretion and power'.

In some cases the courts have confirmed the executive powers of ministers. For example, it was ruled that the determination of refugee status, which in practice was not distinct from consideration of a claim for political asylum, was a matter for the Home Secretary; there was no analogy with cases of illegal entrants where the courts did have the duty to determine on the facts whether an applicant was an illegal entrant (*Times Law Report*, 12 July 1985).

One of the traditional roles of the court is supposedly to prevent arbitrary acts by government. The case of *Congreve* v. *The Home Office* illustrates this role, and also how easily such rulings can be circumvented. Until the end of March 1975 the licence fee for a colour television was £12 for twelve months. From 1 April it was to increase to £18. So some people whose licences expired after 31 March took out new licences before that date, paying £12 and so hoping to postpone the date from which they would have to pay £18. The Home Office then required those persons to pay the extra £6 under threat that the new licences would be revoked. Eventually, on 26 November 1975, the Home Office sent out notices to those who had not paid up, revoking their licences with effect from 1 December. Congreve was a test action for a declaration that the Home Secretary's threat to revoke a television licence, prudently purchased in advance of an increase in the fee, was unlawful. Judges said that ministers must exercise their powers strictly in accordance with the prevailing law. Congreve, then, illustrated the potential role of the judiciary in limiting arbitrary actions by ministers. However, the bad news is that there can be no repeat of this, since the government now announces the increase to come into effect at midnight on the day of the announcement.

Laker Airways Ltd. v. *Department of Trade* involved the courts in defining the powers of a minister to give guidance to a statutory body or 'quango'. Under the Civil Aviation Act 1971, the Civil Aviation Authority was empowered to grant licences to those wishing to operate air transport lines. The Authority granted a licence to Mr Freddy Laker, as he then was, for the period 1973 to 1982 to operate a cheap passenger service known as 'Skytrain' between the United Kingdom and the USA. The Conservative government supported the project, but in February 1976 the Labour government (which had previously supported Mr Laker) announced a change of civil aviation policy. The Act of 1971 empowered the Secretary of State to 'give guidance' to the Authority with respect to their statutory functions. The White Paper purported to contain such guidance, which was that the Authority should not license more than one British airline to serve the same route, with British Airways as the preferred airline to the USA. That prevented Skytrain coming into operation. The Appeal Court held that the minister's statutory power to give 'guidance' to the CAA did not entitle him to set aside the explicit policy objective of encouraging competition in civil aviation. Thus Mr Laker succeeded, and helped to set off a period of cheap transatlantic flights. However, his airline subsequently went into liquidation. The Laker liquidator tried through the American courts to sue a number of airlines for damages for conspiring to put Laker out of business and succeeded in obtaining a settlement. The British government (by now again Conservative) tried to thwart this legal action, as well as persuading the Reagan administration to drop criminal proceedings, in part because it was hoping to sell off shares in British Airways, one of the airlines being sued. The Laker case and the Tameside case considered later in this section indicated a greater willingness of the courts to control ministerial discretion.

One of the most politically important issues decided by the courts was whether the government had been entitled to ban trade unions from GCHQ in Cheltenham as announced in January 1984 without prior consultation of the unions. The government announcement provided a temporary setback to the 'new realism' being promoted by the TUC in its relationship with the Conservative government and led to its temporary withdrawal from the National Economic Development Council. There are two issues involved here: was the government entitled to alter the conditions of its employees in this way, and had it carried out procedures, including consultation, correctly? The initial ruling in July 1984 was that: (1) 'The Crown did have the power to vary at will the terms and conditions of service of civil servants by the exercise of the Royal Prerogative'; (2) 'When a minister was contemplating making a decision that involved the withdrawal of rights relating to membership of trade unions and the right not be unfairly dismissed, the rules of natural justice required that the decision should not be reached until consultation had taken place with the staff or their representatives of the various unions.'

However, the Court of Appeal ruled in August 1984 that courts could not interfere with the ban because it was a decision taken on grounds of national security. The matter then went to the House of Lords, which ruled unanimously in November 1984 that the government did not act illegally in not first consulting the trade unions over the ban because a question of national security was involved. If there had been no question of national security the staff unions would have had a legitimate expectation that they would be consulted before the government made its decision. This decision is important because it indicates that the Crown (i.e. the government) still has important areas of prerogative relating to the civil service and national security—i.e. powers not conferred by statute—though the case also established that these are subject to judicial review. Secondly, it confirms as a legal principle the normal right to consultation (albeit within the government service) before a government decision is made, being overriden in this case only by considerations of national security.

In arriving at judgments in individual cases judges are required to set out their reasons, and these reasons may then form precedents which will be quoted in apparently related cases, and more generally are likely to be regarded as defining the legal position even when no case is being brought to court. Sometimes judges will more explicitly set out rules of general applicability which for all intents and purposes have the same nature as legislation (thus confirming Bell's argument that the policy-shaping role of judges was similar to that of legislation). This is arguably illustrated by the Gillick case (*Gillick* v. *West Norfolk and Wisbech Area Health Authority and the Department of Health and Social Security*). Mrs Victoria Gillick, mother of ten children, sought a declaration that advice from the Department of Health and Social Security which set out circumstances under which doctors could give contraceptive advice to girls under 16 (the age of consent) was unlawful and that contraceptive advice could not be given to her children without her knowledge and consent. Mrs Gillick's action was originally dismissed in July 1983, but the Court of Appeal ruled in December 1984 that the DHSS guidance was unlawful and that none of her children could be given a contraceptive, abortion advice, or treatment except in an emergency or after a court order. This ruling led to the withdrawal of the DHSS advice. However, the matter then went to the House of Lords, which in a majority ruling in October 1985 ruled that the DHSS advice had not been invalid and that a doctor who in exceptional circumstances gave contraceptive advice and treatment to a girl under 16 without her parents' knowledge or consent did not necessarily incur criminal liability or infringe parental rights (*Times Law Report*, 18 October 1985). Lord Fraser, in giving the majority ruling, set out the considerations which a doctor should have in mind when considering any case of a girl under 16 seeking contraceptive advice. With the exception that the language of the ruling is much more easily comprehensible than most statutes, this ruling is clearly 'laying down the law' in the same way as legislation on the subject might have done. More generally, the ruling reaffirmed that parental rights to control a child existed not for the benefit of the parent but for the child, and that as a child grew older the parents had a dwindling right of control. The ruling bears similarity to rulings from the US Supreme Court in the sense that it sets out general tests of what is lawful on a matter of public policy. The DHSS announced that it was reinstating its advice.

In another case involving the behaviour of doctors, the House of Lords ruled in February 1985 that doctors had a legal duty to inform patients of substantial risks involved in treatment, but not every risk, however small. This ruling was made in dismissing a claim for damages, but a rule of general application was established even with the negative ruling in this particular case. This case was the first attempt to introduce into English law the United States doctrine of 'informed consent'.

A number of cases involving the DHSS arose in 1985. In one, a government decision to claw back £14.2m in 'excess' profits on NHS spectacles by cutting opticians' fees was ruled unlawful in the High Court (*Times Law Report*, 17 October 1985). This case related to the minister's powers under a regulation, not to the making of the regulation itself.

Although judges have uniformly accepted the sovereignty of primary legislation (European courts do not have such an inhibition; see 8.4) they have been willing to overturn or comment on secondary legislation. Norman Fowler, Secretary of State for Health and Social Security, was ruled by a High Court judge in May 1985 to have failed in his duty to consult when he rushed through emergency regulations to close a loophole in the housing benefit laws; the case had been brought by the Association of

Metropolitan Counties. The judge ruled that 'There is no degree of urgency which absolves the Secretary of State from the duty to consult'. However, the judge refused to quash the regulations because it was the absence of consultation rather than the content of the regulations which had led the association to complain, and if the regulations were revoked housing authorities would face administrative difficulties.

In a major ruling in December 1985, the Court of Appeal ruled that the Secretary of State for Social Services was not empowered to make regulations enabling himself to fix the maximum amount of supplementary benefit payable to young people in board and lodging accommodation and the geographical limits of the board and lodging areas (*Regina* v. *Secretary of State for Social Services, ex parte Cotton*; *Same* v. *Same, ex parte Waite*). The court also said that the way the new maximum payments were introduced in April 1985 was also unlawful and that Mr Fowler had failed to consult properly his independent advisers, the Social Security Advisory Committee, on the regulations. The DHSS became liable for claims for underpayment during the period in which the overturned regulations were in force. The government had introduced new regulations in an attempt to meet earlier High Court objections, but these in turn came under legal challenge.

Although the British courts cannot overturn primary legislation, their rulings may affect whether the government proceeds with its legislation. In November 1985 the Court of Session in Scotland ruled that the Trustee Savings Bank was owned by its depositors. As a result the government suspended its plans for a stock market flotation of the Trustee Savings Bank as provided for under recently passed legislation. The flotation proceeded in September 1986 after a House of Lords ruling.

Central government has a number of powers to intervene or even take over the affairs of local authorities; for the most part, these are default powers and are rarely used in practice. However, in two cases, one involving a Labour government and a Conservative council over education and another involving a Conservative government and a Labour council over council-house sales, the courts have been asked to rule whether the minister acted correctly in exercising such powers.

In March 1975 the Labour-controlled Tameside Council put forward proposals to the Secretary of State for the reorganization of secondary education along comprehensive lines to come into effect in September 1976. The proposals were approved by the Secretary of State in November 1975. The council made many of the necessary arrangements for the change-over and told pupils which schools they would be going to. At the local elections in May 1976, the Conservatives won control of the council and on 7 June told the Secretary of State that they proposed not to implement the plans for the conversion of the five grammar schools into comprehensive and sixth-form colleges. On 11 June the Secretary of State gave the council a direction under section 68 of the Education Act 1944, requiring them to implement their predecessor's plans. Section 68 provided:

If the Secretary of State is satisfied . . . that any local education authority . . . have acted or are proposing to act unreasonably . . . he may give such directions . . . as appear to him to be expedient.

On 18 June 1976 the Divisional Court ordered the council to comply. On 26 July the Court of Appeal overruled the Divisional Court, and, acting with great speed, the House of Lords upheld the Court of Appeal on 2 August (*Secretary of State for Education and Science* v. *Tameside Metropolitan Borough*). The basis of the House of Lords decision was that the minister could give a valid direction only if he was satisfied that no reasonable local authority could have decided as the Conservative majority did; and that he could not have been so satisfied. Note that since the Secretary of State claimed to be satisfied in his own mind, the House of Lords was in effect ruling on the substantive question of the reasonable-ness or unreasonableness of the council's action. In other words, the House of Lords ruled that the Secretary of State had misdirected himself.

Another, more recent case, *Norwich City Council* v. *Secretary of State for the Environment*, went to the courts in December 1981 when Michael Heseltine, then Secretary of State for the Environment, used his powers under the Housing Act 1980 to take over the management of Norwich City council's housing stock because he was dissatisfied with the speed at which the council was implementing the 'right to buy' provisions of the Act. In the previous year the council had sold only 280 of its 25,000 stock. His department had been involved in detailed review of Norwich's position from May 1981. The Court of Appeal confirmed the decision of a lower court that Mr Heseltine had reached his decision properly under the Act—in this case the minister had not misdirected himself! (It should be noted that the Housing Act conferred greater power on the minister than had the relevant section of the Education Act in the Tameside case.) In arriving at its decision the court said that it did have a concern to protect the individual from the abuse of power by those in authority but that in this case the individuals concerned were the tenants whose right to buy their house had been delayed.

The courts have now become a major method of resolving disputes between central and local government, particularly over central government grants to local government and central government controls over local government finance. In 1981 a joint action by the inner London boroughs which were Labour controlled, led by Camden, led to the High Court ruling that Mr Heseltine, then Secretary of State for the Environment, had to repay several millions of pounds of grants. However, this was something of a Pyrrhic victory, since to comply with the letter of the ruling, Mr Heseltine heard further representations from the boroughs and then reimposed the penalties. Hackney subsequently had its penalty waived on the ground that it had reduced its spending. Camden failed in its subsequent attempts to reclaim the money through the courts.

In March 1984 Hackney failed to win a court judgment against the spending target fixed for it by Patrick Jenkin, Secretary of State for the Environment, which was only four-fifths of what the Labour-controlled council thought it needed to spend. The High Court ruled that Mr Jenkin had acted reasonably in law. The Appeal Court dismissed an appeal against refusal to grant judicial review of the minister's guidance. The judges ruled that the Secretary of State could properly issue guidance based on principles which applied to all authorities notwithstanding that there might be individual authorities which were unable to comply (*Regina* v. *Secretary of State for the Environment, ex parte Hackney London Borough Council, Times Law Report*, 11 May 1985).

1985 saw a number of cases, many of which revolved around tests of how reasonable the Secretary of State had been in listening to representations from councillors. Sheffield City Council failed to be allowed to pursue its challenge against its rate support grant and was refused leave in the Court of Appeal. A private citizen who brought a case against Hackney Borough Council was successful in getting a ruling that the council must set a legal rate as soon as possible.

The Divisional Court granted a declaration to the Inner London Education Authority that the decision of the Secretary of State for Education and Science not to amend the formula for local education authorities' contributions to the advanced further education expenditure pool for the year 1985–6 was unlawful in that, in taking account of rateable value in the formula, he had regard to an 'irrelevant consideration' (*Regina* v. *Secretary of State for Education and Science, ex parte Inner London Education Authority, Times Law Report*, 20 June 1985).

In Scotland the Court of Session ordered Stirling District Council in July 1985 to obey an order by the Secretary of State for Scotland to fix a legal rate. In the same month the Court of Session ordered Edinburgh City Council to revise its rate fund contribution to the housing account, which was more than £5.2 million above the government limit, and as a result the council reduced its rate by 1.8p in the pound.

In December 1985 the House of Lords ruled that government limits on local authority spending, formulated by reference to each authority's previous spending record, are not unlawful on the grounds of discrimination in that although the same principles must be applied to all authorities, their application may reflect differing circumstances (*Nottinghamshire County Council* v. *Secretary of State for the Environment*; *City of Bradford Metropolitan Council* v. *Secretary of State for the Environment, FT Commercial Law Reports*, 13 December 1985). This overturned a ruling of the Court of Appeal which would have resulted in central government having to return millions of pounds to affected authorities.

A resolution of Liverpool City Council to dismiss its teachers followed by their purported dismissal was found to be unlawful because it was a direct consequence of the fixing of an illegal rate, because it was not taken for proper educational purposes, and because its consequences were a breach of the council's duties as an education authority under the Education Act 1944 (*Times Law Report*, 20 November 1985). In March 1986 the Divisional Court ruled that Liverpool and Lambeth councillors were guilty of wilful misconduct by using their votes to defer the setting of a rate the previous year.

It was in Northern Ireland, however, that central government went furthest in financial intervention. Unionist councils were following a policy of adjourning in protest against the Anglo-Irish agreement. In February 1986 a High Court judge ruled that Belfast City Council had been abusing its power by continually adjourning and ordered the council to meet to set a rate. In the end, however, the government had to step in and set rates for eighteen Unionist councils.

In most cases, then, local authorities have been unsuccessful in their attempts to use the courts to overturn central government guidance on finance or the level of central government grant awarded to them. Even when the London boroughs were successful in 1981 the government was able to overcome the problem fairly quickly. The ruling on the arrangements for the further education pool is the one clear defeat for central government.

Not surprisingly, there were a number of cases between the Conservative central government and the Labour GLC, which the government planned to abolish. The results varied in terms of the success of the two sides. The High Court ruled in February 1985 that the Secretary of State for the Environment acted lawfully when he deferred the GLC's proposed amendments to the Greater London Development Plan because of the planned abolition of the GLC in April 1986. In July the High Court ruled that Mr Nicholas Ridley, Secretary of State for Transport, had acted 'illegally, irrationally and unreasonably' in directing that the GLC's night and weekend lorry ban should be dropped unless the GLC held a public inquiry. Mr Ridley lost an appeal at the Court of Appeal (*FT Commercial Law Reports*, 1 November 1985).

The abolition of the GLC and the metropolitan counties at the end of March 1986 was accompanied by a welter of court cases. The House of Lords confirmed a ruling that the GLC could not hand over £40m to the Inner London Education Authority; they held over judgment on plans to distribute £36m to voluntary groups until after the GLC had been abolished, so the money had to be set aside in a special fund to await the ruling. The case had been brought by London boroughs who would benefit from the distribution of funds left after the abolition of the GLC. However, West Midlands County Council was allowed by the courts to transfer £800,000, allocated to Birmingham airport, to a general spending fund. Trafford Borough Council took Greater Manchester Council to court about its plans for distributing funds, but the two councils came to a settlement after an initial ruling in favour of Greater Manchester Council.

As these 'deathbed' cases indicate, cases concerning local government do not necessarily directly involve the central government. One of the most important cases of recent years (*Bromley London Borough Council* v. *Greater London Council*), involving the extent of the GLC's right to subsidize cheap fares on London Transport, was brought against the GLC by the Conservative-controlled Bromley council in 1981. Like the Tameside case, it involved a local authority recently elected with a manifesto pledge, though this time a Labour one. The GLC had made a grant to London Transport to enable it to reduce its fares by 25 per cent and levied a supplementary rate to pay for it in line with an election promise. Bromley was involved because the boroughs were responsible for collecting the rate. The Divisional Court originally ruled in the GLC's favour, but this was overturned by the Appeal Court, and the House of Lords unanimously ruled that the supplementary rate was *ultra vires* the Transport (London) Act 1969. Lord Scarman said that in so acting the GLC had abandoned business principles and that it was a breach of duty owed to ratepayers and was wrong in law. Section 5 of the Act required London Transport to have 'due regard to efficiency, economy and safety', and Section 7 appeared to rule out the deliberate running of a deficit on the revenue account. Further, Lord Wilberforce said, in deciding to make a grant to support the fare reduction, once it became apparent that the ratepayers' burden would be approximately doubled, the GLC acted in breach of its fiduciary duty and failed to hold the balance between the transport users and the ratepayers as they should have done.

This decision was politically controversial since it implied that judges could overturn a key decision of a recently elected council, and a Labour one at that, and that the courts could judge what the appropriate level of subsidy from the GLC to London Transport would be. However, in January 1983 the High Court ruled that a proposed 25 per cent cut in fares (though a smaller cut than the original one because of the different base from which it was calculated) for spring 1983 would be legal. The court ruling was on the relatively narrow ground of whether it was legal for the GLC to instruct London Transport to implement its new fares as part of a balanced package of both transport and other measures: Lord Justice Kerr said that the package 'was done not on the basis of an election manifesto but as a carefully researched strategy for transport in London as a whole, and was subject to full consultation', and in a change in emphasis from the Lords December 1981 ruling, that 'no-one contends that the break-even option is either practicable or the correct answer in law'.

There has been an ironic sequel. The Conservative government subsequently removed London Transport from the GLC and established London Regional Transport, accountable directly to the Department of Transport. London Transport still required a grant to pay for its deficit, and the Minister of Transport, Nicholas Ridley, attempted to levy £281m from the GLC. In January 1985 a judge ruled that this was 'unlawful, irrational and procedurally improper'. The government announced its intention to appeal, but in fact introduced legislation at an accelerated pace to overturn the ruling.

8.3 Is the judiciary political?

The answer to the question of whether the judiciary is 'political' is in part a definitional matter. If we define political as covering issues of political controversy, such as the miners' strike, then clearly the judiciary is involved in political issues, even if the immediate focus is on specific cases of obstruction, assault, etc. Secondly, the role of the judiciary could be said to be political if they have a role in shaping the outcome of the policy process. Clearly, from the cases considered above, they do have such a role. We can go further and argue, following Bell (1983), that in at least some aspects the role of the courts in shaping policy overlaps with that played by elected politicians.

There is one sense, however, in which judges have become less political. Fewer of them have been actively involved in party politics prior to their appointment (Griffith, 1985, 27). Judges do still, however, come from a narrow range of social backgrounds, overwhelmingly upper and upper-middle class. The overwhelming bulk of judges have been to public schools and Oxford or Cambridge (Griffith, 1985, 25–7).

In his controversial book, *The Politics of the Judiciary*, J. A. G.

Griffith (1985) makes a number of serious accusations of bias in the judiciary. These accusations are of two types. First, he alleges prejudice in dealing with certain types of cases. Griffith argues that judges are prejudiced against trade unions (including disputes between trade unions and their members). He argues that there is a willingness to set aside habeas corpus on policy, not legal grounds. He argues that there is a bias towards owners seeking to evict squatters, towards property owners but not individuals in planning cases, and against students when upholding the actions of universities and colleges (contrasting with the alleged bias towards trade unionists in dispute with their trade unions). There is certainly evidence to support some of these points, but Griffith spoils his case by failing to distinguish between what he personally does not like on policy grounds and what is bad *law* or judicial decision-making. For example, Griffith clearly does not like any constraint on trade unions, but to criticize judges for upholding Conservative industrial relations law is not evidence that they are not doing their work properly—on the contrary.

Secondly, and rather more subtly, Griffith implies a pro-Conservative, anti-Labour bias in the judiciary. Griffith refers to the period of judicial activism or intervention which began in the early 1960s and writes:

How far this development has been inspired or assisted by the fact that between 1964 and 1979 Labour governments were in office for all but four years is an open question. Perhaps all that can be said is that Labour governments are more likely than Conservative governments to act in ways which offend the judicial sense of rightness, the judicial view of where the public interest lies. (Griffith, 1985, 238.)

Two points can now be made about this. First, as Griffith himself notes, the courts exercised restraint in intervening during the 1945–51 Labour government. Secondly, the pattern of judicial intervention continued under the 1979 Conservative government, with that government both winning and losing cases.

One interesting feature of recent cases involving public policy is that cases have been brought by both the traditional main parties against each other, with varying results. Thus, despite the uproar over the original London Fares decision (see 8.2), it appears that Labour local authorities, far from ignoring the courts as an instrument of Tory interference in Labour policies, are themselves prepared to go to court against Conservative decisions, and they by no means always lose when cases are brought against them by Conservative authorities.

More generally, it is important to bear in mind that there are a large number of court cases involving disputes between public bodies which have no party political connotations, as when the Clyde River Purification Board prosecuted British Steel over pollution. It is interesting that this instrument for resolution is used rather than a system of referring such disputes up to ministers.

Judges and courts are sometimes given the aura of impartiality, of being above the considerations which affect government and Parliament. Griffith is quite right in arguing that this impartiality is a myth, if by impartiality we mean a refusal to support politically inspired legislation. Judges are, as Griffith points out, part of the machinery for enforcing *party political* law. Griffith (1985, 204) clearly dislikes some of the consequences of this: he states 'So the National Industrial Relations Courts in 1972 forced the judiciary to take up a position on the government's side of industrial disputes which divided the country.' However, this seems to reflect Griffith's dislike of Conservative industrial relations legislation rather than being a fair criticism of the judges. The Conservatives might be criticized for placing judges in this position, but it does not seem fair to criticize judges for carrying out their job in a position in which they were placed. This is, of course, a separate issue from whether judges make bad legal decisions in the context of the legislation. Griffith's views about the relationship between the judiciary and the executive in making public policy seem rather confused. At times he argues that judges are thwarting the thrust of legislation (if not necessarily the letter). At other times he says that judges share the same values as the executive. Since it is the executive which effectively makes most legislation (see chapter 5), these arguments seem rather contradictory.

How far can judges be seen as maintainers of the established economic and political order? While some judges have shown a degree of creativity in attempting to emphasize individual claims against the government, for the most part judges do act to maintain the existing distribution of property rights. As Griffith (1985, 203) puts it, 'The law protects legal rights as they are. Its function, and that of the judiciary, is to maintain the existing state of affairs.'

As noted earlier, a period of judicial activism and intervention in public policy decisions by ministers and public authorities began in the early 1960s and has continued. However, there are signs that at least some judges are sensitive to the dangers of the courts becoming embroiled in disputes involving disagreement over decisions taken for party political reasons and have made statements to this effect in court.

In April 1982 Mr Justice McNeill of the Divisional Court dismissed a challenge by Conservative councillors from Kensington Borough Council to the GLC's 1982–3 budget and in doing so criticized attempts to use the courts for party political purposes (*The Times*, 3 April 1982). He complained of 'issues for the hustings and not for the court', and of 'party superficialities dressed up as points of law'. He added: 'The proper remedy on such issues is the ballot box, not the court.' Similarly in the same month the Divisional Court dismissed an application by the district auditor for London to declare illegal the payments made by Camden Labour council to some of their employees over the national average to settle a strike during the 1978–9 'winter of discontent'. Both the judges in the case made remarks about the proper limits of the courts' involvement in issues best left to the discretion of councils. Lord Justice Ormrod said that the test of whether a council's actions were reasonable was a much broader principle than recent cases might have suggested. He said: 'It is not for this court to pass judgement on the wisdom of the settlement.' The issue was not whether Camden had a bad bargain: that was for the electorate to decide. It should be noted with reference to Griffith's imputation of political bias that this judicial reluctance in these two cases arose not as a result of attacks on Conservative councils or ministers but as a result of cases against *Labour* councils.

However, judges have also indicated the limits of the role of the courts in cases brought by Labour councils against the Conservative central government. In refusing to allow Sheffield City Council to challenge its rate-capping by the Secretary of State for the Environment, Mr Justice Woolf said that the High Court had jurisdiction, but that it was right for matters involving political judgement to be left to 'debate through the democratic processes rather than debate before the courts' (*The Times*, 3 April 1985). In concurring with the House of Lords decision in December 1985 to uphold the government's rate support grant system in a case originally brought by Bradford City Council and Nottingham County Council, Lord Scarman indicated the limits of judicial review of ministerial decisions (see also 8.2). He stated that where legislation indicated that the approval of the House of Commons for a ministerial decision was required and that approval had been given then it was not open to the courts to intervene unless the minister and the House had misconstrued the statute.

However, the view that judges should not become involved in ruling on such matters can itself be regarded as political. This point was neatly made by Lord Hailsham in 1978, before he went on to become Lord Chancellor in the 1979 Conservative government:

Judges cannot choose the work they do; they have to come to a decision one way or another on all litigation which is brought before them. If they assume jurisdiction, they are in politics; if they decline jurisdiction, they are in politics. (*House of Lords Debates*, 29 November 1978, col. 1384.)

In Lord Hailsham's view judging is a political activity, involving definite stands on political issues, where all that can be expected is an openness to argument.

8.4 The European dimension

There are actually two main European dimensions to adjudication which can have important effects in shaping public policy. The first is through Britain's adherence to the European Convention on Human Rights and the second arises through Britain's membership of the European Communities.

8.4.1 The European Convention on Human Rights

The United Kingdom ratified the European Convention on Human Rights in 1951 but it was 1965 before individuals were granted a right of petition to the European Commission and Court in Strasburg. There is a three-stage process affecting the consideration of complaints made by British residents (see Zander, 1985). First, the European Commission on Human Rights determines whether it considers the case admissible. The bulk of complaints fail at this stage, with only 3.3 per cent of applications passing this hurdle between 1955 and 1984. If the complaint is held to be admissible, the Commission investigates it, a process which can take two or more years. If no settlement is reached, the Commission draws up a report, stating whether the facts appear to disclose a breach of the Convention. The case can then be brought to the European Court of Human Rights by the Commission or by one of the parties to the dispute. In total, for all countries, by the end of 1984 there had been 11,000 complaints; only about 3 per cent went to the Court and the Court found forty-six violations (Rutherford, 1985).

Though individual British citizens have the right to take cases direct to the Commission, unlike all other signatories except Sweden (which has a written constitution, unlike Britain), Britain has not made it possible to sue for a breach of Convention in its own domestic courts. The result of this combination of individual right of direct access and not incorporating the Convention into British law is that Britain appears to be in frequent breach of the Convention. About 25 per cent of the 320 cases ruled admissible in the thirty years since the Commission was set up were British applications (*The Times*, 18 March 1985). In 1984 there were 800 complaints from British citizens to the Commission. Up to the beginning of 1986 there were a dozen European Court rulings against the United Kingdom government, out of fifteen cases brought, leading to legislative reforms in telephone tapping, the law of contempt and freedom of expression, sex discrimination against immigrants, prisoners' and mental patients' rights. Some of these cases are discussed in more detail below.

From time to time there have been proposals to incorporate Convention into *British* law—if it were, British courts could handle cases alleging breach of Convention (see Zander, 1985). If the Convention was incorporated as a Bill of Rights it would give British judges the power to rule on the acceptability of Westminster legislation. Even if the Convention was incorporated in normal law, judges would be involved in rulings about possible conflict between that Act and other Acts of Parliament and in overruling the actions of ministers. Britain's adherence to the Convention comes up for periodic renewal, and during 1985 Lord Hailsham, the Lord Chancellor, pressed in Cabinet for key elements of the Convention to be incorporated into British law to avoid the irritating judgments against the government by an international court. However, this was not accepted. In October 1985 the government announced that it was to renew for a further five years the right of private citizens, due to lapse in January, to take the government to the European Court of Human Rights. In December 1985 Lord Scarman introduced the Human Rights and Fundamental Freedoms Bill in the House of Lords. The bill was designed to incorporate the European Convention on Human Rights into British domestic law, enforceable by British courts. The bill received its second reading in the House of Lords, but did not have the support of the government.

One of the most famous cases relating to Britain handled by the European Court related to whether the *Sunday Times* could be banned from publishing its findings on the adverse consequenes of the drug thalidomide. The British courts had ruled that the newspaper's findings about the effects of the drug could not be published because they might be prejudicial to legal actions still pending. The newspaper went to the European Court and its right to publish was eventually upheld. The British government reacted to the Strasburg ruling by introducing the Contempt of Court Act 1981, which was designed to facilitate the publication of articles that might previously have been regarded as prejudicial to legal proceedings.

In August 1984 the European Court of Human Rights judged that British laws about telephone tapping and the interception of mail were too vague and needed clarification. In February 1985 the government published a White Paper setting out a proposed new statutory framework, which included provision for an independent tribunal to hear complaints against the government, and the subsequent Interception of Communications Act 1985 came into force in April 1986.

In May 1985 the Court ruled that immigration rules introduced in 1980 amounted to sex discrimination. The case was brought by three women, born abroad but legally settled in Britain, who had been refused permission for their foreign husbands to live with them in Britain. Men, whether British citizens or not, had the right to bring in foreign wives. The Court ruled that this difference of treatment between men and women amounted to sex discrimination, which could not be justified by what is considered to be the British government's 'unconvincing' arguments about the impact on the domestic labour market at a time of high unemployment. It was estimated that about 2,000 couples a year could be affected. The British government accepted that it would need to change the immigration rules to comply with the ruling, but indicated that it might do so by tightening the rules on entry of wives to Britain.

The British government does not accept that rulings by the European Court of Human Rights automatically become part of British law. However, Britain had up to 1985 always altered its legislation to conform to Court rulings. However, when the House of Lords replaced a clause allowing parents to opt out of corporal punishment with one abolishing corporal punishment completely the government abandoned the bill. The Commons voted to ban corporal punishment in 1986.

The British government did win a case before the Commission in August 1985 when the Commission ruled that abolition of the GLC would not be a violation of human rights. It also decided that the government's cancellation of elections due for all GLC seats in May 1985 was not a denial of human rights. The Commission ruled that the GLC's powers were subordinate to those of Parliament and were 'exercised subject to that Parliament's ultimate control'.

The British government was also successful in a case brought by the Duke of Westminster claiming that the Leasehold Reform Act 1967 as amended by the Housing Act 1974 was a breach of human rights. The Act gave tenants in houses held on long leases who met certain conditions the right to purchase compulsorily the freehold of the house at a price set by a formula in the Act. The Duke claimed that he had been forced to sell houses at a loss running into millions of pounds. In February 1986 the Court ruled that while the taking of property for no reason other than to confer a private benefit could not be in the public interest, the compulsory transfer of property from one individual to another might constitute a legitimate means for promoting the public interest (*Times European Law Report*, 22 February 1986). A wide margin of interpretation should be available to the legislature in implementing social and economic policies, and the legislature's judgment about what served the public had to be respected unless it was manifestly without reasonable foundation. Further, the Court ruled that the Convention did not guarantee the right to full compensation in all circumstances and that legitimate objective of public interest such as economic reforms or righting social disequilibria might call for less than full reimbursement of the market value.

8.4.2 Adjudication through the European Communities

Four aspects of how Britain's membership of the European Communities affects adjudication will be touched on: (1) the incorporation of the Treaty of Rome into the framework of British law; (2) rulings by the European Court of Justice (a European Communities body based in Luxemburg) on the legality of actions of the British government or laws passed by the British Parliament; (3) rulings on the legality of the actions of other governments which affect Britain; (4) rulings on the legality of actions of European Communities organizations which affect Britain. The European Court relies on the conformity of Community institutions and national governments—the Court lacks direct enforcement mechanisms.

The workload of the European Court of Justice showed a marked increase in 1985, with the number of cases coming before the Court increasing to over 400 a year, compared with 312 cases in 1984 and an annual average of 159 since the Court's inception in 1953 as part of the European Coal and Steel Community (Hughes, 1985b). In contrast to the European Court of Human Rights, British cases do not constitute a disproportionate number of those considered by the Court. The UK courts had referred fifty-five cases to the European Court up to the end of 1985 for rulings on the interpretation of Community law. British courts were for years after accession reluctant to refer cases to the European Court, though this attitude has changed. Those cases which have been referred by Britain have tended to give the European judges some of their knottiest problems (Hughes, 1985b). In terms of cases taken directly to the European Court, up to the end of October 1985 Britain had brought 7 cases and been the respondent in 18, of which 17 were for alleged treaty breaches. Britain was found to be in default in eleven of these cases; the resulting percentage default rate of 64 per cent was the highest in the Community, but was based on a much smaller number of cases than the much more frequently defaulting Italy (73 cases in breach of the treaties between 1961 and 1985).

1. One aspect of the European dimension is that the Treaty of

the European Economic Community (Treaty of Rome) and Regulations issued by the Commission have themselves become incorporated into the British legal framework (in contrast to the Convention of Human Rights discussed above). Thus British judges may refer to the Treaty of Rome in judging the actions of ministers. The Court of Appeal did this in ruling that a government scheme was unlawful if its object or effect was to reduce or exclude competition from imported drugs which had the same effect as UK drugs but had been manufactured more cheaply in other EEC countries. Drug importers had offered more generous discounts to chemists than British wholesalers, but the government had altered its scheme so as to penalize chemists who bought at discounts of between 12 and 20 per cent of the 'drug tariff' agreed by the DHSS. It was this scheme which was ruled unlawful (*FT Commercial Law Reports*, 6 December 1985).

In February 1986 the Court of Appeal ruled that proposed tax concessions to Shell and Esso at the Mossmorran project in Fife and to British Petroleum at Grangemouth would breach both the 1982 Finance Act and also be an illegal subsidy or 'aid' under the Treaty of Rome (*Times Law Report*, 27 February 1986). The case had been brought by ICI, which claimed that the government was favouring its competitors. The court ruled that any agreement already made between the Inland Revenue and the oil companies was invalid.

2. The European Court of Justice ruled in July 1982 that the British government would have to amend its equal pay laws to bring them into line with the EEC's equal pay directive, so that women would be able to claim equal pay for work of equal value even when the work was of a different kind. The government introduced legislation to implement this ruling, and the new criterion has been invoked in a number of firms. In another ruling on sex discrimination in 1985 the European Court judged that the British government was wrong to exempt firms of fewer than five employees from the provisions of the Sex Discrimination Act. The British government published a bill in February 1986 to give effect to this ruling. In February 1986 the Court ruled in a case brought by a former health authority employee that public authorities which force women employees to retire earlier than their male colleagues were in breach of a 1976 Community directive (*Times European Law Report*, 27 February 1980). Britain had not brought

in domestic law to implement the directive, but the Court ruled that an individual employed by the state can rely on the directive itself in bringing a case. This did not apply to those in the private sector. In April 1986 the British government announced that it would introduce legislation making it illegal to have a different retirement age for women in both the public and private sectors. However, this would not affect state pensions (available at 60 for women and 65 for men), or private pension schemes. The European Court of Justice has effectively become the source of equal opportunities policy for Britain.

In what must be the most bizarre case considered by the European Court, it ruled that the British Customs and Excise had acted wrongly in banning the import and seizing of certain goods imported from West Germany by Conegate Ltd.; 'the goods consisted essentially of inflatable dolls, which were clearly of a sexual nature, and other erotic articles' (*Times European Law Report*, 12 March 1986). Member states are allowed to ban imports on the grounds of public morality. However, the manufacture and sale of inflatable sex dolls are not themselves illegal in Britain. Accordingly, the Court ruled that the public morality grounds for banning imports could not be used where the same goods could be manufactured and sold within the member state.

The Ministry of Agriculture imposed a ban on French turkey imports in 1981, saying that it was to prevent the introduction of disease into Britain. However, the European Court ruled in July 1982 that the ban was a breach of the Treaty of Rome and that the real aim of the ban had been to block turkey imports for commercial and economic reasons. The British government allowed the resumption of French imports in November 1982. However, in July 1985 the English Court of Appeal ruled that the French producers were not entitled to claim damages from the Ministry of Agriculture for losses they suffered during the period of the ban (*FT Commercial Law Reports*, 9 August 1985).

Since January 1979 Britain has been operating a ban on oil sales to Israel. This ban has never been written into British law. The government asked oil companies to comply with a policy statement which authorized exports only to European Communities states, member states of the International Energy Agency, and countries with which there was an existing pattern of trade; although not mentioned by name, the effect of this was to exclude Israel and

South Africa. In a case brought by a company which had been refused the supply of a cargo when it had been learned that the destination would be Israel, the European Court ruled that the ban was not illegal under the terms of a European Community Agreement with Israel (*FT Commercial Law Reports*, 21 February 1986). However, the Court did rule that Britain should have informed the Commission and its Community partners before introducing the ban, though failure to do this did not of itself confer individual rights which national courts must protect.

The European Commission has taken a number of member countries to court because of what it considered to be taxation of alcohol of different strengths which had the effect of discriminating against alcohol imported from other member countries. In the case of Britain, the Commission contended that the government was protecting beer by under-taxing it in relation to wine. The government fought the case but lost. The Chancellor of the Exchequer implemented the judgment in his Budget of 14 March 1984 by raising beer by the minimum amount necessary to comply with the judgment and maintain revenue (2p on a typical pint), and at the same time reducing the duty on table wine by the equivalent of about 18p a bottle.

3. At the same time as announcing the cut in duty in wine, the Chancellor of the Exchequer told the House of Commons that the government of Italy had, after discussions, given the British government an undertaking that they would comply with an earlier Court ruling on discrimination against Scotch whisky.

Britain and British citizens can be affected by rulings which are in an immediate sense targeted at other countries. In September 1985 the Court ruled that the Commission had acted correctly in refusing to exempt Ford of Germany's car distribution system from the EEC's competition regulations. This arose from an instruction from Ford to its West German dealers in 1982 not to supply any more right-hand drive cars to British customers at low pre-tax prices; pre-tax prices were higher in Britain. The decision had been overtaken by events by the time it was made, since EEC regulations which came into effect in July 1985 insisted that customers can buy cars anywhere in the EEC at the local pre-tax price without undue difficulty or delay.

4. In May 1985 the European Court gave a judgment on a case brought by the European Parliament against member states for

failing to carry out their obligations under the Treaty of Rome to bring in a common transport policy. The Court rejected many of the detailed charges brought by the Parliament, but it did agree that the Council of Ministers had failed to allow transport services to be offered freely throughout the community and that it had failed to allow EEC nationals to set up a transport business anywhere in the Community. The Court's ruling contained no means of enforcement against the Council of Ministers, but it did provide political ammunition for Britain's campaign within the Community for greater liberalization of air services. During 1986 the British government successfully pursued a case through the European Court arguing that the Communities' budget approved by the European Parliament was illegal.

8.5 Tribunals

The growth of the use of tribunals can be explained both by the need to offset the disadvantages of court proceedings (limited scope, cost, formality of proceedings) and to relieve the courts of a potentially very heavy workload in specialized fields (Ridley, 1984, 11–12; Harlow and Rawlings, 1984, 73). In total, tribunals handle several hundred thousand cases a year. These tribunals do not constitute a uniform or universal system. As Ridley (1984, 12) puts it, 'Different tribunals were established at different times, differently composed and with different procedures.' Only some areas of public policy (particularly social security, immigration, and tax) are covered by tribunals. For the most part, tribunals are concerned with the details of the eligibility of individual applicants. From time to time, however, they do make rulings of more general policy significance.

An industrial tribunal was responsible for a change in civil service recruitment policy. A woman who had married early and left employment to bring up her young family later qualified as a mature student and applied at the age of 32 to the civil service for a job as an executive officer. The civil service refused her entry at that level because of its age limit of 28. The industrial tribunal found this limit 'indirectly' sex discriminatory because more women than men rear children during the traditional civil service recruitment years. The civil service subsequently raised the age limit to 45. An industrial tribunal in Sheffield also ruled in August

1985 that married women were entitled to take part in the Manpower Services Commission's Community Programme for the long-term unemployed. In October 1984 the Department of Employment had changed regulations so as to prevent those not receiving benefit from taking part in the scheme. The idea was that the gross cost of the Programme would be partly offset by the benefits which would have been paid in benefit anyway. However, the tribunal ruled that an unemployed wife had been entitled to a place on the Programme although she was not receiving benefit. Similarly, in March 1986 an industrial tribunal found that the University Grants Committee's 'new blood' scheme to encourage the appointment of lecturers up to 35 years old to reduce imbalance in the career structure was in breach of the Sex Discrimination Act; a woman had been turned down for a post under the scheme because she was 39.

In August 1985 the government announced that it would change the social security regulations to protect the benefit entitlement of students who were having their social security benefits cut because they were receiving income from parents under covenant. Decisions by the independent adjudicating authorities at the Oxford office of the DHSS and proposals by the Chief Adjudicating Officer had resulted in reduced benefits because of the covenant payments. The government wanted to amend the regulations to restore the previous intention.

In September 1985 a DHSS tribunal ruled that rules imposing cash limits on supplementary benefit payments for bed and breakfast accommodation were void, and that the couple whose case was being considered should have their charges paid in full by the department (see 8.2 for the court cases affecting the supplementary benefit regulations in 1985).

In October 1985 the Social Security Commissioners ruled unlawful the DHSS's system for deciding whether to make extra payments towards fuel bills when the weather was exceptionally severe. The system used a complex formula based on trigger points using 'degree days' calculated on the temperature at a number of weather stations and meant that weather that was regarded as exceptionally severe in the south of England would trigger a payment but would not be regarded as exceptionally severe in the north of Scotland. The system had been described earlier in the year by Mr Tony Newton, Minister for Social Security, as 'weird and wonderful' and was already under review following protests in the winter of 1984–5 (emphasizing that political routes in Britain are often more important than legal ones in leading to a review of policies).

The government's policy on enterprise zones received a setback in 1986 when a lands tribunal in Swansea ruled that rates on industrial property close to the city's enterprise zone should be cut by up to 20 per cent because of the impact of the enterprise zone in lowering rents in nearby industrial property. This decision would result in a considerable reduction in local government income, substantially adding to the cost to government of the enterprise zones, as well as drawing attention to the side-effects of the policy.

A Council on Tribunals was established in 1958 to keep the constitution, organization, and procedure of tribunals under continuous review (see Harlow and Rawlings, 1984, ch. 6; Stacey, 1975, 176–7). Originally, the Council on Tribunals could investigate only statutory tribunals and statutory inquiries, but a 1966 Act gave the Lord Chancellor the power to bring discretionary tribunals within the jurisdiction of the Council on Tribunals, and this power has been used to bring a number of types of inquiry within the Council's remit. By the mid-1980s the Council, itself a 'shoestring' operation, was responsible for overseeing the work of about 2,000 tribunals of about sixty different types. The Council has no power to recommend the creation of new tribunals, which means that it cannot fill in gaps in the rather patchwork coverage of review by existing tribunals. The Council is, however, informally consulted by departments in the preparation of legislation. The Council does not have any appeal function in respect of individual cases considered by tribunal systems, nor can it be regarded as an effective 'ombudsman' for the treatment of individual cases by tribunals.

8.6 Ombudsmen

The national ombudsman was established in 1967 (see Stacey, 1975, 182–90; Gwyn, 1982; Ridley, 1984, 14–19). The ombudsman cannot investigate cases which raise questions about the legality of an issue or whether the best assessment of facts was made or the best conclusion drawn from them. He is concerned only with grievances which arise from defects in the way the decision was arrived at, such as delay, incompetence, or arbitrariness. The ombudsman can investigate most matters for which a minister is responsible, though this excludes a number of matters such as cases relating to taxation, cases which are subject to judicial review, commercial contracts of government, and personnel matters relating to the civil service.

The correct title of the national ombudsman is the Parliamentary Commissioner for Administration. This reflects the persistence of a number of mythological aspects of the British Constitution, namely that ministers are responsible for the conduct of their officials (see 4.1) and that Members of Parliament are the main focus for the protection of citizens. Thus the ombudsman is technically an officer of Parliament, reporting to a parliamentary committee. In order not to undermine the position of MPs, citizens have no direct right of access to the ombudsman; if anyone does write directly to the ombudsman, the ombudsman asks the constituency MP whether he may proceed with the case. Though the ombudsman has extensive powers of investigation, he has no independent enforcement powers and if his recommendations are ignored by a ministry, it is supposedly up to Parliament (in which the government normally has a majority) to press them further. In practice, there are unlikely to be debates on the floor of the Commons about individual grievances identified by the ombudsman. Only in the cases of Sachsenhausen, which involved a group of former prisoners of war, and the Court Line affair (see also 4.1), which involved a large number of would-be holiday-makers who had lost money, were the issues taken up by Parliament (see Ridley, 1984, 18).

From the perspective of the individual citizen, the advantage of investigation by the ombudsman rather than through court or tribunal hearings is that no charge is made for his services and no legal representation is required. The ombudsman's staff themselves take on the responsibility of conducting the investigation. Despite these advantages, only 800 to 1,000 complaints are received by the ombudsman each year, only a minority of which are accepted as appropriate for investigation, a very small number in relation to the total scale of government activity and the inevitable maladministration which accompanies it. About 30 per cent of complaints concern the Department of Health and Social Security and another 15 per cent concern the Inland Revenue. The ombudsman upholds complaints in about 10 per cent of the cases he considers, and in another 10 per cent makes criticisms of a department's practices, though not upholding the complaint. However, the impact of the ombudsman can be much wider than these figures would suggest, since many thousands of citizens have been helped by changes in administrative practices and procedures resulting entirely or in part from his investigations and reports (Gwyn, 1982).

The local ombudsmen were established in 1974. They can investigate most local government matters, but this excludes the conduct of individual police officers (for which there is now an independent Police Complaints Authority), and internal school affairs such as curricula and discipline (see Ridley, 1984, 18–19). The local ombudsmen have similar powers of investigation to the national ombudsman. Although a citizen with a complaint must approach a local councillor first, he can subsequently complain to the local ombudsman if he is not satisfied, since all councillors technically have an executive role in local government, and thus cannot be expected to be the defender of the citizen against the executive in the same way as Members of Parliament supposedly are.

In the majority of cases where there are adverse findings against them by the local ombudsman, the councils comply with the terms of his findings and any recommendations he makes. However, in a minority of cases councils refuse to accept the findings or fail to take effective action to deal with the recommendations, even when the ombudsman then issues a second report. The local ombudsmen have no powers of enforcement of their own and there is no provision in law for councils to be forced to abide by them or for the original complainant or the council to appeal against them if they disagree with the findings. Central government has refused to introduce changes to the law so that councils would be forced to accept findings and pay compensation in relevant cases on the grounds that only a few cases go badly wrong. In 1984, 9 per cent of the more than 3,000 cases referred to the English local ombudsmen reached the stage of a report to the council concerned (Clayton, 1985). The others were abandoned because they were outside the remit of the ombudsmen or were settled before report stage. In the first ten years of the local ombudsman system in England, there were more than 1,500 cases in which a ruling of injustice was made. In all but 92 of those cases (6 per cent) the councils took action which satisfied the ombudsman.

The National Health Service also has its own ombudsman, though rather confusingly he is in fact the same person as the Parliamentary Commissioner for Administration operating under different rules and with a different staff. Citizens may appeal directly to the NHS ombudsman. However, he is excluded from investigating the clinical judgements of doctors (reflecting the success of doctors in maintaining control of review of their own actions), and this effectively reduces the value of the NHS ombudsman, since many of the complaints about the NHS are in fact about faulty medical treatment in hospital. The case-load of the ombudsman in his NHS capacity has increased from 493 in 1974–5 to 815 in 1984–5.

Overall, as Ridley (1984, 19) points out, ombudsmen are not the routine route for handling citizens' grievances. They deal with relatively few cases, though the recommendations they make on those cases may have wider impact on the future handling of similar cases and the very knowledge of potential investigation by the ombudsmen may encourage officials to be more careful. The continuing evidence of those cases actually investigated by the ombudsmen encourages some scepticism about this last point, however.

Chapter 9

Impact and Evaluation

9.1 The outcome of issues

Policies have both substantive policy impacts and political consequences. This introductory section outlines the main possible
consequences in terms of political reaction to policies. Section 9.2
looks at problems of assessing variations in impact and the
following section analyses sources of variation in impact. Section
9.4 looks at how far the outcome of policies is evaluated in Britain,
while section 9.5 concludes the chapter and the book by asking
whether there are signs that British government has become
somewhat less complacent about the effectiveness of its policies.

One possible consequence of government action or inaction is
that the *issue subsides*. For example, there was concern about a
possible manpower shortage in the mid-1960s; it was never there,
and the issue naturally subsided when this became apparent.
Balance of payments used to be a continuing concern of
governments in the 1960s; partly as a result of the floating of the
pound and oil revenues, but partly also because of a change in
perceptions of what are the important economic problems, this
issue is now much less prominent. Some issues may only appear to
subside: devolution to Scotland occupied a considerable amount of
the time and attention of the Labour government between 1974
and 1979. Since then the issue appears from a Westminster
perspective to have disappeared from the political agenda.
However, the underlying political pressures still exist, and it would
be surprising if the issue did not re-emerge in Westminster in the
late 1980s or early 1990s.

Some policies may result in *dissatisfaction with the government
response,* and continuing pressure to take more effective action.
For example, the introduction of Family Income Supplement by
the Conservatives and of child benefit by Labour failed to satisfy
the 'poverty lobby', in the first case because the nature of the

policy was disliked and in the second because the level was considered to be too low and was subsequently eroded by inflation. The dissatisfaction may stem from a perception that the original policy was inadequate to start with. Dissatisfaction may disappear, only to reappear later after perceived results become manifest; for example, although the British electorate voted to remain in the European Communities in 1975, dissatisfaction with its policies and institutions subsequently grew. Note that it is *perceived* results that matter, and the coincidence of joining the Communities with a period of reduced growth led to the two developments being associated. However, people may be dissatisfied with a policy for opposite reasons, with some feeling that payments to the unemployed are too high, and others thinking that they are too low (see also 9.4). Lack of any expressed dissatisfaction does not necessarily equate to satisfaction, however; those dissatisfied may see the problem as one of how they are treated as individuals rather than the nature of the policy or may not have the resources or inclination to mobilize politically to try to get a policy changed.

Naturally, grumbles about inadequacies receive political attention, whereas *satisfaction with government responses*, at least in relative terms, may never be articulated. One way of trying to get at relative satisfaction or dissatisfaction among the general public is through surveys, and section 9.4 represents findings about a number of social policies.

One perverse political outcome is the *displacement* of the initial issue by a new one related to the government response: the policy itself becomes perceived to be a problem (Hogwood and Peters, 1985). For example, a programme of whooping cough vaccine leads to concern about brain damage from the vaccinations; a policy of fluoridation of the water supply to improve dental care leads to concern about the right of government to add chemicals to the general water supply; policies to control inflation lead to incomes constraint being regarded as the problem by those whose income is constrained; slum clearance programmes lead to the creation of peripheral council-housing estates with desparate social problems. Such issue displacement reminds us of the point made in chapters 1 and 2 that issues do not come in neat self-contained packages.

9.2 Analysing variations in impact

Despite the emphasis often placed on the unitary and centralized nature of decision-making in Britain, there are in fact often substantial variations in the delivery and impact of public policy in different geographical areas and between different categories of people. These variations occur even in public policies which are administered by central government and even in policies such as the administration of criminal justice which one might expect to be applied evenly throughout the country.

For example, defendants in Dorset are twelve times more likely to be remanded in custody than their counterparts in Bedfordshire (Prison Reform Trust, 1986). The National Audit Office found that while 127 out of every 1,000 women were screened for cervical cancer in the Mersey region, 260 were screened in the neighbouring North-West region (HC 229, 1985–6). Comparatively very high proportions of those accepted into university come from families with professional and 'intermediate' occupations: 22.1 per cent of those accepted in 1984 came from professional families and only 1.1 per cent from unskilled family backgrounds (*Social Trends*, 1986, 55). Often the distribution of social and economic characteristics itself produces apparent territorial variations: the Department of Education and Science (1983) has argued that it is social class differences rather than spending on secondary schools which are the main reason for the wide variations in examination results of English education authorities.

Government is often ignorant about the existence and causes of variations in policy impact. The government is particularly ignorant about the overall impact of its policies on a particular area or group of people. A report from the government's Central Policy Review Staff (1975, 5), called *A Joint Framework for Social Policies*, stated that: 'there are wide variations not only in local standards of service, but in Whitehall's knowledge of these variations.' When we look at detailed variations within an individual local authority area, we may find that the local authority does not have information about the extent to which citizens benefit differently from services in different parts of the city. The much ridiculed job creation project which involved counting lamp-posts was not as daft as it seemed at first sight.

In looking at variations in the impact of public policy, it is very easy to slip into the habit of using only figures which are relatively easily available, are relatively hard, and allow ready comparisons, for example, public expenditure per head variations between Scotland and England. However, variation in expenditure is only one measure of variation. As a result of variations in efficiency and cost, a given amount of expenditure may result in different numbers of teachers, doctors, or houses.

These are still *quantitative* measures. More difficult to measure and to assess are *qualitative* differences. For example, the arrangements for administering health, education, and industry policy are different in Scotland compared to England. Does this represent a difference in the quality of the service delivered? Certainly, it produces observable differences, for example in the schools examination system, but it may be difficult to *specify* the form which the difference takes, and it may be impossible to come up with a *valid* quantitative measure of the extent of the difference.

A second example, also from education, is that Northern Ireland still operates a largely selective school system, whereas the rest of the UK has moved towards a comprehensive system. This is clearly a qualitative difference, though which is the 'better' than the other is a matter for political and educational judgement. Some qualitative differences may be susceptible to quantitative measures of coverage; for example, we can measure the percentage of pupils in a region going to comprehensive schools. But when we want to evaluate the extent to which comprehensive schools are more something than non-comprehensive schools we would have to use verbal as well as numerical measures.

In measuring variations in policy we may well want to use a *mixture* of qualitative and quantitative measures. For example, if we wanted to examine differences in the extent to which government policies had improved the visual qualities of the environment we might use figures of expenditure, number of projects completed, number of trees planted, etc. However, this would literally not give us the complete picture, since different amounts of expenditure, trees, etc. can be used in various ways. Therefore we might want to make a more qualitative, perhaps subjective, assessment-based, say, on examinations of photographs of different areas before and after, or by on-site inspection. One can get a good idea of some territorial variations in policy impact in any large city simply by walking around.

Wherever possible, we will want to use numerical measures of variations; however, we should use them only if they are valid (i.e. true) measures of the differences we are actually interested in. For example, variation in pupil–teacher ratios is not a valid measure of the quality of education. We should not neglect other types of variation simply because they are difficult to pin numbers on, either because of conceptual problems or because the figures simply are not available.

The term 'outputs' occurs quite a lot in the literature on local authority variations in public policy. However, on closer examination we find that the authors are normally referring to *expenditure* on various functions. Arguably expenditure (except in the case of cash benefits) is not an output at all, since it still has to be transformed into the goods and services which actually constitute the outputs. Similarly, even if we move along the policy delivery process and measure, say, the number of teachers employed or number of hospital beds used, we are still measuring the resources used in a particular policy area rather than the actual output, which in the case of schools would be the amount and quality of teaching, and in the case of hospitals would be the amount and quality of health care. Variations in the resources used may not reflect variations in the final output, because of greater efficiency in the use of resources or because of some other feature not measured by the indicator of resources used. That is not to say that we are not concerned with measures used—they are of considerable interest because they are of key importance in decision-making about policies—but we should be quite clear just what it is that we are measuring.

Unfortunately, we often do not have data about outputs in the strict sense, either because of conceptual problems—how do you measure 'amount of health care'?—or because suitable data are not available. We may therefore have to fall back on subjective judgements or measures of resources used and approximate indicators, but, again, we should always be aware about what it is we are trying to do, and the reliability of the measures we are using.

Apart from variations in the resources used and variations in the outputs of policies, we may also be concerned with variations in the outcomes of policies, that is the effects of the policies. For example, our concern in a particular policy may not be to ensure equality of *outputs* as a measure of equality of service but to ensure equality of *outcomes*. That is, the government would be providing the same service to all regions when regions have equal unemployment, equal health, etc. Since problems vary between areas, expenditure and outputs would also have to vary to ensure equality of service in this sense.

Even where data about policy variations exist, there may be problems about allocating figures to each area to enable a fair comparison to be made. In other words an expenditure may be incurred or a service provided in one area, but be of benefit to a different area. An example here would be treatment of patients from outside the district in which the hospital is located; this is especially likely to be true of specialist hospitals. Another example would be the distribution of local authority services within an area, for example, variations in availability and use of library facilities between wards. Only very limited information is available on this. One study in Coventry first calculated the population within a one-mile radius of libraries, then calculated the number in each ward, and then calculated expenditure in each ward; then a sample of users was taken, plotted by ward, and expenditure on wards was calculated on the basis of use (Randall, Lomas, and Newton, 1973). The findings were that not only were there substantial differences between different wards, but that there was little correlation between standards of supply and usage in individual wards. This shows (1) the complex calculations often needed to make comparisons between areas; (2) the importance of distinguishing between indicators of *supply* and indicators of *use*.

Comparisons about public policy can be made on the basis of any size of unit, ranging from very broad areas containing millions of people, down to areas of towns which may contain only a few streets. Some policies are focused on areas smaller than local authority areas; for example, Housing Action Areas; Educational Priority Areas. Information about such areas is necessary both for policy delivery and analysis.

However, information may be available about 'needs' indicators but not current resources allocated or standards of service. A study was carried out in one small area of Liverpool in 1973/4 which produced some striking results (see Hambleton, 1978, 250–1). Although Liverpool had adopted an education policy of positive discrimination in favour of deprived groups some years earlier, it was found that this area received *less* than its share of the education budget compared to its share of population despite the fact that it was a deprived area. This largely reflected low spending on further education. We may also be interested in the overall impact of all public policies on a particular area. Unfortunately, apart from very limited specific studies, such information is not available.

The appropriate level of aggregation for looking at geographical variations in impact will depend on the policy being examined and the purpose of the comparison. The area used for policy delivery purposes is an obvious candidate, partly because there are good theoretical reasons for assuming this to be significant, and partly because statistics are likely to be available at this level. However, we may also be concerned with variations in the delivery of policy within the area (e.g. Liverpool) or to look for broader patterns (e.g. proportions of public sector housing in different regions). Frequently, it will be appropriate to make comparisons at more than one level. This will help us to avoid the trap of assuming that causes of variation operate at only one level.

9.3 Factors producing or maintaining variations in impact

Having established that there are variations in policy impact and that these occur in all types of policy and at all levels of aggregation, it is important to look at possible causes of such variations, and at the difficulties in attempting to analyse these causes. Our problem is not a lack of explanation of variations, but a variety of them. Many of these explanations are interrelated. In a sense it is misleading to go through each factor separately, since a number of them may occur in combination. A particular factor may not actually cause variation in public policy until it is triggered off by another, such as political demands.

Some relevant factors are more highly visible than others. Areas may vary considerably in their *physical* characteristics, including their topography. Variations in hilliness and soil quality can result in variations in expenditure on different kinds of agricultural support. Overall, expenditure on agriculture is likely to be higher per capita where there is a greater acreage of farmland.

Related to purely physical factors are those arising from the *man-made environment*, especially the degree of urbanization.

Some expenditures, such as on public housing, are likely to be higher in urban areas. Urban areas may also have social and other problems in a particularly concentrated form. Also large cities, because of their concentrated population, are likely to provide certain facilities, such as museums and art galleries, for their own and surrounding populations (Sharpe and Newton, 1984, ch. 6). In some cases, it is difficult to determine a priori in which direction urbanization would influence policy. In the case of transport urban areas might need expensive commuter services and urban motorways, but rural areas might need public transport subsidies and long roads linking dispersed populations, so that per capita expenditure there might also be high.

Regions and areas within regions vary in economic characteristics, of which the most politically significant is unemployment. Northern Ireland, Scotland, Wales, the North, the North-West, and now the West Midlands have unemployment rates above the UK average. We would therefore expect expenditure under the headings of employment, industry, and social security to be higher in those regions, and the statistics for the 1970s bear this out (Short, 1981). At industry level, the distribution of factories varies in different parts of the country, so that if the government intervenes to help an industry such as shipbuilding or the car industry this will have a differential impact; indeed it may be precisely because of this concentration that government intervened in the first place. Related to the existence of variations in economic characteristics is the issue of variations between areas in the resources they can devote to public policy. To some extent in Britain this variation in resources is offset by the role of the centre in reallocation through the rate support grant (see 6.6).

Variations in *social* characteristics may be related to economic variations, though not in a uniform manner. For example, regions and social groups vary in the extent to which pupils stay on at school after the minimum leaving age. The north of England and East Anglia were well below the English average in 1982 and the south-east of England was well above.

Even policies which had as a major objective the provision of equal access reveal substantial variations between social classes and between areas. Until resource reallocation formulas were put into effect from the mid-1970s to bring about a gradual equalization of resources (difficult at a time of financial restraint), variations between regions in the National Health Service reflected differ-ences stemming from before the establishment of the NHS (Buxton and Klein, 1978). At first sight, those from manual occupations appear to receive most benefit from the National Health Service (see Table 9.1). However, once account is taken of the fact that people in those social groups tend to be of poor health, it emerges that it is non-manual and professional people who get the biggest amount of NHS resources devoted to them per capita.

On education, those from professional, employer, and mana-gerial families actually received rather less than the average per capita public expenditure up to school-leaving age (presumably because they make greater use of private education), and there is an approximation to equality of resources per capita among the other socio-economic groups, both manual and non-manual (Le Grand, 1982, ch. 4). However, post-compulsory education over-whelmingly goes to those from non-manual household backgrounds (*Social Trends*, 1986, 55), resulting in the non-manual groups receiving about 50 per cent more than the manual groups in terms of per capita public expenditure on all education. This pattern predates the decline in the real value of student support from the late 1970s; indeed, the expansion of opportunities for higher education from the early 1960s did *not* result in an increased percentage of those from manual household backgrounds going to university.

Table 9.1 Public expenditure on health care by socio-economic group (England and Wales, 1972)

Socio-economic group	Expenditure per person: % of mean	Expenditure per person reporting illness: % of mean
Professionals, employers, and managers	94	120
Intermediate and junior non-manual	104	114
Skilled manual	92	97
Semi- and unskilled manual	114	85

Source: Le Grand (1982).

Demographic variations have important implications for variations in the distribution of policy, particularly variation over time
between areas in the size and structure of the population. So, for
example, the population of Scotland was relatively static between
1961 and 1982 while that of East Anglia rose from 1.4m to 1.9m.
Variations may also result from differences in the population
structure, i.e. the proportion in each age group. At a local level,
this can be reflected in extreme form; seaside towns notoriously
have a high proportion of retired people, which can cause severe
strains on social services (East Sussex, which includes Brighton
and Eastbourne, had 28.1 per cent of its population over
retirement age, whereas only 13.8 per cent of Buckinghamshire's
population was over retirement age). New towns and new housing
estates have much higher proportions of young children in the
early phases of their development, leading to a demographic bulge
as they work their way through the system.

Even if there are variations in objective indicators of physical,
economic, social, and demographic characteristics, these will be
reflected in expenditure patterns only if these characteristics are
defined as 'needs' and are effectively translated into *political*
demands or structural biases in distribution are allowed to develop
or remain. There are a wide variety of political processes through
which such political demands are articulated, and we miss out if we
simply conflate them all under the heading of 'politics'.

One obvious source of variation is *central government political
views*. The ideology of the party in power may stress certain public
policies which tend to favour one area or social group rather than
another. Thus a Conservative government stressing the need to
build up defence will benefit areas with plants producing defence
equipment. A belief in the importance of home ownership and of
tax subsidies to support it is inevitably of benefit to those who are
able to afford to buy their own home (see Le Grand, 1982, ch. 4).
Further, within that category mortgage tax relief goes in larger
amounts to those with larger mortgages (up to £30,000) or higher
rates of tax. Policies to build urban roads and restrict passenger
transport subsidies will benefit most those who drive rather than
those who have to use public transport, and vice versa. It might
seem obvious that it will be the less well off who will benefit most
from the subsidy of public transport. In practice, most rail
subsidies benefit those in better-off occupations; subsidies to

commuter lines have been of considerable value to middle-class commuters from the suburbs and of little use to inner city areas with social problems (see Le Grand, 1982, ch. 6). Thus, even when it is not a specific objective, policies have distributional impacts, and impacts which on reflection policy-makers might accept are perverse.

Territorial justice and social justice are themselves political values and some aspects of the distribution of policies, such as regional policy and urban policy, are at least in part a reflection of a genuine feeling of a need for evenhandedness or a social justice role for government in rectifying the problems of areas or social groups with perceived disadvantages.

Secondly, there is *central government vote catching and maintenance*. It would seem rational for a political party which obtains the reins of government to allocate resources (*a*) to some extent to areas which it clearly won as a reward to its supporters; (*b*) with special concentration on marginal areas. It would seem foolish, on this rationale, to spend more on policies mainly benefiting areas where the opposing party was strong. Unfortunately, our evidence to support this hypothesis is inevitably anecdotal. A particularly blatant example occurred at the time of the Grimsby by-election, which was due to be held on 28 April 1977. On 14 April Grimsby was one of three areas raised to Development Area status to counter unemployment there. Other areas with similar unemployment were not redesignated. Labour held the seat at the by-election there while losing to the Conservatives a seat which had a much larger Labour majority. In June 1985 the Conservative government announced a reprieve from closure of a military training camp in the constituency of Brecon and Radnor during the by-election campaign there.

Arguably, much of Labour government industrial policy in Scotland in the mid-1970s, for example the rescue of Chrysler at the end of 1975, was directed at reducing the threat then thought to be posed by the SNP, particularly in the west of Scotland. Often we have to infer political manipulation on the basis of figures (or consider them a peculiar coincidence). For example, before 1976 there were 125 parliamentary constituencies containing education colleges in England (Johnston, 1979, 118–19). Various closure possibilities were considered, with a final leaked list suggesting closures affecting 34 constituencies. Although there were more marginal seats among the 125 than among all 516 English constituencies, the constituencies affected by the closures were clearly not the marginals.

Another factor influencing the distribution of policy is the *maintenance of civil order*. Obviously this affects the distribution of defence and law and order expenditure, particularly to Northern Ireland, but it can also affect other expenditures, such as on industrial subsidies. Again, this applies most obviously to Northern Ireland, but one of the considerations behind the decision to rescue the yards which had formerly been part of the Upper Clyde Shipbuilders until it was liquidated in 1971 was concern about possible civil disturbances (Hogwood, 1979b, 162). What matters is not necessarily the actual occurrence of civil disorder, but a perception that it could be a problem.

A related concern is *maintenance of support for government*. Here support is not meant in terms of party political support at the next election but 'supports' as an element in the systems model set out in 1.3. Government would have difficulty in managing a recalcitrant population. This is reflected in remarks subsequently made by John Davies, who was Secretary of State for Trade and Industry in the Conservative government at the time of the Upper Clyde Shipbuilders liquidation in 1971:

one had to face the problem that this was not an issue which could be considered on its own industrial merits, that it, in fact, affected the whole of the attitude of mind of West Central Scotland with its growing problem of unemployment. (Interviewed in Open University programme, cited in Hogwood, 1979b, 162.)

Again, it is the government's perception that matters.

Local authority political views can be of importance in producing different resource allocations to policies and the final impact of the policies. Different parties in power may mean different priorities in total expenditure or emphasis on comprehensivization or council housing. There are a number of problems in trying to assess the significance of political views at local level, including trying to separate out the effect of different parties if they alternate in power, disentangling central–local interaction, and dealing with the interaction between political and other factors. For example, areas of housing need are also more likely to vote Labour, so which factor is responsible for more expenditure on council housing? Sharpe and Newton (1984) found 'from their study of counties and county boroughs between 1960 and 1973 that parties of the left in local government did tend to spend more on redistributive and ameliorative services and that parties of the right did spend more on police and highways. They also found that the more competitive the local party system the more similar the expenditure pattern of authorities, irrespective of party control at the time. Conversely, the larger the majority a party enjoyed, the greater party ideology showed itself in quantitative terms.

Finally, we should note that the existing pattern of policy impacts may not reflect the current effect of any of the influences discussed above, but the impact of their past influence, since it may take several years to 'turn round' a policy—or no one may try.

9.4 Evaluation in practice in Britain

Unlike the United States, where up to 1 per cent of expenditure on some programmes may be set aside for research and where one 1976 estimate of the amount of federal funds going into evaluation research was around one billion dollars, there has been relatively little systematic evaluation research in Britain (see Glennerster, 1975, 191–47; Rossi, 1979). The comparison is not all to the advantage of the United States: estimates of the valid and relevant proportion of evaluation research vary between 5 per cent and 20 per cent. The bulk of evaluation research is never directly utilized in redesigning policies, though it may have more subtle effects in altering the appreciative climate in which future proposals for policy change will be considered.

The comparison is, of course, in relative terms. British government and the broader public sector does carry out evaluative research itself and commissions and consumes research conducted elsewhere. Examples of 'in-house' research from the Home Office between 1981 and 1983 include 'Evaluation of experimental schemes for providing alternative means of coping with simple drunkenness without recourse to arrest', and 'An evaluation of the voluntary small grants scheme designed to promote local voluntary activity and community self-help'. The Department of Trade and Industry has a particular interest in the evaluation of regional policy (tricky because the multiplicity of programmes directed at it over the years), both in reviewing the academic evidence

(Marquand, 1980) and in sponsoring research into both the general and specific aspects of regional policy (FMU, 1985).

One example of an evaluation commissioned by the government which fed directly into decision-making concerned the seat-belt legislation, and illustrates the use of evaluation to justify the continuation of an initially experimental programme. Parliament had approved the compulsory wearing of seat-belts for drivers and front-seat passengers for an experimental period of three years. To provide supporting evidence for making the legislation permanent from 1986, the Department of Transport commissioned an evaluation of the effectiveness of legislation (Department of Transport, 1985), including an assessment from academics at the London School of Economics. The analysis claimed that the compulsory wearing of seat-belts had prevented an estimated 200 deaths and 7,000 injuries each year. This conclusion was challenged by Adams (1985), who claimed that the reduction in deaths of drivers and front-seat passengers could be attributed to the introduction of a new type of breath-testing machine in 1983 and a consequent drop in drunken driving. He further claimed that the reported increase in deaths of rear-seat passengers, pedestrians, and cyclists could be attributed to a change in driver behaviour because the drivers felt safer wearing a seat-belt and therefore compensated by driving worse. This indicates the way in which the same basic evidence can be interpreted in different ways, particularly if more than one policy change was introduced at the same time. In a debate in January 1986 which referred both to the Department of Transport Report and the 'risk compensation' approach advocated by Adams, the House of Commons approved making the seat-belt legislation permanent.

While much less use is made of large-scale policy experiments in Britain than in the United States, an exception was a five-year electricity pricing experiment initiated in 1966 by the Electricity Council (see Ferber and Hirsch, 1982, 142–63). In each of six Area Boards, about 1,500 households were included in experiments which applied different electricity rates during the summer and winter, and during the day. The Technical and Vocational Educational Initiative launched by the Manpower Services Commission is another example of an experimental programme originally operating only in selected areas and subject to a formal evaluation (though concern with adjusting the delivery of the programme may conflict with the requirements of effective evaluation). However, as a result of policy initiatives at local level the opportunity can arise for 'happenstancical experiments' which, if carefully evaluated, can provide guidance for further diffusion. An example here would be the initially slow start to health centres in England and Wales, which provided an opportunity for studying early examples (see Hall *et al.*, 1975, ch. 11).

The MSC has commissioned a number of evaluations of its programmes. This reflects both a greater focus on clearly designated programmes in the American manner, and the initially short-term or experimental nature of many of the programmes, so that evaluations could be used to justify continuation or extension of the MSC's activities.

Much of the research commissioned by government is, however, *ad hoc* and fragmentary in nature. Arguably, systematic evaluation requires the accumulation of evidence. Relatively little of the research conducted or commissioned by government is evaluatively orientated; it is mainly concerned with demand or need. Some research originally sponsored by government may turn out to be embarrassing to it; for example, the Centre for Environmental Studies had its funding withdrawn by the Department of the Environment following research findings which by implication were critical of existing policy; the Black Report on Inequalities in Health, which showed the failure of health policy to achieve a major objective, was not published in the usual way (though it was subsequently published by Penguin).

There is an obvious link with academic research in that much of the government-sponsored research is commissioned from academics (though management consultants are also commissioned). One potential problem facing academics accepting such commissions is whether the terms of reference restrict them from tackling what they feel are the intellectually interesting questions or from using what they feel are the most reputable methods (Bulmer, 1982). Much policy research conducted by academics is independent of direct government sponsorship (though some is funded through the Economic and Social Research Council). However, much of social science research is not concerned with policy issues in an immediate sense, and even where it is it may not constitute a systematic evaluation of the effectiveness of government policy. One example of academic evaluation of British social policies on one criterion only, the promotion of equality, is Le Grand (1982), who concluded that health, education, housing, and transport policies had all failed on this criterion.

British academia, perhaps because of the lack of massive funding as in the United States, has not geared itself up to establish a specifically policy evaluation focus. In the United States evaluation has become a specialism in itself, with a large number of books and journals on evaluation; the results both in terms of useful findings and intellectual interest have, however, been mixed.

From the central government perspective, Whitehall departments are often cut off from the organizations actually delivering the policy. Inspectorates, for example in education, give departments direct access to the real world of policy delivery. Inspectors can collect information (normally fairly fast), for example, on the extent and nature of difficulties faced by schools teaching immigrant children, or the extent and nature of violence in schools. However, as these examples show, this may be a useful method of problem definition and of monitoring the delivery of a policy, but it is not designed to tackle more fundamental evaluations of policy, which would require the purposes of, for example, school education to be clearly set out in the first place.

One of the traditional roles which Parliament is supposed to carry out is the scrutiny of government activity. Its capacity for doing so has been strengthened by the transformation of the Exchequer and Audit Department into the National Audit Office in 1984 and by the establishment in 1979 of specialist committees of the Commons covering most aspects of government activity (see Drewry, 1985). The Public Accounts Committee and the specialist select committees do indeed carry out useful though spasmodic and unsystematic scrutinies of particular policies (incidentally generating much published evidence which may be used by academics). Committees are, however, often concerned with the efficiency of the delivery of policies (i.e. monitoring) rather than with the evaluation of policy designs. Committees are especially important for spotting failures rather than successes. The reports of committees are rarely debated on the floor of the House of Commons, but may have an indirect impact through press coverage and because civil servants do appear to treat their committee appearances with some apprehension (see also 3.7).

The monitoring and evaluative roles of parliamentary committees would be enhanced if periodically but systematically they reviewed policies (or their replacements) which had been the subject of previous reviews.

In terms of policy delivery at local level and broader issues of central–local relations, the establishment of the Audit Commission in 1983 led to a number of sharply critical reports not only of some aspects of 'waste' in local authority policy delivery but of the central government's system for distributing grants to local government and of central government housing policy. The Commission appears to have taken a robust and independent perspective, though it has no means of ensuring that its policy recommendations (as opposed to penalizing illegal behaviour by councillors) are followed through. For the most part the Commission's reports are concerned with cost savings rather than with the purposes of policies or alternative methods for achieving them.

There is a considerable amount of information available, some of it published, including by the government, about results associated with particular policies. This might seem to open the way to evaluation through measurement by results. However, the example of education illustrates the problems of using such information. The delivery of education policy is only one of the impacts on patterns of examination results (home environment being another major one). Further, consideration of examination results focuses attention on what is measurable rather than on what (else) might be important. This again leads us back to the thorny problem: what are the objectives of education (or any other policy)? By what criteria can we judge success in meeting these objectives? Which of the criteria are measurable?

Britain has been in the forefront of producing policy-relevant social statistics (see Carley, 1981). The original aspirations of those promoting the development of social indicators included the hope that these could be used in a system of social accounting, which would include the measurement of the results of policy— just as the success of a firm can be measured by its profitability. However, these aspirations have to confront the difficulty of separating out influences on the indicator other than the programme which is of interest. That said, health indicators have actually been used in Britain to make changes at the margin in health expenditure.

Media, group, and public interest, whether through investigative journalism or symbolic 'events' like the Year of the Disabled, may involve or may trigger investigation of existing policies. However, much of this coverage is likely to be anecdotal and concerned with whether the policy is being correctly delivered rather than reappraisal of policy design.

There are a number of avenues for the redress of grievances felt by citizens, through MPs, the various ombudsmen, and the courts (see chapter 8). However, these *ad hoc* investigations fail by their nature to find successes or identify systematic failures of policy design.

Finally, one might look at the behaviour and attitudes of the policy's target group as one form of client or customer evaluation. This raises the broader question of whether the client's self-perceived interests should be a criterion for evaluation. One crude form of such client assessment is where the target groups fail to take advantage of policy outputs directed at them (e.g. 'difficult to let' council housing). At the extreme, potential clients may 'exit' from or decline to take advantage of a policy output even when it is normally free, as when private education or health care is purchased. However, 'exit' as an indicator does not constitute an evaluation of a policy as a whole, though perhaps constituting an indication of a degree of dissatisfaction with a programme which should therefore be subject to systematic evaluation.

The available evidence suggests that there is substantial dis-satisfaction with the service provided by the 'civil service' and 'local government' in general terms (Goodhardt, 1985, 43–4). When questions are asked about specific public services the level of satisfaction, with the exception of British Rail, tends to be higher (see Table 9.2).

Satisfaction is, of course, a relative rather than an absolute attitude, and Table 9.3 shows that few people are 'very satisfied' with the National Health Service; even fewer were 'very dissatisfied' (Bosanquet, 1984). There are considerable variations between regions in the level of satisfaction, with 34 per cent dissatisfied in Greater London and only 43 per cent satisfied, while in Scotland only 18 per cent were dissatisfied and 66 per cent satisfied. Interestingly, with the exception of out-patient treatment, there was a much lower level of dissatisfaction with particular services in the NHS than there was with the NHS as a whole (see Table 9.4).

Table 9.2 Citizen satisfaction with public services (%)

	Satisfied	Not satisfied
Local doctor	84	13
Telephone service	80	16
Police	79	17
Postal service	75	22
BBC	66	30
(Independent TV and radio	76	21)
Civil service	53	42
British Rail	52	42
Local government	49	47

Source: Goodhardt (1985, 44).

Table 9.3 Degrees of citizen satisfaction with the NHS (%)

Very satisfied	11
Quite satisfied	44
Neither	20
Quite dissatisfied	18
Very dissatisfied	7

Source: Bosanquet (1984, 86).

Table 9.4 Percentage expressing dissatisfaction with way in which particular parts of the NHS are run

Local doctors or GPs	13
NHS dentists	10
Health visitors	6
District nurses	2
Being in hospital as an in-patient	7
Attending hospital as an out-patient	21

Source: Bosanquet (1984, 87).

Of course, where there is dissatisfaction, different people may be dissatisfied for opposite reasons, as is illustrated by Table 9.5, which shows that a majority are not happy with the level of benefits for the unemployed (Bosanquet, 1984). However, they are split between those who think benefits are too low and cause hardship (46 per cent of the total) and those who think benefits are too high and discourage people from finding jobs. Not surprisingly, there are substantial differences between supporters of different

Table 9.5 Views about benefits for the unemployed (%)

	Total	Cons.	Alliance	Labour
Benefits for the unemployed are:				
Too low and cause hardship	46	30	50	64
Too high and discourage people				
from finding jobs	35	50	26	23
Neither	13	13	17	9

Source: Bosanquet (1984, 82).

political parties in the way they split on their views. There are also considerable differences in view according to age (61 per cent of those under 25 thought that benefits were too low but only 32 per cent of those 65 and older did so) and employment status (76 per cent of unemployed thought benefits were too low, but only 46 per cent of employees and 26 per cent of self-employed thought so). Bosanquet (1984, 82) notes that there appears to be a much greater division of attitudes in the population towards the level of cash benefits than there is towards social services in kind. In such circumstances it is obviously difficult to come up with an 'objective' evaluation of how well a policy is working.

9.5 An end to complacency?

In chapter 2 it was concluded that while a crisis would help to place an issue on the agenda, it was not the only route by which an issue could receive serious political attention in Britain. In chapter 3 we saw that considerable effort went into processing issues both between government and groups and within Whitehall, though the emphasis is largely on achieving a politically acceptable solution rather than necessarily a rigorously analysed one. Chapter 4 pointed out that few issues were discussed or decided by the full Cabinet, while the following chapter showed that despite an increased role in shaping public policy parliament's role was largely to legitimate rather than make policy itself. Chapter 6 showed how policy can be continuously remade through budgetary decisions but suggested that public expenditure decision-making now focused primarily on financing public expenditure rather than delivering specified volumes of public policy. Chapter 7 showed that for many types of policy creative shaping takes place during the process of implementation, but that many policy failures do occur at implementation stage, sometimes over a period of decades, suggesting that government is often complacent about what happens to policies once they have been legislated on. In recent years, as chapter 8 showed, government's complacency has often been rudely shaken by the willingness of both British and European courts to review and often overrule the actions of ministers or other public authorities.

The material in this final chapter has drawn attention to the way in which government is often ignorant about the impact of its policies, that those policies often have substantial distributional impacts, sometimes intended and sometimes unintended and perverse, and that up to the mid-1980s there was a lack of systematic evaluation of the whole range of government policies. This implies a considerable degree of complacency about just what public policy achieves. The reason why the heading to this final section raises the question of whether this complacency might be coming to an end is that sections of the government machinery are themselves aware of these problems and are making attempts to pursue more systematic and effective evaluation of government policies. A report from the Financial Management Unit (FMU) of the Manpower and Personnel Office in the Cabinet Office and the Treasury submitted in January 1985 neatly summarizes many of the deficiencies of the British policy process in practice:

valuable progress is being made and good practice established in assessing the performance of programmes but there is scope for very considerable further improvement. In many areas:

—policy aims or purposes, where stated, are not expressed with sufficient precision to allow assessment of whether these purposes are being achieved or not;

—assumptions about the nature of the problems or conditions with which the policy is intended to deal are not made explicit and therefore not systematically tracked to see whether the assumptions remain valid; and

—assumptions about the link between policy and impacts on the world outside are not made explicit and therefore not systematically tested.

The Joint Management Unit (JMU), which replaced the FMU in February 1985, had as one of its main tasks the development of more systematic evaluation within British government. The JMU is itself something of a shoestring operation, with one under-secretary, one assistant secretary, and one principal, and with other co-ordinating tasks besides evaluation. The JMU has suggested a limited and developmental approach to evaluation, believing that government does not know how to do evaluation in many areas. It is also recognized that there can be particular difficulty in evaluating policies which central government is not itself directly responsible for delivering.

The FMU report had argued that the best time to build in provision for evaluation was when options were being considered and a decision made. The JMU followed this up by proposing that provision for evaluation should be *mandatory* for all new policy initiatives and for all policy reviews, however carried out, and should be *encouraged* for Public Expenditure Survey bids, which currently focus on resource inputs (see 8.2), and for current programmes and policies. The mandatory requirement for new initiatives and policy reviews was agreed by ministers. In order to implement these recommendations a requirement was introduced in 1985 that all cabinet papers (including those going to cabinet committees) containing proposals with value for money implications should state: (1) What is to be achieved? (2) By when? (3) At what cost? (4) How is improvement to be measured? Treasury expenditure divisions have the power to prevent a paper going to Cabinet if it does not cover these points, though they have the discretion to allow it through even if it does not. However, as we saw in chapter 4, far from all government decisions are put up for formal discussion within Cabinet or cabinet committee.

In terms of *how* evaluation should be conducted, the JMU is proceeding by commissioning of case studies of current evaluation in practice within government. By searching for examples of current good practice, the JMU can point out to departments that good evaluation can be done since it is already being done elsewhere in Whitehall. The JMU is deliberately refraining from public criticism (even within Whitehall) of what it considers to be inadequacies of evaluations which have been conducted. Based partly on the experience of examples of current good practice, a guide to evaluation will be produced and seminars held for policy managers. It can be seen that the operation is very much an 'insider job', with it being envisaged that departments themselves would carry out most of the evaluations. The initiative on evaluation itself came from inside Whitehall and was introduced in a publicly unheralded way; this is likely to increase its chances of securing acceptance throughout Whitehall.

However, there are a number of difficulties and potential dangers with the proposed drive to improved evaluation in British government, some relating to the specific form of this initiative and some problems intrinsic to the nature of evaluation. First, it is doubtful whether the skills necessary for proper evaluation are widespread within Whitehall. It appears that what may count as acceptable reviews of policy under the proposed system may not always meet the standards aspired to by the policy analysis approach to evaluation—but then they are rarely achieved in the United States anyway (see Hogwood and Gunn, 1984, ch. 12).

Secondly, there are potential dangers in allowing departments to evaluate their own proposals or to propose how they should be evaluated; it will be very difficult for them to resist the temptation to propose evaluation criteria or methods which show the department in the best possible light; some form of external audit of the departmental evaluations, either from an expanded JMU within Whitehall or the National Audit Office, would help to overcome this problem.

Thirdly, by concentrating evaluation of new initiatives and policy reviews there is a danger, as with the PES system (see 6.2), that the great bulk of programmes will roll ahead for years to come without being evaluated. However, it is simply impracticable to evaluate all programmes at once, so a long-term perspective is inevitable.

Fourthly, evaluation itself costs money (the JMU cites the half of 1 per cent cost of evaluating one programme); evaluation may save money by drawing attention to ineffective programmes, but it may also lead to more effective programmes at the same cost or even more expensive ones. The idea of evaluation is being promoted at a time of financial and manpower restraints.

Finally, Whitehall has seen off a number of policy analysis initiatives before, including the Central Policy Review Staff and Programme Analysis and Review (PAR) (see Gray and Jenkins, 1985). The JMU is aware of these precedents and is trying to develop a management style which will ensure understanding and acceptance of the change and avoid defensive reactions and token acceptance by departments.

There are a number of more general problems in making

increased use of formal evaluations, such as lack of information in a suitable form, ambiguous or multiple objectives, separating programme impact from other influences, identifying side effects and assessing whether it is meaningful to look at the impact of a single programme in isolation (see Hogwood and Gunn, 1984, 222–8). Further, the monitoring and evaluation of public policy may be politically sensitive if they are perceived by those delivering the policy as a threat to individuals or to preferred methods of delivering policy.

So Whitehall is getting itself into a messy business in attempting to improve the evaluation of policy. Success, if it occurs, will consist of steady improvements over a decade rather than an instant brave new policy world. In particular it should be borne in mind that the requirement from 1985 onwards was for provision for evaluation to be built in; the evaluations might not be completed until the programme had been running for some years, and any resulting policy change might take even longer to be introduced.

There are a number of pointers to watch for to see if the initiative does lead to a new style of policy-making. First, if a report on developments in evaluation is published in 1987, this will mark a public commitment. Secondly, will evaluation reports be published, whether at the initiative of Whitehall or under pressure from parliamentary committees? If not, then evaluation can be seen as a development within the existing pattern where the meaningful shaping of options on many issues takes place in private discussions. Finally, by the early 1990s there ought to be indications that policies are being adjusted in the light of evaluation findings.

If none of these developments materialize then British government will be seen to be doubly complacent, since having identified its previous complacency about the outcomes of policy it will be complacent enough to continue in this state.

References

Adams, J. (1985), Seat belts, drink and statistics, *Financial Times*, 20 December 1985.

Alexander, A. (1982), *Local Government since Reorganisation*. London: Allen & Unwin.

Anderson, J. E. (1979), *Public Policy Making*, 2nd ed. New York: Nelson.

Baldwin, N. D. J. (1985), A new professionalism and a more independent House. In P. Norton (ed.), *Parliament in the 1980s*. Oxford: Basil Blackwell.

Barber, J. (1976), *Who Makes British Foreign Policy?* Milton Keynes: Open University Press.

Barker, A. (1982), *Quangos in Britain*. London: Macmillan.

Barnett, J. (1982), *Inside the Treasury*. London: André Deutsch.

Barrett, S. and C. Fudge (1981), *Policy and Action*. London: Methuen.

Bell, J. (1983), *Policy Arguments in Judicial Decisions*. Oxford: Oxford University Press.

Benn, T. (1980), Manifestos and mandarins. In Royal Institute of Public Administration, *Policy and Practice: The Experience of Government*. London: Royal Institute of Public Administration.

Bennett, R. J. (1982), *Central Grants to Local Governments*. Cambridge: Cambridge University Press.

Benson, J. K. (1982), A framework for policy analysis. In D. L. Rogers and D. A. Whetten (eds.), *Interorganizational Coordination: Theory, Research, and Implementation*. Ames, Iowa: Iowa University Press.

Booth, S. A. S., D. C. Pitt, and W. J. Money (1982), Organizational redundancy? A critical appraisal of the GEAR project, *Public Administration*, 60, 56–72.

Bosanquet, N. (1984), Social policy and the welfare state. In R. Jowell and C. Airey (eds.), *British Social Attitudes: The 1984 Report*. Aldershot: Gower.

Brookes, S. K., A. G. Jordan, R. H. Kimber, and J. J. Richardson (1976), The growth of the environment as a political issue in Britain, *British Journal of Political Science*, 6, 245–55.

Bruce-Gardyne, J. and N. Lawson (1976), *The Power Game*. London: Macmillan.

Bulmer, M. (ed.) (1980), *Social Research and Royal Commissions*. London: Allen & Unwin.

—— (1982), *The Uses of Social Research: Social Investigation in Public Policy-making*. London: Allen & Unwin.

—— (1983), *Royal Commissions and Departmental Committees of Inquiry*. London: Royal Institute of Public Administration.

Burch, M. (1983), Mrs Thatcher's approach to leadership in government: 1979–June 1983, *Parliamentary Affairs*, 36, 399–416.

—— and B. Wood (1983), *Public Policy in Britain*. Oxford: Martin Robertson.

Burton, I. and G. Drewry (1983), Public legislation: a survey of the session 1980/81, *Parliamentary Affairs*, 36, 436–59.

—— —— (1985), Public legislation: a survey of the sessions 1981/82 and 1982/83, *Parliamentary Affairs*, 38, 219–52.

Butler, D. and D. Stokes (1969), *Political Change in Britain*. Harmondsworth, Middlesex: Penguin.

—— and A. Sloman (1980), *British Political Facts 1900–79*, 5th ed. London: Macmillan.

Butler, Lord and Lord Crowther-Hunt (1965), Reflections on cabinet government, *The Listener*, 16 September 1965. Reprinted in V. Herman and J. Alt (eds.), *Cabinet Studies: A Reader*. London: Macmillan, 1975.

Buxton, M. J. and R. E. Klein (1978), *Allocating Health Resources: A Commentary on the Report of the Resource Allocation Working Party*, Research Paper Number 3, Royal Commission on the National Health Service. London: HMSO.

Campbell, C. (1983), *Governments under Stress: Political Executives and Key Bureaucrats in Washington, London and Ottawa*. Toronto: University of Toronto Press.

Cardona, G. (1981), One step ahead of 'Yes Minister', *The Times*, 11 December 1981.

Carley, M. (1981), *Social Measurement and Social Indicators*. London: Allen & Unwin.

Cartwright, T. J. (1974), *Royal Commissions and Departmental Committees in Britain*. London: University of London Press.

Central Policy Review Staff (1975), *A Joint Framework for Social Policies*. London: HMSO.

Chapman, R. A. (ed.) (1973), *The Role of Commissions in Policy-Making*. London: Allen & Unwin.

Clarke, R. (1971), *New Trends in Government*, Civil Service College Studies no. 1. London: HMSO.

Clayton, H. (1985), Injustices that go unresolved, *The Times*, 27 November 1985.

Clutterbuck, R. (1985), Judicial review of executive action: the approach of the courts, *Catalyst*, 1(4), 31–40.

Cmnd. 4506 (1970), *The Reorganization of Central Government*. London: HMSO.

Cmnd. 9702 (1986), *The Government's Expenditure Plans 1986–87 to 1988–89*. London: HMSO.

Cobb, R. W. and C. D. Elder (1972), *Participation in American Politics: The Dynamics of Agenda-Building*. Baltimore: Johns Hopkins.

Coplin, W. D. and M. K. O'Leary (1978), *Analyzing Public Policy Issues*, Learning Packages in the Policy Sciences PS 17. Croton-on-Hudson, NY: Policy Studies Associates.

Crenson, M. (1971), *The Unpolitics of Air Pollution*. Baltimore: Johns Hopkins.

Crossman, R. (1975), *The Diaries of a Cabinet Minister: Volume One: Minister of Housing 1964–66*. London: Hamish Hamilton and Jonathan Cape.

—— (1976), *The Diaries of a Cabinet Minister: Volume Two: Lord President of the Council and Leader of the House of Commons 1966–68*. London: Hamish Hamilton and Jonathan Cape.

Danziger, J. N. (1978), *Making Budgets: Public Resource Allocation*. Beverly Hills, Calif.: Sage.

Davies, M. (1985), *Politics of Pressure*. London: BBC.

Dell, E. (1973), *Political Responsibility and Industry*. London: Allen & Unwin.

Department of Education and Science (1983), *Statistical Bulletin 16/83: Schools Standards and Spending*. London: Department of Education and Science.

Department of Transport (1985), *Compulsory Seat Belt Wearing*. London: HMSO.

Downs, A. (1972), Up and down with ecology—the issue attention cycle, *The Public Interest*, 28, 38–50.

Downs, S. J. (1985), Select committees: experiment and establishment. In P. Norton (ed.), *Parliament in the 1980s*. Oxford: Basil Blackwell.

Drewry, G. (1981), Legislation. In S. A. Walkland and M. Ryle (eds.), *The Commons Today*. London: Fontana.

—— (ed.) (1985), *The New Select Committees*. Oxford: Oxford University Press.

Dunleavy, P. (1982), Quasi-governmental sector professionalism: some implications for public policy-making in Britain. In A. Barker (ed.), *Quangos in Britain*. London: Macmillan.

Easton, D. (1965), *A Systems Analysis of Political Life*. Chicago: Chicago University Press.

Englefield, D. (1985), *Whitehall and Westminster*. London: Longman.

Fay, S. and H. Young (1976), *The Fall of Heath*. London: The Sunday Times.

Ferber, R. and W. Z. Hirsch (1982), *Social Experimentation and Economic Policy*. Cambridge: Cambridge University Press.

FMU (1985), *Policy Work and the FMI*. London: HM Treasury.

Giddings, P. (1985), What has been achieved? In G. Drewry (ed.), *The New Select Committees*. Oxford: Oxford University Press.

Glennerster, H. (1975), *Social Service Budgets and Social Policy: British and American Experience*. London: Allen & Unwin.

Goodhardt, G. (1985), Prices, incomes and consumer issues. In R. Jowell and S. Witherspoon (eds.), *British Social Attitudes: The 1985 Report*. Aldershot: Gower.

Gowing, M. (1974), *Independence and Deterrence: Britain and Atomic Energy, 1945–52: Volume 1: Policy Making*. London: Macmillan.

Granada Television (1973), *The State of the Nation: Parliament*. London and Manchester: Granada Television.

—— (1977), *Inside British Politics*. London and Manchester: Granada Television.

Gray, A. and B. Jenkins (1982), Policy analysis in British central government: the experience of PAR, *Public Administration*, 60, 429–50.

—— and W. Jenkins (1985), *Administrative Politics in British Government*. Brighton: Wheatsheaf.

Greenwood, R. (1983), Changing patterns of budgeting in English local government, *Public Administration*, 61, 149–68.

Griffith, J. A. G. (1974), *Parliamentary Scrutiny of Government Bills*. London: Allen & Unwin.

—— (1985), *The Politics of the Judiciary*, 3rd ed. London: Fontana.

Gunn, L. A. (1978), Why is implementation so difficult? *Management Services in Government*, 33, 169–76.

Gwyn, W. B. (1982), The ombudsman in Britain: a qualified success in government reform, *Public Administration*, 60, 177–95.

Hall, P., H. Land, R. Parker, and A. Webb (1975), *Change, Choice and Conflict in Social Policy*. London: Heinemann.

Ham, C. and M. Hill (1984), *The Policy Process in the Modern Capitalist State*. Brighton: Wheatsheaf.

Hambleton, R. (1978), *Policy Planning and Local Government*. London: Hutchinson.

Harlow, C. and R. Rawlings (1984), *Law and Administration*. London: Weidenfeld & Nicolson.

Harrison, A. (1984), Economic policy and expectations. In R. Jowell and

C. Airey (eds.), *British Social Attitudes: The 1984 Report*. Aldershot: Gower.

Haywood, S. C. and H. J. Elcock (1982), Regional Health Authorities: regional government or central agencies? In B. W. Hogwood and M. Keating (eds.), *Regional Government in England*. Oxford: Oxford University Press.

HC 69 (1975–6), *Select Committee on Expenditure: 1st Report: The Financing of Public Expenditure*. London: HMSO.

HC 229 (1985–6), *National Health Service: Preventive Medicine*. London: HMSO.

Headey, B. (1974), *British Cabinet Ministers*. London: Allen & Unwin.

Heclo, H. (1978), Issue networks and the executive establishment. In A. King (ed.), *The New American Political System*. Washington DC: American Enterprise Institute.

—— and A. Wildavsky (1981), *The Private Government of Public Money*, 2nd ed. London: Macmillan.

Hennessy, P. (1980), Committee decided Callaghan economic policy, *The Times*, 17 March 1980.

—— (1982), Document access inquiry troubles Whitehall, *The Times*, 13 November 1982.

—— (1983a), Is tradition of cabinet government on the wane? *The Times*, 16 May 1983.

—— (1983b), Shades of a Home Counties Boudicca, *The Times*, 17 May 1983.

—— (1984), Whitehall's real power house, *The Times*, 30 April 1984.

—— (1985a), The quality of cabinet government in Britain, *Policy Studies*, 6(2), 15–45.

—— (1985b), The secret world of cabinet committees, *Social Studies Review*, 1(2), 7–11.

—— (1986), Why Heseltine finally snapped, *The Times*, 10 January 1986.

Hogwood, B. W. (1979a), Analysing industrial policy: a multi-perspective approach, *Public Administration Bulletin*, 29, 18–42.

—— (1979b), *Government and Shipbuilding*. Farnborough, Hants: Saxon House.

—— (1982), In search of accountability: the territorial dimension of industrial policy, *Public Administration Bulletin*, 38, 22–39.

—— and L. A. Gunn (1984), *Policy Analysis for the Real World*. Oxford: Oxford University Press.

—— and T. T. Mackie (1985), The United Kingdom: decision-sifting in a secret garden. In T. T. Mackie and B. W. Hogwood (eds.), *Unlocking the Cabinet: Cabinet Structures in Comparative Perspective*. London: Sage.

—— and B. G. Peters (1983), *Policy Dynamics*. Brighton: Wheatsheaf and New York: St Martin's Press.

—— —— (1985), *The Pathology of Public Policy*. Oxford: Oxford University Press.

Hood, C. (1976), *The Limits of Administration*. London: Wiley.

—— (1981), Axeperson, spare that quango . . . In C. Hood and M. Wright (eds.), *Big Government in Hard Times*. Oxford: Martin Robertson.

—— (1983), *The Tools of Government*. London: Macmillan.

Howell, D. (1970), *A New Style of Government*. London: Conservative Political Centre.

Hughes, R. (1985a), A string of court rulings for future disputes, *Financial Times*, 4 March 1985.

—— (1985b), Surge of litigation puts pressure on European Court, *Financial Times*, 13 December 1985.

Irwin, A. (1985), *Risk and the Control of Technology*. Manchester: Manchester University Press.

Jenkins, R. (1971), On being a minister, *Sunday Times*, 17 January 1971. Reprinted in V. Herman and J. Alt (eds.), *Cabinet Studies: A Reader*. London: Macmillan, 1975.

Johnston, R. J. (1979), *Political, Electoral and Spatial Systems*. Oxford: Oxford University Press.

Johnstone, D. (1975), *A Tax Shall be Charged*. London: HMSO.

Jones, G. (1975), Development of the cabinet. In W. Thornhill (ed.), *The Modernization of British Government*. London: Pitman.

Jordan, A. G. (1981), Iron triangles, woolly corporatism, or elastic nets: images of the policy process, *Journal of Public Policy*, 1, 95–123.

—— (1985), Consultation processes as de facto legislation: Britain. Paper presented to International Political Science Association World Congress. Paris, July 1985.

—— and J. Richardson (1982), The British policy style or the logic of negotiation? In J. J. Richardson (ed.), *Policy Styles in Western Europe*. London: Allen & Unwin.

—— —— and R. H. Kimber (1977), The origins of the Water Act of 1973, *Public Administration*, 55, 317–34.

Kaufman, G. (1980), *How to be a Minister*. London: Sidgwick & Jackson.

Kimber, R. *et al.* (1974), The Deposit of Poisonous Waste Act 1972: a case of government by reaction? *Public Law*, Autumn 1974, 148–219.

King, A. (1976), The problem of overload. In A. King (ed.), *Why is Britain Becoming Harder to Govern?* London: BBC.

Kogan, M. (1971), *The Politics of Education: Edward Boyle and Anthony Crosland in Conversation with Maurice Kogan*. Harmondsworth, Middlesex: Penguin.

Larkey, P. D., C. Stolp, and M. Winer (1981), Theorizing about the growth of government, *Journal of Public Policy*, 1, 157–220.

Le Grand, J. (1982), *The Strategy of Equality: Redistribution and the Social Services*. London: Allen & Unwin.

Lock, G. (1985), Resources and operations of select committees: a survey of the statistics. In G. Drewry (ed.), *The New Select Committees*. Oxford: Oxford University Press.

Lukes, S. (1974), *Power*. London: Macmillan.

Mackintosh, J. P. (1977), *The British Cabinet*. London: Stevens.

March, J. G. and J. P. Olsen (1976), *Ambiguity and Choice in Organizations*. Bergen: Universitetsforlaget.

Marquand, J. (1980), *Measuring the Effects and Costs of Regional Incentives*, Government Economic Service Working Paper no. 32. London: Department of Industry.

Meadows, J. (1985), The changing pattern of central–local fiscal relations 1979–83. In P. Jackson (ed.), *Implementing Government Policy Initiatives: The Thatcher Administration 1979–83*. London: RIPA.

Moon, J. and J. J. Richardson (1984a), Policy-making with a difference? the Technical and Vocational Initiative, *Public Administration*, 62, 23–33.

—— —— (1984b), The unemployment industry, *Policy and Politics*, 12, 391–411.

Morris, J. (1984), There to rule on the law—not to make it, *The Times*, 23 November 1984.

Morrison, H. (1954), *Government and Parliament: A View from the Inside*. Oxford: Oxford University Press.

Niskanen, W. A. (1973), *Bureaucracy: Servant or Master?* London: Institute of Economic Affairs.

Norton, P. (1980), *Dissension in the House of Commons 1974–1979*. Oxford: Oxford University Press.

—— (1985), Behavioural changes: backbench independence in the 1980s. In P. Norton (ed.), *Parliament in the 1980s*. Oxford: Basil Blackwell.

—— (1985b), Appendix 1: Recent structural and procedural changes in the House of Commons. In P. Norton (ed.), *Parliament in the 1980s*. Oxford: Basil Blackwell.

Page, B. (1978), The secret constitution, *New Statesman*, 21 July 1978.

Parker, R. A. (1967), Social administration and scarcity: the problem of rationing, *Social Work*, 24(2), 9–14. Reprinted in E. Butterworth and R. Holman, *Social Welfare in Modern Britain*. London: Fontana, 1975.

Pliatzky, L. (1982), *Getting and Spending: Public Expenditure, Employment and Inflation*. Oxford: Basil Blackwell.

—— (1985), *Paying and Choosing: The Intelligent Person's Guide to the Mixed Economy*. Oxford: Basil Blackwell.

Pollitt, C. (1977), The Public Expenditure Survey, *Public Administration*, 55, 127–42.

Polsby, N. W. (1980), *Community Power and Political Theory*. New Haven: Yale University Press.

Pressman, J. L. and A. B. Wildavsky (1973), *Implementation*. Berkeley: University of California Press.

Prest, A. R. (1980), Royal Commission reporting. In M. Bulmer (ed.), *Social Research and Royal Commissions*. London: Allen & Unwin, 180–8.

Prison Reform Trust (1986), *The Bail Lottery*. London: Prison Reform Trust.

Randall, G. W., K. W. Lomas, and T. Newton (1973), Area distribution of resources in Coventry, *Local Government Finance*, 11, 396–400.

Rhodes, G. (1975), *Committees of Inquiry*. London: Allen & Unwin.

Rhodes, R. (1981), *Control and Power in Central–Local Government Relations*. Farnborough: Gower.

—— (1985), Power-dependence, policy communities and intergovernmental networks, *Public Administration Bulletin*, 49, 4–31.

Richardson, J. J. and A. G. Jordan (1979), *Governing under Pressure*. Oxford: Martin Robertson.

—— and J. Moon (1984), The politics of unemployment in Britain, *Political Quarterly*, 55, 29–37.

Riddell, P. (1985), Wakeham marshals the government patronage corps, *Financial Times*, 26 June 1985.

Ridley, F. F. (1984), The citizen against authority: British approaches to the redress of grievances, *Parliamentary Affairs*, 37, 1–32.

RIPA (1980), *Policy and Practice: The Experience of Government*. London: RIPA.

Robinson, A. and C. Sandford (1983), *Tax Policy-Making in the United Kingdom*. London: Heinemann.

—— (1985a), The Treasury and Civil Service Committee. In G. Drewry (ed.), *The New Select Committees*. Oxford: Oxford University Press.

—— (1985b), The financial work of the new select committees. In G. Drewry (ed.), *The New Select Committees*. Oxford: Oxford University Press.

Rose, R. (1973), Comparing public policy: an overview, *European Journal of Political Research*, 1, 67–94.

—— (1980), Government against subgovernments: a European perspective. In R. Rose and E. Suleiman (eds.), *Presidents and Prime Ministers*. Washington DC: American Enterprise Institute.

—— (1984), *Do Parties Make a Difference?* 2nd ed. London: Macmillan.

Rossi, P. H. (1979), Past, present and future prospects of evaluation research. In L.-E. Datta and R. Perloff (eds), *Improving Evaluations*. Beverly Hills, Calif.: Sage.

Rush, M. (1985), The Education, Science and Arts Committee. In G. Drewry (ed.), *The New Select Committees*. Oxford: Oxford University Press.

Rutherford, M. (1985), Human rights: time for Britain to catch up, *Financial Times*, 13 December 1985.

Sandbach, F. (1980), *Environment, Ideology and Policy*. Oxford: Basil Blackwell.

Schwartz, J. E. (1980), Exploring a new role in policy making: the British House of Commons in the 1970s, *American Political Science Review*, 74, 23–37.

Seldon, A. (1981), *Churchill's Indian Summer: The Conservative Government, 1951–55*. London: Hodder & Stoughton.

Seymour-Ure, C. (1971), The disintegration of the cabinet and the neglected question of cabinet reform, *Parliamentary Affairs*, 24, 196–207.

—— (1984), British 'war cabinets' in limited wars: Korea, Suez and the Falklands, *Public Administration*, 62, 181–200.

Sharpe, L. J. and K. Newton (1984), *Does Politics Matter?* Oxford: Oxford University Press.

—— (1985), Central coordination and the policy network, *Political Studies*, 33, 361–81.

Shell, D. R. (1985), The House of Lords and the Thatcher government, *Parliamentary Affairs*, 38, 16–32.

Short, J. (1981), *Public Expenditure and Taxation in the UK Regions*. Farnborough: Gower.

Solesbury, W. (1976), The environmental agenda, *Public Administration*, 54, 379–97.

Stacey, F. (1975), *British Government 1966–1975: Years of Reform*. Oxford: Oxford University Press.

Stringer, J. K. and J. J. Richardson (1980), Managing the political agenda: problem definition and policy making in Britain, *Parliamentary Affairs*, 23, 23–39.

Thain, C. (1985), The education of the Treasury: the Medium-Term Financial Strategy 1980–84, *Public Administration*, 63, 261–85.

Theakston, K. (1984), Junior ministers in British government. Ph.D. thesis, London School of Economics.

Treasury (1983a), Making a budget—1: the decisions, *Economic Progress Report*, 153, 1–3.

—— (1983b), Parliament's new 'Supply' procedure, *Economic Progress Report*, 154, 1–2.

Turner, P. W. (1980), The implementation of government policy with particular reference to education and schools. Paper delivered to Public Administration Committee Annual Conference, 1–3 September 1980, University of York.

Vickers, G. (1965), *The Art of Judgement*. London: Chapman & Hall.

Walker, P. Gordon (1972), *The Cabinet*, rev. ed. Glasgow and London: Collins and Fontana.

Walkland, S. A. (1968), *The Legislative Process in Great Britain*. London: Allen & Unwin.

Wallace, H. (1984), Implementation across national boundaries. In D. Lewis and H. Wallace (eds.), *Policies into Practice*. London: Heinemann.

Wallace, W. (1975), *The Foreign Policy Process in Britain*. London: RIIA.

Ward, T. (1985), The implications and problems of planning public expenditure on a cash basis. Paper presented to ESRC public sector group, London, April 1985.

Weiner, L. (1976), Future scanning for trade groups and companies, *Harvard Business Review*, September/October, 14 and 174–6.

Whittington, G. (1974), *Company Taxation and Dividends*. London: Institute for Fiscal Studies.

Wildavsky, A. (1973), If planning is everything, maybe it's nothing, *Policy Sciences*, 4, 127–53.

—— (1975), *Budgeting: A Comparative Theory of Budgetary Processes* Boston: Little, Brown.

—— (1980), *The Art and Craft of Policy Analysis*. London: Macmillan.

Williams, R. (1980), *The Nuclear Power Decisions*. London: Croom Helm.

Wilson, H. (1976), *The Governance of Britain*. London: Weidenfeld & Nicolson and Michael Joseph.

Wright, M. (1977), Public expenditure in Britain: the crisis of control, *Public Administration*, 55, 143–69.

Young, H. and A. Sloman (1982), *No, Minister: An Inquiry into the Civil Service*. London: BBC.

—— —— (1984), *But, Chancellor: An Inquiry into the Treasury*. London: BBC.

Zander, M. (1985), The United Kingdom and the Bill of Rights debate, *Catalyst*, 1(4), 13–21.

Index